INTERCULTURAL EDUCATION

Ethnographic and Religious Approaches

Eleanor Nesbitt

sussex
ACADEMIC
PRESS

BRIGHTON • PORTLAND

The right of Eleanor Nesbitt to be identified as Author of this work has been asserted in accordance with the Copyright, Designs and Patents Act 1988.

2 4 6 8 10 9 7 5 3 1

First published 2004 in Great Britain by
SUSSEX ACADEMIC PRESS
PO Box 2950
Brighton BN2 5SP

and in the United States of America by
SUSSEX ACADEMIC PRESS
920 NE 58th Ave   Suite 300
Portland, Oregon 97213–3786

British Library Cataloguing in Publication Data
A CIP catalogue record for this book is available from the British Library.

Library of Congress Cataloging-in-Publication Data
Nesbitt, Eleanor M.
    Intercultural education : ethnographic and
    religious approaches / Eleanor Nesbitt.
        p. cm.
    Includes bibliographical references and index.
    ISBN 1-84519-033-5 (hardcover : alk. paper)
    — ISBN 1-84519-034-3 (pbk.)
        1.   Religious education—Great Britain.
        2.   Multicultural education—Great Britain.
    I.   Title.
    BL42.5.G7N47 2004
    200′.71′041—dc22   2004007346
                                                CIP

Typeset and designed by G&G Editorial, Brighton
Printed by MPG Books, Ltd, Bodmin, Cornwall
This book is printed on acid-free paper.

INTERCULTURAL
EDUCATION

For Rajeev, Rajni and Rita
with love

Contents

Acknowledgements

The University of Warwick made it possible for me to write this book by giving me a term's study leave in 2003. The Leverhulme Trust generously funded three projects: Hindu Nurture in Coventry, Punjabi Hindu Nurture, A Longitudinal Study of Young British Hindus' Perceptions of their Religious Tradition, and the Economic and Social Research Council funded Ethnography and Religious Education (Project No. R00232489). I am grateful for all this support and to all the many individuals who made the research possible through their willingness to be interviewed and for welcoming me into their homes and communities. Professor Jackson has encouraged and counselled me through thick and thin and I thank him and my many other colleagues past and present for their support, in various ways, in this and other endeavours. By naming a few: Janet Ainley, Elisabeth Arweck, Carol Aubrey, Jim Campbell, Elizabeth Coates, Judith Everington, Mary Hayward, Ann Henderson, Geoff Lindsay, Ursula McKenna, Joe Winston, Peter Woodward and Richard Yeomans, I am no doubt appearing to overlook others. I am certainly not implicating them in any of the book's shortcomings – for these I am solely responsible. Thank you to Anthony Grahame and his colleagues at Sussex Academic Press for their impressive efficiency.

Parts of this book are revised versions of material that has appeared elsewhere. My thanks go to Taylor and Francis for permission to reproduce material which first appeared in articles. These are: 'British, Asian and Hindu: identity, self-narration and the ethnographic interview', Eleanor Nesbitt, *Journal of Beliefs and Values* (1998) vol. 19, no. 2, pp. 189–200 (the journal can be accessed at http://www. tandf.co.uk/ journals/carfax/13617672.html); 'Splashed with Goodness: The Many Meanings of *Amrit* for Young British Sikhs', E. N., *Journal of Contemporary Religion*, (1997) vol. 12, no. 1 (The journal's web site is http://www.tandf.co.uk/ journals/ carfax/13537903.html). Thanks also to Professor Robert Jackson, in his capacity as Editor of the *British Journal of Religious Education*, for permission to use in modified form material which appeared in Robert Jackson and E. N. (1992), 'The Diversity of Experience in the Religious Upbringing of Children from Christian Families in Britain', vol. 15, no. 1, pp. 19–28; E. N. and Robert Jackson

(1995) 'Sikh Children's Use of "God": Ethnographic Fieldwork and Religious Education', vol. 17, no. 2, pp. 108–20; and E. N. (1998), 'Bridging the Gap between Young People's Experience of their Religious Traditions at Home and School: The Contribution of Ethnographic Research', vol. 20, no. 2, pp. 102–14.

The first version of part of chapter 5 appeared as E. N. (1998), 'How Culture Changes: British Sikh Children and the Vaisakhi Festival' in the *Journal of Sikh Studies*, vol. 12, no. 1, pp. 95–118. For permission to use this material I thank Dr Balwant Singh Dhillon, Editor of the *Journal*. I acknowledge the *International Journal of Punjab Studies* for permission to use in modified form the article, 'We are All Equal: Young British Punjabis' and Gujaratis' Perceptions of Caste' which appeared in vol. 4, no. 2, 1997 (the journal's website is http://www.stile.coventry.ac. uk/punjab/index.html). Part of chapter 2 has been revised from E. N. (1995), 'Many Happy Returns: Some British South Asian Children's Birthday Parties' and part of chapter 4 appeared in E. N. (1993), 'Drawing on the Ethnic Diversity of Christian Tradition in Britain'. These articles appeared in *Multicultural Teaching* in vol. 14, no. 1, pp. 34–5 and 40 and vol. 11, no. 2, pp. 9–11 respectively. I gratefully acknowledge Trentham Books Limited for permission to use these.

I thank Dr Michael J. Rainer and LIT Verlag Münster and the editors for kind permission to use a modified version of my chapter 'What Young British Hindus Believe: Some Issues for the Researcher and the RE Teacher' from H-G. Heimbrock, C. Scheilke and P. Schreiner (eds), *Towards Religious Competence: Diversity as a Challenge for Education in Europe*, Münster, Lit-verlag, pp. 50–62. Peeters Publishers has kindly permitted me to use a modified version of the chapter 'Transmission of Christian Tradition in an Ethnically Diverse Society', which was originally published in Rohit Barot (ed.) (1993), *Religion and Ethnicity: Minorities and Social Change in the Metropolis*, Kampen: Kok Pharos, pp. 156–69. I thank Professor Kim Knott (monograph series editor) and the Community Religions Project, Department of Theology and Religious Studies, University of Leeds for permission to use in modified form material which first appeared in E. N. (2000), *The Religious Lives of Sikh Children: A Coventry Based Study*. Thank you to Professor T. S. Rukmani for permission to adapt for chapter 3 my chapter '"Being Religious Shows in your Food": Young British Hindus and Vegetarianism', which first appeared in T. S. Rukmani (ed.), *Hindu Diaspora: Global Perspectives*, Montreal: Chair Hindu Studies, Concordia University, pp. 397–426.

Finally, my husband, Mr Ram Krishan (Prashar), has helped me to keep a sense of perspective and has provided the sustenance and refreshment that have allowed me to maintain momentum. I am flouting the one-time conventions of my community-by-marriage by both naming and thanking him.

A Note on Transliteration

This book includes many words from languages other than English, and these are explained in the glossary. The majority of these words are from languages which originate in North India, and especially Punjabi, Gujarati and Hindi. Letters of the roman alphabet have been used consistently to represent the sounds of the original language, but scholarly diacritics (dots and dashes) have not been included in this volume (diacritics are used by linguists in order to distinguish, for example, a 'd' or a 't' pronounced with the tongue rolled back against the palate from a 'd' or a 't' with the tongue touching the front teeth).

Where Indic words occur in the course of a sentence, the plurals have been made by adding a final 's', as in English. However, this is not the way in which they are formed in the original language.

In the spirit of *Intercultural Education*, readers are encouraged, if the opportunity arises, to draw the book to the attention of speakers of any of the languages concerned, and to listen to their pronunciation of the relevant words.

Introduction: Cultural Diversity and Intercultural Education

Joe Winston, a specialist in drama education, was working with a class of year 4 (8–9 year-old) children in a north Coventry school on an adaptation of *The Tempest* (in this version Prospero and Miranda were exiled on another planet). As he worked with the children Winston noted their commentary on the dramatic situations and relationships (2003). Eighty per cent of the class were from Punjabi families – Muslim families with roots in Pakistan, Sikh and Hindu families from North India. Winston wondered whether the children's insights into relationships, and ideas about magic, drew upon their families' South Asian culture – at least as much as they drew on Harry Potter. Or, did apparent resonances with Punjab's oral and literary tradition of honour, shame and romantic ballads point to his own academically trained inquisitiveness, which too readily perceived these children as different from their 'English' peers?

During the 1990s Barbara Easton, a secondary school teacher in a Wolverhampton school with a predominantly Punjabi catchment area, noted the patterns of solidarity and friction among sixth formers. She began to realise that division along hereditary caste lines was a key factor in parental anger, and young people's anxieties, when pupil x from the Jat community and pupil y from the Chamar community became too close (Easton 1999). In order to inform and sensitise her professionalism in pastoral care (as well as in religious education) Easton decided to pursue an MA in Religious Education through which she could investigate the caste-specific experience of British Jats and Chamars.

These two examples illustrate in part the rationale of this book. Pupils' religious and cultural backgrounds connect with the curriculum and they also influence their relationships. Faith and family are formative of school experience. Sensitive classroom practice respects and taps pupils' resources of experience and supports the connections (of emotion and information) that appear in their creativity and imagination. At the same time competent pastoral care is informed by discovering the dynamics of local social norms. Teachers need, I argue, to take account of these in counselling pupils and liaising with their families.

A third illustration (literally) flags up a third cluster of reasons for writing this book and for its relevance to teachers. In November 2001 the cover of *The Teacher* showed 'a child at a multiracial memorial rally, attended by New York school children, for the victims of the September 11 terrorist attacks' (2001: 3). The photographic image consisted of a hazy paternal figure holding an infant next to the stars and stripes. The child's hair was caught up on the top of his head in a bun covered by a little white hand-kerchief. As a matter of religious principle, Sikhs (or at least Sikhs who accept the discipline of the Khalsa, the order of committed Sikhs) do not shorten their hair. Many infant Sikh boys' hair is kept tidy in the manner of the child in the cover photograph. Two months previously the interna-tional news had reported the killing of a Sikh in the United States in the wake of the assault on the twin towers by al-Qaeda. Sikh Americans were vulnerable to attack because fellow Americans assumed that their turbans identified them with Afghans/ the Taliban/ al-Qaeda. On British campuses at the time of writing, Sikhs still report being greeted in public places by shouts of 'Osama bin Laden' (personal communication 2003 from officer in Sikh student organisation) and 'at least two hundred Sikhs have been victims of hate crimes in America simply because they happened to be wearing a turban' (N.-G. K. Singh 2003).

When I invited a class of trainee primary school teachers to comment on the message of the photograph the best that the bravest could venture was to guess that the photo was drawing attention to the currently uneasy relationship between 'Muslims' and 'Americans'. The fact that the class was in Coventry, a city with one of the highest numbers of Sikhs in the UK – nearly 14,000 according to the 2001 UK Census – increased my concern at the trainees' innocence of the clues available in the diverse society which they will influence as teachers (Census 2001, 2004).

As future teachers in primary schools in England and Wales these trainees will be delivering a curriculum in which religious education is a statutory requirement. Sikhism is one of the 'principal religions' which they are likely to be teaching (UK Government 1988). As primary school teachers they will be seeking to establish supportive relationships with their pupils' families. An ability to read indicators (such as the infant's head covering) can contribute to building relationships of trust and respect.

But there are also dangers in stereotyping on the basis of such details. Some members of the American public had jumped to the conclusion that all turban-wearers are Afghans, coupled with the assumption that all Afghans are terrorists. It was these leaps of association which gave the cover image its intended poignancy and irony. Stereotyping involves both perceiving groups to be homogeneous and 'different' and representing them as such – in religious education lessons, for example. It is all too often at the level of 'Hindus have a red spot on their foreheads', or (as I over-heard in a hospital waiting room) the sort of logic that a man who had walked through wearing a short sheathed sword (a Sikh in fact) must be a Gurkha. The implications both of blindness to difference on the one hand and over-emphasis of it on the other are teased out in this book, with a wealth of examples, from a series of ethnographic studies.

To return to that cover picture, its irony – and intended impact – presumably depended on readers (teachers) making connections between recent events and social groups in a particular international context. As Robert Jackson (2004a, b) has pointed out, since 2001 further global atrocities have 'put religion on political, social and educational agendas internationally': Jackson provides examples of international initiatives, in response to such events, to add 'the dimension of religious diversity to intercultural education'.

By law in England and Wales, since 2001, secondary schools have been providing citizenship education. Primary schools have also increased their (non-statutory) provision. Citizenship education is intended to include understanding diversity, and the interrelationship between local community, international events and global issues, between the vulnerability of a Sikh family in a European town and events in Afghanistan, Baghdad or New York (see especially Jackson 2003). In the United States, Canada and other countries the legal framework is different and the curriculum is differently constructed, but the issues which this book addresses are transnational.

They are crucial to the provision of a fully reflective intercultural education – using 'intercultural' for what British authors frequently call 'multicultural education' or, more recently, 'multicultural antiracist education'. This refers not only to the fact that schools – and society more widely – comprise individuals from culturally diverse communities, but also indicates a set of educational ideals, in terms of the educational goals and implications of promoting constructive, creative, mutually respectful interrelationships between these culturally diverse individuals and groups (Figueroa 1998: 122–3).

Religious and cultural literacy

If society is to progress smartly from stereotyping to alert receptivity, both religious education and citizenship education require of us not only a theoretical, distanced, broad brush understanding of religions and cultures but also a fine-grained, close-up awareness. Teachers and others can share the insights provided by in-depth, nuanced studies which draw on the ethnographic skills of participant observation (and listening) and interviews (structured and less structured) of individuals and groups. My hope is that teachers, and those in other professions, are able to share some of the wealth of detail – the fine grain of human diversity – in what follows.

At a time when, as recommended by the Cantle Report, 'community cohesion' requires that educational programmes promote cross-cultural contact (Home Office 2001a, para. 5.8.18: 36), pupils need to be educated to identify the dimensions of their own identities and to understand society as both global and as locally diverse. In this enterprise ethnography can be enabling for educationists and others. By ethnography I mean both published reporting of in depth studies of communities and also the methodological approach involved. This approach is one of attentive listening and observation and entails an unflagging readiness to rethink one's earlier assumptions rather than to make unsubstantiated generalisations.

Invitations from not only University Departments of Education and Local Education Authorities, but also from churches, constabularies, social services, lawyers in the UK and the USA (to give expert advice on cultural issues) and from co-ordinators of post-graduate training for medical students, have demonstrated for me the relevance of ethnographic detail and insight to professionals in the broadest sense both in and beyond the UK and its education service.

A prime purpose of this book is to sharpen our sensitivity to children's and young people's cultural and religious diversity and to hone the ways in which we represent diversity. Our capacity to make our pupils religiously and culturally literate depends upon how we represent difference. By religious and cultural literacy I mean being conversant with the processes that produce what we call religion and culture and having a sense of their dynamics. Andrew Wright defines religious literacy differently as 'learn[ing] to engage in informed conversation about their beliefs, and the beliefs of others' (2000: 183). Wright's definition assumes the 'distinctive identities' of 'specific spiritual traditions' (2000: 175). The difference between the sense in which I use 'religious literacy' and Wright's sense is analogous to the difference between linguistics (or language awareness) and learning some French and German, as an English speaker, and then discussing the differences between these two languages.

A religious literacy that is informed by ethnographic insights takes us beyond, on the one hand, multiculturalism and, on the other, antiracism. Both have been critiqued extensively (see Leicester 1992 and Rex 1997). Both Mal Leicester (1992) and Ali Rattansi (1992) argued for the two approaches to be combined. Multiculturalism takes account of and, indeed, celebrates diversity, but by essentialising cultures leads to tokenism and disempowerment (Troyna 1983). Antiracism centers on power imbalance; it challenges structures of inequality but has frequently disregarded the diversity within 'black', 'Asian' etc. and leaves 'faith' out of account. In this regard the Canadian anthropologist Dhooleka S. Raj has summarised recent unpacking of ethnicity (2003: 9). Earlier Avtar Brah (1996) and others had deconstructed 'Asian' as a category. 'Asian' in fact subsumes (or disguises) multiple differences of religious, national, regional and linguistic identity between, for example, a UK Sylheti-speaking Bangladeshi Muslim family and a UK Gujarati-speaking Hindu family with roots in Kenya and India and relatives in areas including North America and mainland Europe. Portmanteau terms certainly give no hint of the fine grain of diversity recorded in the present volume.

Releasing the inner ethnographer

The word 'ethnography' is used here for an approach to understanding others which relies on a discipline of deep listening and close, reflective observation. Its purpose is to understand human behaviour at ever increasing depth, and to communicate this deepening understanding sensitively to others. Ethnographers recognise too the part that interpretation necessarily plays in these processes. Typically ethnographers make use of the methods of conducting interviews and of being a participant observer. The interviews are usually structured, but not rigidly so. Such interviews avoid constraining the interviewee whilst allowing for comparison to take place during the analysis of the data. The balance between being an observer and being a participant varies considerably from one situation to another. Manuals abound: Fetterman (1998) and Hammersley and Atkinson (1995) are excellent examples.

In advocating an ethnographic approach I recognise that there is insufficient time for teachers (and others) themselves to double up as ethnographers in the sense of full time anthropologists, immersed in understanding a community. But as you read this book you may realise not only that you can become an ethnographer – but even that you already are an ethnographer in your sympathetic receptivity and critical attentiveness to the patterning of individuals' and groups' concepts and activities. Opening up ethnography to the 'amateur' need by no means ignore the essentials of 'ideal' ethnography for fuller time ethnographic researchers. These include having an extended period of time in the field, paying attention to a total social context and coming to understand situations 'from the native's point of view' (Stringer 1999: 13 quoting Malinowski 1922: 25). Jackson (1997a: 30–48) provides a helpful discussion of the debates within ethnographic interpretation.

Undeterred by the unattainability of the ideal, for ten years I have been training postgraduate educationists (mainly primary and secondary school teachers) in the conduct of field studies at the interface between faith communities and education. Their testimonies to the transformative and empowering impact of the exercise on their approach to their work drive my contention in chapter 10 that the adoption of 'an ethnographic stance' is vital to being educators.

The discussion of recent decades has compelled the ethnographer to think through the ethics of conducting studies of communities and to take seriously the dimension of 'reflexivity'. In other words how far do the researcher's preconceptions affect the interpretation of what is being studied and vice versa? Reflexive awareness requires probing reflection on the extent to which one is an insider or an outsider to the community which one is observing. In her account of her relationship, as a Canadian from a Punjabi Hindu family, with her research community of London (UK) Punjabi Hindu families, Raj provides one recent example of this sort of self-analysis (2003: 11–12) in which any polarising of insider and outsider is evidently simplistic and unhelpful. The Quaker sociologist of religion, Ben Pink Dandelion, provides a useful typology in which one can be an insider to a particular group, as well as to its wider context, or an insider only to the wider context (1996: 37–50). So, for example, the person for whom religious faith is a reality, may be an insider to the wider context of faith – a fact which may be significant in entering sympathetically into contact with members of a particular group (Plymouth Brethren, Baptists, Baha'is or Buddhists) to which one is an outsider.

Teachers who have tried their hands at being ethnographers can become more aware of their personal 'lenses', of their hunches and prejudices, and of the uncommonness of common sense and they can become more sensitive to others' differences of priority and perception. Reading the ethnography of others, too, can unsettle a few taken for granted assumptions.

In keeping with what I have already advocated regarding a transparent reflexivity it is appropriate to acknowledge some of the ways in which my personal experience connects me to the communities discussed in this volume. In religious terms the strongest influence on my childhood was Anglican. In terms of ethnicity and culture I am English. For over 30 years I have been part of the Religious Society of Friends (Quakers) and Nesbitt (2002) explores the relevance of this to my ethnography. Through marriage my family is Hindu, with its roots in the North Indian state of Punjab. Professionally a major part of my work in religious studies prior to the fieldwork reported in this book had been concerned with the Sikh tradition.

So, in bringing together the following essays on UK field studies, my hope is that they contribute to heightening in readers this 'ethnographic awareness' which needs to permeate all levels of education. The issue is important because school ethos and pastoral care, as well as the content and presentation of the curriculum, will as a result be more informed, self-questioning and challenging. Gradually our schools will be better matched to an increasingly fluid, plural, multiply interactive society. This 'ethnographic awareness' involves an alertness to those individuals and groups that separate themselves out, or are marginalised, and it discerns potential points of connection, overlap and communication between communities.

Advocating an 'ethnographic approach' also carries a health warning.

Bearing the burden of its etymology, as the writing (inscribing) of an *ethnos* (people), it is all too easy for ethnography to create and crystallise 'ethnic' distinctions and distinctiveness. This hazard persists, despite recent decades of energetic debate, attack and (usually by 'western' practitioners) self-flagellation. Michel Foucault and Edward Said especially raised anthropologists' awareness of the pernicious effects of dominant societies defining weaker societies as 'the other' (Foucault 1971; Said 1989). Robert Jackson provides one senior educationist's overview of their contribution to ethnography's journey from colonial ethnology (and the gentleman anthropologist's veranda) to a more reflexive, gender-aware and poly-phonic ethnography (1997a: 55-7). At a further remove from the veranda is Rosen's advocacy of schools as 'ethnographic centres' (1998, cited in Gardner 2001: 47). It is just this emphasis on 'listening' that requires emphasis, and it is what Blair and Bourne identify as a prerequisite for a successful multi-ethnic school (1998). This listening applies to other insti-tutional milieux as well as to schools; it applies to all schools – not only to those which are 'multi-ethnic'.

Why focus on 'religions'?

The studies on which this volume is based focus upon young people from Christian, Hindu and Sikh communities in the Midlands of Britain. In the first studies the age range was 8 to 13 – see Nesbitt (2001a) for an overview. A 'longitudinal study' returned to some of these young people when they were aged 16 to 23 (see Nesbitt 1998a, 1999a and b). The research raised substantial methodological issues (Nesbitt 2001a). Of these one concerns the choice of a conceptual framework in which religion (allegiance to a faith or at least a willingness in certain contexts to be identified with it) was a primary category. So, young people were selected for the Warwick studies from those who attended activities explicitly linked to a faith community. They identified themselves as Christian, Hindu and Sikh, at least in certain contexts.

It may be objected that the focus of these studies means that the young people concerned do not include members of that substantial group of young people – in some UK schools the vast majority – who are unaligned with any religion, and so answer 'I am nothing' to the question 'What is your religion?' (Rudge 1998). But the ethnographic approach adopted here applies to the unaligned as much as to those who are committed to particular faiths.

A further cautionary note is required: Mary Searle-Chatterjee's swingeing critique of the 'world religions' and 'ethnic groups' paradigm needs to be read by all who are concerned with religions in education (2000). She rightly highlights the danger of 'isolating out a Hindu sample, rather than studying an existing social matrix' (2000: 503). The isolating of a Hindu sample is

> problematic, since it involves starting with the conceptions both of religion and Hinduism as separable phenomena, as well as with the conception of 'Hindu' as a pre-existing identity. (2000: 503)

In other words, Searle-Chatterjee contends, we damage our understanding of society by defining and selecting out 'religion' and its assumed bearers.

The anthropologist Gert Baumann suggests pizzas and shish kebabs as fruitful subjects for future cultural research, in order to avoid the pitfalls of singling out local 'communities' defined by their ethnicity or religion (1999). Baumann's theorising is grounded in his fieldwork in Southall (1996) which provided the basis for his deconstruction of the identities of Sikh, Hindu, Muslim and other communities by attending to the types of discourse in which individuals and organisations use these and other ('cross-cutting') designations of themselves or others. The exploitation of religious (and so emotive) terms by political aspirants can, as Baumann and Searle-Chatterjee saw, be served by researchers whose paradigm is uncritically one of 'religions'. The reification of 'religions' feeds into competition for resources, which are – in the UK – increasingly being designated for constituencies that are defined by their religious allegiance. The government recognises and mobilises faith communities in its bid for 'community cohesion' (Home Office 2001a and 2001b) and recommends national and local consultation with religious groups regarding policy and initiatives (Home Office Faith Communites Unit 2004).

Baumann does, however, concede that:

> One can certainly limit one's study to, let us say, 'Sikhs in Middletown' without reducing all their actions and words to a symptom of Sikhness. Neither does such a study have to treat ethnicity as if it were the same phenomenon in all situations. (1996: 203)

For 'ethnicity' one must also read 'religion'.

To provide some historical background for the University of Warwick studies, it was the process of working within the framework of religious education in the UK, a subject with syllabuses predicated on 'world religions', which initially led to research projects that were based on this paradigm. Yet, ironically, it was this very experience which precipitated my – and my colleague Robert Jackson's – formulation of critiques of the world religions framework which defines not only school-based religious education but also much of the religious studies syllabus in higher education. Our critiques were based on just the grounded concerns that Baumann and Searle-Chatterjee articulate. 'Religion' can only artificially be separated from 'culture' and 'society'. As noted, the essentialising of either religion or culture provides potentially dangerous resources for those with political and personal agendas, and these are particularly dangerous if those involved in religious education remain in ignorance of this political dimension, locally, nationally and internationally. Parita Mukta gave a wake-up call for religious educationists with an impassioned plea to wise up regarding the agenda and bedfellows of a Hindu organisation, the Vishwa Hindu Parishad (1997). More recently the Centre for Applied South Asian Studies has carried these concerns forward through its website, conferences and consultancies.[1]

Additionally, the mounting data from the University of Warwick studies undermines any conceptualising of religions as bounded or discrete – a key assumption of religious education syllabuses (see SCAA 1994). Ron Geaves (1998a) and Roger Ballard (1999, 2003) based their challenges to the 'boundaries between the religions' on their field work in Punjab. The Warwick University studies of communities in the Midlands leaves no doubt that some imagined boundaries (notably between 'Sikh' and 'Hindu') are arbitrary and porous (e.g. Nesbitt 1990a, 1991).

At the same time, for Hindus, Muslims and Sikhs of South Asian origin, and for other minority ethnic groups, religion has become an increasingly evident form of self-identification (Weller 2004: 5, citing Modood, Beishon and Virdee 1994; Modood et al. 1997). For this reason, UK government discourse and strategy have shown an upsurge of interest in faiths. Increasing concern for religious discrimination, too, lends a legitimacy to the religious paradigm, but only if it is used with due caution. In this situation distrust of easy categories that are all too readily treated as homogeneous communities becomes all the more imperative.

Why focus on particular 'religions'?

Given that the studies reported in this volume have used (as well as challenged) a religious paradigm, the reader may wonder why the focus is so selective. Why are young Christians, Hindus and Sikhs centre stage, with only more incidental reference to Jewish, Muslim and other constituencies? The constraints of academic specialism, time and resources are in large part responsible. However, whilst conducting and reporting my own field studies I have looked to other scholars' studies in Jewish and Muslim contexts for illuminating insights. Their observation (about, for example, identity) has sharpened my questioning of my own data. Similarly, the chapters which follow raise issues and suggest nuancing for reading other local, religious and ethnic communities.

For readers wishing to read ethnographies of Jewish schools I commend Bullivant (1978) and Scholefield (2004). Those concerned with Muslim pupils in common schools in the UK can refer to Haw (1998) and Parker-Jenkins (1995), and to Bhatti (1999) and Shain (2003), both of whose samples were predominantly Muslim. Østberg's discussion of the 'integrated plural identity' of young Pakistani Muslims in Oslo is a particularly rich ethnography (2003). Among the increasing numbers of scholars who are focusing upon Muslim diaspora groups, the UK-based studies of Jacobson (1998), Joly (1995), Lewis (1994) and Shaw (1994 and 2000) provide analytical context for understanding the experience of Muslims in the education system.

The very abundance of studies of young Muslims, and the public preoccupation with Islam, also provide a strong justification for adding to the much more meagre literature on young people for whom being a Christian, a Hindu or a Sikh shapes their experience.

Overview of contents

The bulk of the text offers analytical reflection on the experience of interpreting and communicating empirical data from successive studies focused on local Sikh, Hindu and Christian communities over two decades in the Midlands. These local groups are multiply constituted of smaller 'membership groups' (Jackson 1997a), corresponding to (inter alia) gender, generation, socio-economic group, 'caste' (see chapter 8), devotional orientation and denomination. Through in-depth semi-structured interviewing (in some studies over a period of eight years) individual young people's creative 'cultural repertoires' emerge – responsive to and formative of multiple interacting influences.

No chapter should be generalised to other locations or times. Each is a representation of particular young people at particular points in time and place (usually Coventry). As such this ethnography belongs to the UK's social history and cultural geography.

Chapter 1 focuses on birthdays – the celebration of which (with cake, the blowing out of candles, giving of presents, playing of party games etc.) is widely assumed to be cross-cultural. In fact the configurations and reconfigurations of 'English' and 'Asian' elements give rise to a spectrum of birthday celebrations in the UK. Some are religious in character, some are secular or a combination of both. Teachers' and pupils' assumptions about birthdays may marginalise the experience of children who do not fit a dominant model.

Chapter 2 is concerned with the complex relationship between being Hindu and being vegetarian. Vegetarianism and Hinduism are frequently linked in popular and academic discourse. For instance, '(all) Hindus are vegetarian', 'Hindus should be vegetarian' or 'this person is vegetarian because s/he is Hindu'. Longitudinal study of young Hindu adults, who look back on their own schooldays, suggests far more complex patterns of continuity, change, aspiration, rhetoric and practice. The multiple factors involved include those that are neither underpinned by religious tradition nor community-specific. Hindus too watch mainstream television.

Chapter 3 explores intrafaith diversity and individual plurality and raises questions for the representation of religions in religious education as more monolithic, and thus more exclusive, than the faith traditions actually are.

The three festivals of Christmas, Divali and Vaisakhi provide the basis for chapter 4's consideration of the multiple meanings of festivals. In particular the role of UK schools in acknowledging, perpetuating and fashioning 'tradition' is examined.

Most accounts of Sikh 'belief' and 'practice', whether by insiders or outsiders to Sikh tradition, afford no suggestion of the complexity of Sikhs' variegated use of the word 'God' or of their use of holy water (*amrit*). This complexity is unravelled in chapter 5.

Chapter 6 shifts the spotlight on 'belief' to four areas of young British Hindus' beliefs, including reflection on what if anything makes one idea a 'belief' (and so the stuff of religious education texts) and another a 'superstition'. Much that is written about late or post-modernity emphasises the unprecedented scale of unavoidable individual choice. Chapter 6 asks to what extent young people *choose* their beliefs. Analysis of young British Hindus' ways of articulating their views on religious, cultural and ethical issues provides examples of the convictions and assumptions which they manage to maintain. The chapter alerts to contributory factors in forming their beliefs and illustrates the ways in which young people incorporate or reject alternative views.

Chapter 7 challenges the representation of one faith community by contrast with another – in particular the distinctions frequently made between Sikh and Hindu practice. The challenge is mounted by bringing ethnographic data to bear on widespread representation of Sikhs as being less caste-conscious (e.g. in relation to finding spouses for their children) than Hindus. Writers of religious education curriculum materials and religious education teachers echo the Sikh preachers' rhetoric that the Gurus abolished the caste system as far as their followers, the Sikhs, are concerned. Once caste is understood as both vertical (hereditary and diachronic) and horizontal (synchronic, uniting and dividing contemporaries) the gap becomes evident between Sikh families' experience and religious education's tendency to oversimplify caste.

Chapter 8 attends to the multiple identities of young British Hindus. Plenty of publications, both scholarly and popular, use the idiom of culture conflict and culture clash. In line with a smaller – though growing – body of literature, chapter 8 paints a more complex picture. With reference to a recent study of young Muslims' identity, I shall argue that the young Hindus identify themselves as Hindu, not as an assertion of a return to true teachings (as distinct from the ethnic interpretations of their elders), but as an assertion of family continuities.

In order to counter any impression that 'faiths' need to be deciphered in terms of visible behaviour and appearance (externals), chapter 9 presents the view that at heart 'religion' expresses individuals' 'spirituality'. Young Christians', Hindus' and Sikhs' experience of God, of Spirit, of inner peace raise questions for schools' provision for 'spiritual development' – provision which is an area for government inspection in British schools (Ofsted 1994). Young people's religious experience also suggests issues for the way in which religions are represented in the curriculum. In particular, data on the affective aspect of Sikh devotion for primary school age children are called upon to contest the dominant portrayal of Sikhism, with its emphasis on externals, in school curricula.

Chapter 10 returns to considering ways in which ethnography can benefit professional practice in schools. Particular ethnographic studies provide data that may be a source of insight, they also make us look afresh at assumptions of what 'religion' and 'culture' are. The school's role in the perpetuation, as well as in the representation, of religion and culture comes under scrutiny. 'Process' is a key word, both in relation to the way in which individual identity forms and in relation to ethnography itself. The chapter concludes with endorsement of an approach to religious education that encourages the skills of interpretation and dialogue.

The Appendix summarises practical advice for teachers, from early years to secondary, on such matters as calendars and celebrations and liaising with pupils' parents, and offers pointers to making the whole curriculum more culturally inclusive.

Words from several languages are used in the text. These are in most cases defined on their first occurrence, and then listed in the comprehensive Glossary.

An ethnographic approach entails receptivity to new vocabulary!

Note

1 See http://www.art.man.ac.uk/CASAS/ (accessed 12 December 2003).

Birthdays – A Spectrum of Difference

Unnoticed variations

'We treat them all the same', a deputy head of a culturally diverse London primary school assured me in response to my questioning him about the school's recognition of cultural difference. Respect (equal respect) for individuals and their families requires educationists and all school staff to sensitise themselves to diversity. At the same time this awareness, a readiness to learn and to respond, needs to be coupled with awareness of the active part which schools are playing, whether this is the intention or not, in precipitating cultural change.

Birthdays provide our focus. The context is the primary school, including the foundation stage (i.e. provision for three- to five-year olds) (Nesbitt 1995a). The reasons for the focus on birthdays are the frequency of reference in schools to birthdays; together with a dominant perception (by teachers and many pupils) of what constitutes a birthday celebration (involving the sharing of a birthday cake and the giving of presents, and – increasingly – themed parties in special venues); plus the fact that families in a diverse society regard birthdays very differently. Families may never previously have marked them but may be ready to start doing so. The resultant celebrations may differ markedly from the teachers', or the majority of the pupils', assumptions. Parents may, deliberately or less self-consciously, develop a form of celebration which emphasises certain religious/cultural aspects of their inherited minority tradition. Their children may not be able to articulate easily in English what happens. Alternatively, parents may have strong reasons for avoiding the celebration of birthdays. Teachers may not know what these reasons are, or they may not wish either to know them or to evince respect for this alternative perspective in their dealings with their class. In a number of Christian communities, both Catholic and Orthodox, name days feature alongside or instead of birthdays as a child's annual day. The relative weighting of birthday and name day will vary from community to community and, within these, from family to family. Of course, families' economic circumstances affect the manner and scale of birthday celebration and need to be borne in mind as another axis of difference.

The present chapter introduces examples of the spectrum of parental attitude towards birthdays (and children's experience of birthdays) and, on the basis of field studies in Coventry, illustrates the diversity – and evolution – of practice in some families of South Asian background. On the basis of the experiences of these Sikh families it goes on to advocate heightening attention to other assumed cultural norms in the interests of actually 'treating them all the same', in the sense of showing equal respect and growing understanding rather than mistakenly assuming commonalities of experience. We begin by considering some parents' reasons for not wishing their children to celebrate birthdays.

Not celebrating birthdays

More research is needed on Christian sects such as Jehovah's Witnesses and Exclusive Brethren, which adhere to a distinctive discipline, including reservations about birthday celebrations. Jehovah's Witness parents usually insist on their children's exclusion from the marking of birthdays in school.

> Jehovah's Witness children can be made to feel unnecessarily isolated from their classmates when they have to decline invitations to birthday parties, and non-Witness relatives can be unnecessarily offended by the refusal of JW relatives to send them birthday or Christmas cards. (McCann 2002: 4)

The reasons which McCann gives for Jehovah's Witnesses' rejection of birthdays are that birthdays are (a) 'pagan' and (b) associated with negative events (in fact murder) on the two occasions when they are explicitly mentioned in the Bible. Genesis 40: 20–22 tells how on his birthday Pharaoh hanged his chief baker and Matthew 14: 6–10 reports Herod's decapitation of John the Baptist.

Christian sects are not alone in not marking birthdays. Muslim parents less often object to their children participating in class when birthdays are being celebrated, and many Muslim children do have a party, but the marking of the day is in many families a response to living in the UK, not (in most cases) a continuation of family tradition. Thus, information on a 'diversity in health' website informs practitioners that among Kurds 'Birthdays are not widely celebrated' and that in the Somali community 'Birthdays are not celebrated' (diversity in health, 2003). Further information includes the explanation that

> Somalis are historically nomads. The consequence is that Somalis may not know their exact date of birth. (Diversity in Health 2003)

But resistance to birthdays is not simply a matter of being a nomad or not keeping a record of birth dates – the latter was also the case for many South Asian families in previous generations. Some Muslim parents, no less than Jehovah's Witnesses, base their resistance to celebrating birthdays on explicitly religious tradition. For example:

> Celebrating birthdays has no source whatever in the pure shariah [divine law]. In fact it is an innovation, since the Messenger of Allah (peace be upon him) said, 'Whoever introduces anything into this matter of ours that does not belong to it shall have that action rejected.' (Shaikh 'Abdul 'Aziz bin 'Abdullah bib Baaz 2003)

The Shaikh's ruling concurs with the exposition by Shaikh Muhammed Salih Al-Munajjid (available on the same website). Others ask why anyone should celebrate having one year fewer to live.

Name days

In other communities the lack of emphasis on birthdays results from a (Christian) focus on the child's name day, rather than on the birthday, which is the case in some Catholic as well as Orthodox communities. The name day is the feast day of the saint whose name a family member has assumed at either baptism or confirmation. In some devout Catholic families the celebration of name days is a deliberate means of 'bring[ing] this liturgical life of the church into the life of the family' (Fournier: 1997-2003). There may be an ethnic or nationalistic dimension: for example, the official Slovak calendar assigns a name to each day of the year on which people bearing this name will celebrate, although birthdays are given more importance (Slovensko.com: 2003). This calendar does not in every case allocate the days to the names listed in either Protestant or Catholic religious calendars, but it has been created with reference to these ecclesiastical traditions.

Among Orthodox families (e.g. Greek, Russian, Serbian, Ukrainian) in the UK the traditional emphasis on name days often continues strongly (see Roman 2003), with the child concerned at the centre of a celebratory rite in front of the congregation. In church on the Sunday nearest to their name day (e.g. St Anastasia for a boy whose name was Anastasias) children with the same name as the saint concerned receive a special type of bread:

> We have special saints' days for each name, each person has a special saint's name. You get your icon, the icon with the saint's name – that's your name – on it, and you have a table in the middle near the altar, and it's got holy water on it and, I think, palm leaves. And you walk around the table with the priest holding

the icon three times. You'll all hold the icon (if there's about three of you), and afterwards the priest gives you a loaf of home made bread and you go outside and cut it and give it to everyone as they go in. (13 year-old Cypriot Greek Orthodox boy)

Birthdays as religious occasions

Rather than regarding the birthday as an unwelcome cultural accretion, however, many minority families welcome an opportunity to reinforce religious and cultural tradition.

Birthday celebrations are not intrinsically Jewish, although (among Chasidic Jews) a boy's third Hebrew birthday is marked by his first haircut and a festive meal (Miller and Widener 2003: 3). The Hebrew birthday is calculated by the Jewish calendar (see www.jewfaq.org/ calendar.htm). Once they have passed their twelfth and thirteenth Hebrew birthdays, respectively, girls and boys attain religious maturity. For boys this coming of age is marked by the Bar Mitzvah which entails being called to read from the Torah (scripture) in the Shabbat (Sabbath) congregation. In many Orthodox Jewish families a Bat Chayil celebration (often on a Sunday afternoon) takes place in the synagogue, and increasing numbers of Jewish girls – especially from Progressive families – take part in a Bat Mitzvah which parallels the Bar Mitzvah. Despite the lack of traditional authority for celebrating birthdays, Lisa Farber Miller and Sandra Widener ask 'Why not create your own Jewish traditions and customs to celebrate your child's birthday?' given that 'under the influence of secular culture, birthday celebrations have become a fact of family life' (2003: 1). They suggest introducing a spiritual, reflective element and 'adapt[ing] old rituals' by planting a tree.

Some adaptations of religious tradition are less calculated. As I write these words, a one year-old Punjabi girl's first birthday celebration has just ended. It consisted of her parents and grandparents hosting a continuous 24-hour reading (an *akhand path*) of the *Ramayana*, the Hindu epic, in their house. The event involved generous hospitality to the friends and relatives who attended and to three Brahmins who were invited to read during the night. Fieldwork in Coventry showed that some Sikh children, too, are familiar with birthday parties modelled on the devotional gathering or *satsang*. The family hosts a reading of the Guru Granth Sahib, the Sikh scriptures, with the intention of bringing the child future 'luck' or blessing. The reading may be either a continuous 48-hour reading of the entire volume (an *akhand path*) or a Sukhmani *path*, i.e. the reading of the Sukhmani Sahib (Hymn of Peace), a favourite composition, and the reading (*path*) may be held in either the gurdwara (Sikh place of worship) or at home.

In the latter case the house is cleaned, strictly vegetarian food is prepared for the anticipated congregation, the living room is cleared of furniture, white sheets are spread over the carpet, a canopy is suspended from the ceiling and the requisite *chauri* (a sign of authority consisting of a handle in which a switch of white horse or yak tail hair is embedded) and cushions for the holy volume are set in place. A copy of the Guru Granth Sahib is borrowed from the gurdwara for the occasion. It is carried into the house ceremonially on the bearer's covered head, while someone else sprinkles purificatory water on the floor ahead of him, before being installed on the cushions below the canopy. While a reader sits behind the book, reading the verses aloud, guests continue to enter, kneel before the Guru Granth Sahib, touch the floor with their foreheads, make an offering, then move back and sit cross-legged on the floor.

At the end of the reading that marked one Coventry Sikh boy's eleventh birthday, there was hymn-singing to an accompaniment of harmonium and percussion. The boy was presented with a red cloth, as a sign of honour. Otherwise he was hardly in evidence. (Contrast the 'western' birthday party in which, usually, the birthday child is centre stage.) After this everyone received *karah prashad* (the sacred mixture of wheat flour, clarified butter, sugar and water), then the equally vegetarian, but more innovative, butterscotch and plums which someone had donated, and then came the shared meal, a savoury course followed by sweets.

The celebration was an all-age religious event, of just the same type as marks other important events such as moving house (see the illustrations in Bennett 1989). As is the case at these other junctures, the 11 year-old's family had a serious, long-term purpose in organising this occasion. In this instance it was to gain the blessing of the boy's success at school.

Birthdays as 'secular' events

However, not all Sikh children's birthdays strike such a religious note. Recalling his fieldwork in Southall (West London) Gert Baumann graphically described one Sikh family's 'secular' party: the informal segregation of the participants according to gender – with only the men drinking alcohol; the videoing of the 'core ritual' of feeding the birthday boys with cake and unwrapping the presents; and, finally, the all-age dancing to *bhangra* recordings until late evening (1992).

These activities mirror other family festivities – notably those involved in marriages. In Coventry an eight year-old girl summarised just such a birthday party:

> We celebrate a lot and then we start dancing in the garden sometimes – Indian [dancing]. The people in our religion – well not religion – family, they live quite close to us and we call those over. (Baumann 1992)

Different party norms

Both the religious and the more secular styles of partying point up the processes of cultural change underway in British birthday parties – in these cases South Asian (and more specifically) Punjabi Sikh ones. In most cases it is only after their settlement in the UK that families take to decorating the house with balloons and giving presents – brightly wrapped presents to be opened in the presence of the givers – or organising parties in restaurants, leisure complexes or cinemas that offer this facility.

One example of divergence from 'mainstream' birthday practice is the South Asians' tendency to invite members of the family and 'community' (or what the girl quoted above referred to as her 'religion') to an all-age function, rather than inviting the child's peers. Moreover, alongside the cake there may be Indian sweets and savouries (samosas, pakoras etc.) and the entertainment may consist of dancing to cassettes of bhangra music rather than of organised party games. Incidentally, as Baumann (an ethnomusicologist) pointed out, this music is not so much part of earlier rural Punjabi tradition as a post-migration fusion of musical styles (1992: 108).

Less immediately apparent as a divergence from Anglo-European custom is the varying importance accorded to particular years for celebration (Baumann 1992: 108) and the gender factor. In many South Asian families the first birthday is celebrated on a particularly impressive scale. In some families, too, it appears that boys' birthdays merit more prominence and expenditure than girls'. This is what underlies one Sikh woman writer's exhortation that 'the celebration of a girl's birthday should be on the same scale as that of a boy's birthday' (Kaur-Singh 1994: 156).

Children in South Asian families also learn from experience that if a close relative has died recently there may well be no birthday celebrations (see Barratt 1994a: 8).

Cutting into the cake

The birthday cake – both how it is dealt with and what it consists of – provides a metaphor for the complex processes of cultural fusion and discrimination that are in progress. A glance at two books of pictures and accompanying text for five to seven year olds immediately shows up culturally divergent ways of sharing out the cake. Bailey has a cake being cut and served out to children seated around a table (1989: 20). Barratt, on the other hand, shows Sana, a Muslim girl, feeding her dad with some of the birthday cake, after her mum has fed her a piece of it (1994: 22).

Here is what Ruth, a ten year-old English Roman Catholic girl described, when I asked her to tell me more about people from 'other religions'.

My friend across the road . . . when it was her birthday, we went to her birthday, me and my sisters. First of all they cut the cake – they cut a small piece off and the mum gives her some cake and gives her a hug. She holds it in her hands and puts it in her [i.e. the daughter's] mouth, and then her dad does it and then her sister done it. Then they just gave out the rest of the cake to us.

Guests at similar birthday parties – and at some South Asian wedding receptions – will be able to picture the mother, followed by jostling, joking relatives, each trying laughingly to post a chunk of sponge cake into the birthday girl's mouth. As for the cake's composition: less evident to the outsider is the dilemma that a British birthday cake's usual recipe poses for those Sikhs and Hindus (and others) who are strictly vegetarian. Whereas all present can share *mithai* (the sweetmeats – made of milk, sugar, chickpea flour and other vegetarian ingredients – that have traditionally been distributed on festive occasions) the eggs in cakes can present a problem. Sikh and Hindu children talk about 'eggless cake', and about how some relatives avoid eating cake because they are vegetarian. (Children's descriptions of the birthdays of 'Babas' [spiritual teachers] also centred on eggless birthday cakes; Nesbitt 1995a expands on this.) The provision of eggless cakes shows concern not to offend anyone's scruples.

Yet, despite this difficulty, both children and adults clearly see a cake as central to appropriate birthday celebrations. It symbolises not only birthdays but also 'Englishness'. To quote a nine year-old Sikh lad:

We just celebrate like an English person, because that's more kind of celebrated, because in an Indian way, you don't have cake.

Blowing out candles has become unquestioned practice, alien as extinguishing – rather than lighting – candles is to traditional understandings of auspicious events.

Birthdays, diversity and the teacher

It is usually at school or, earlier, at a pre-school nursery, that children and their parents start to feel the pressure to conform by having a birthday party and inviting some or all of their class. There is pressure too for those in whose families birthday parties have featured in previous generations. As the writer of a BBC webpage on parenting acknowledges; regarding children of four to seven years old, 'You may feel the pressure to "go one better" than the several generous birthday bashes your daughter has attended through the year' (BBC 2003a: 1). Those pupils whose parents' beliefs (or poverty) make the prospect of having a party untenable may be acutely sensitive to the whole subject.

What does 'treating them all the same' (in the socially inclusive sense of affirming every family and respecting every individual's experience) require? Careful primary school teachers will have tried to check with parents whether they have reservations about birthdays. In any case, good practice benefits from communications of this sort with parents. It also means avoiding making assumptions that because a parent has a particular religious allegiance (e.g. Jehovah's Witness) the children will definitely not be allowed to participate in birthday celebrations. Conversation with parents leads to further opportunities for deepening knowledge of children's out-of-school experience.

The teacher may (if he or she shows interest) be invited to a family's celebration of birthday or name day, for example, by attending Sunday morning liturgy in the Orthodox church with a child's family. Alert teachers will be wary of statements that imply that all families do (or should) recognise birthdays. There may be occasions for introducing pupils to alternative viewpoints on the subject of birthdays.

Religious Education offers one context for referring (for example) to the story of Pharaoh's dream in the biblical book of Genesis (40: 20–22) which has contributed to the refusal of Jehovah's Witnesses (and the reluctance in the past of many Jews) to look favourably on birthdays (Miller and Widener 2003; McCann 2003). The teachers' concern with 'special occasions' as a link for introducing topics in religious education need not commence with the assumption that everyone observes birthdays.

Awareness of the need to widen pupils' appreciation of diversity can influence the selection of reading material. To books that reinforce images of the classic British birthday party (e.g. Bailey 1989) less stereotypical titles can be added. One such is Beryl Dhanjal's excellently non-stereotypical *Sarah's Birthday Surprise* (1987), a bilingual Punjabi–English picture book about a Sikh family going to the zoo and adopting an elephant. One play for young children, *Birthday Surprise*, inches towards inclusiveness by mentioning Jaswinder (a girl with a Sikh name) in the text and by featuring two children of African and Asian appearance respectively in its illustrations (Donaldson 1994). Is this the extent to which inclusive texts should go? Would focus on a (UK minority) style of birthday party widen horizons or foster stereotypes of difference? Are these questions only for schools with culturally diverse intakes; are they less – or more – compelling for 'monocultural' schools?

Reflection on the range of attitude and experience presented above gives cause for further reflection on the role of the school (children's teachers, their peers, their experience in collective worship and circle time and the displays on the walls) in both (mis)representing and precipitating cultural transformations. Families' attitudes to birthdays, and observance of them, are just one index of a cultural diversity and of continuing changes that escape general notice.

Young Hindus and Vegetarianism

Reducing difference to 'religion'

Stereotyping different communities involves making assumptions that (all) members behave in a certain way. It is easy to assume that there is a strong correlation between a particular religion or culture and particular preferences and practices. Related to this is a tendency to explain some behaviour in terms of a community's culture or religion, without considering the possible interplay of other factors, or that the same decisive influences may be at work in society as a whole. For example, Sikhs are sometimes stereotyped as being marked by the 'five Ks', and Muslim girls as wearing a headscarf and (in some cases) as either repressed and submissive or – another reading – as needlessly confrontational (Henley 2003). The present chapter will concentrate in detail on Hindus and the frequently assumed corollary of vegetarianism. The complexities that are unravelled are intended as a signal to expect similar fluidity, nuancing and surprise in the Sikh, Muslim, Jewish and every other 'ethnic' or 'religious' constituency. Findings from field studies can help us not to over-simplify the factors that are involved in behaviour. The data can challenge any tendency to reduce behaviour to a family's 'religion', 'culture' or ethnicity.

Ethnography reveals multiple slippages between the preacher's (and the religious education text book's) norm and individuals' actual practice. Sticking with the theme of diet (practice and exhortation), Scholefield's observations in a Jewish secondary school in London include the place of McDonald's alongside the bagel in Jewish pupils' identity formation (2004). Or, to return to the experiences of Muslim pupils, teachers and children alike can learn from a narrative – intended for 'early years' readers – which helps them to understand that a non-vegetarian Muslim girl might declare herself 'vegetarian' in school, not because she was lying but because the canteen did not serve *halal* food (Ward 2001).

Of course, vegetarianism and Hinduism are frequently linked in both popular and academic discourse. We hear (or say) that '(All) Hindus are vegetarian'. Some Hindus state that 'Hindus should be vegetarian', some religious education materials suggest that they are, and when a Hindu happens to abstain from meat someone may explain that 'He/she is a vegetarian because he/she is a Hindu'.

In fact a longitudinal study of young Hindus in Coventry disclosed the far more complex patterns of continuity and change, and of both convergence and divergence between aspiration, rhetoric and dietary practice. The multiple factors involved include those that are neither underpinned by characteristically Hindu religious tradition nor specific to the Hindu community. After all, like their peers, Hindus too watch mainstream television and join in debates in school. At the same time, fieldwork provides ample basis for understanding the origins of widespread assumptions of community-specific difference, just as exploration of birthdays can be used to provide arguments for emphasising their importance for the majority of the population as well as for challenging generalisations.

In what follows, a brief reference to studies of vegetarianism and some Hindu statements about dietary norms, preface the reporting of the Coventry findings. As will become clear, Hindus' dietary attitudes and practices constitute a spectrum and there is no clear-cut vegetarian/non-vegetarian divide, whether one looks at individuals' lives diachronically or at communities more synchronically. The complex picture includes variations in diet on certain days (see the section on *vrat* below), so explaining why a pupil may say in school, 'Yes, I eat meat, but not today', or – as we shall see – why a distressed sixth former requested to withdraw from a dissection in her biology class.

The Hindu focus of this chapter illustrates a considerable dietary diversity, which could equally have been illustrated by, for example, Jewish or Muslim pupils' patterns of principle, avoidance and compromise and expectation of future change.

Vegetarianism: conversion or lifelong practice?

The data which follow suggest that the linked assumptions that (a) Hindus are vegetarian, that (b) this practice is life-long, and (c) that it is the result of tradition and does not involve 'reflection' or 'conversion' are misleadingly simple. Hindus' marginalisation – as far as studies of vegetarianism in predominantly western societies have been concerned – is symptomatic of a more pervasive inadequate conceptualisation of cultures as reified, homogeneous, discrete and static (Jackson 1997). Hindus too reflect and 'convert', and these processes often get well underway during their school days.

Yet, when introducing their survey of the motivation to be vegetarian 'in western cultures', Beardsworth and Keil distinguished sharply between 'life-long practitioners' and 'converts' whose 'dietary practices have been established as a result of more or less explicit processes of reflection' (1992: 253). Two decades earlier, when Dwyer and others studied '100 young adults who had converted to vegetarianism after adolescence', they distinguished between 'joiners', whose vegetarianism was associated with membership of a relevant group or network, and 'loners' whose vegetarianism was more individualistic. The 'joiners', however, did not include members of 'ethnic minorities in which *some form of vegetarianism was an element of customary or religious practice* [my italics] since the primary concern of the study was to examine the experiences of respondents who had undergone a process of *reflection* and *conversion*' [my italics] (1974: 261).

Twigg argues, in the case of western vegetarians, that vegetarianism is associated with such ideas as 'wholeness' and with 'the ethical and utopian wing of socialism' and 'renewal' (1979). For western vegetarians 'the change to the vegetarian diet becomes a daily reiteration of commitment to these values of reform and a freeing of the self from bonds of accepting tradition' (1979: 29). On this understanding, the vegetarianism of UK Hindus from families of South Asian background is, by contrast with westerners, an acceptance of the bonds of tradition rather than a chosen assertion of freedom.

What Hindu spokespeople say

Although some books presenting the Hindu tradition mention that many Hindus are non-vegetarian (Brockington 1981: 3; Kanitkar and Cole 1995: 57) the very fact that vegetarianism is consistently mentioned – which is not the case with accounts of, for example, Christianity – contributes to an impression that vegetarianism is integral to Hinduism, or at least that it is an issue. Consistently with the assumptions about Hindus that are discernible in literature on 'western' vegetarianism, some works presenting the Hindu tradition give a cumulative impression that the majority of Hindus are vegetarian, or at least that vegetarianism is expected of and approved by Hindus, and that this state of affairs is consistent with central Hindu 'beliefs'. Thus Werner Menski points out that Hindu belief in rebirth and reincarnation has implications for dietary rules (1996). Similarly Hemant Kanitkar (1991: 108) and Sugirtharajah (1997: 42) relate vegetarianism to the concept of *ahimsa* (non-violence), which has 'ethical and ecological implications'.

Hindu religious teachers writing in English are unequivocal about vegetarianism as essential to their religious tradition. To take a single example:

Hindus teach vegetarianism as a way to live with a minimum of hurt to other beings, for to consume meat, fish, fowl or eggs is to participate indirectly in acts of cruelty and violence against the animal kingdom. (Subramuniyaswami 1993: 201)

Indeed, the writings and oral teachings of other Hindu *sampradayas* (movements following a succession of gurus) in Britain emphasise vegetarianism. For example, the International Society of Krishna Consciousness (ISKCON) requires this of devotees, argues the case and produces books of recipes (e.g. Adiraja dasa 1984). Abstinence from meat is the first of the five primary vows taken by lay initiates into the 'Swaminarayan religion', and vegetarianism is defended on the grounds that it avoids killing, promotes a state of mind conducive to right conduct and is good for health (Williams 1984: 136ff). If one looks at the South Indian 'god-man', Sathya Sai Baba, and his disciples, at the Pushtimargis (a Gujarati devotional grouping) or at the Arya Samaj (a group which began as a late nineteenth-century reform movement) one encounters the same message.

Longitudinal study findings

The 22 young people (10 men and 12 women) whose experience is the basis for the present chapter, participated over nine years in a longitudinal ethnographic study in Coventry of young British Hindus' perceptions of their religious tradition. When interviewed each was initially aged between eight and 13 years, and the last three interviews took place when they ranged in age from 16 to 23. Eight of the young people were from Punjabi families, 14 were Gujarati, and a range of *jatis* (castes), including Brahmins and – in Indian terms – the much 'lower' Scheduled Castes, was represented. (For the reader who is interested in possible connections between individuals' *jati* and their diet, Nesbitt [1999] provides the caste identification of each of the young people quoted in this chapter.) Six of the young people were still studying at school, 12 had moved on to university and four were already in full-time paid employment. In both phases of the longitudinal study all were interviewed in depth on many areas of experience and the subject of diet often came to the fore.

As a 12 year-old, one Gujarati had articulated the centrality of food when she said:

If you're Hindu being religious or not shows in your food, what you cook, not in [not] cutting your hair.

In other words, in her experience diet was as decisive a marker of Hindu identity as maintaining uncut hair (*kesh*) was of Sikh identity. Similarly, in order to illustrate what she meant by calling her (Pushtimargi) grandmother 'very religious', she outlined not ritual observance but her discipline in maintaining the purity of her food:

She doesn't let anybody eat on her plate, she doesn't let anybody touch her plate . . . whether she eats [her food] before us or not, she takes it out of the pan and keeps it separate from ours.

What she is describing is the implications of avoiding eating food which is *jutha* (i.e. rendered impure through contact with what another uses in eating).

From this first phase of the research, diet emerged as salient in children's understanding of Hindu tradition. Vegetarianism was stressed in the supplementary classes which some attended, such as one run by ISKCON (see p. 000). In the home, children became familiar with distinctively Hindu practice e.g. a Punjabi girl emulating her mother's fasting (*vrat*) on the October/November day of Karva Chauth, when wives fast for their husbands' welfare in the year ahead (see Jackson and Nesbitt 1993: 57–73).

As children, many of the young people had mentioned the consumption of meat as what they 'would notice most in a non-Hindu home'. Even more of them had said that beef should be avoided; and some condemned the killing of animals for food, referring to the cruelty of killing animals and the possibly determining effect on a person's future incarnation. Nevertheless many of the children and their immediate relatives ate meat. The young people's actual dietary practice ranged from frequent consumption of meats other than beef to total avoidance of meat, fish and anything which might contain egg or animal fat. The 12 year-old girl quoted above (who herself ate meat outside the house) was fully aware of the strict 'Vaishnav' practice of her family. As Pushtimargis – followers of (literally) 'the way of grace' – they were devotees of Krishna, and referred to themselves simply as 'Vaishnav', i.e. devotees of Vishnu, the form of God of which Krishna was an *avatar* or incarnation. Pushtimargi discipline also excluded such pungent or reddish coloured items as onion, garlic, carrots and red water-melon.

What was also evident was that periodically, at least, some non-vegetarians – in almost all the young Hindus' families – would abstain from all non-vegetarian food and all were aware of family members who periodically observed further restrictions (for example, no grain, no acidic foods such as tomatoes or no salt). This was to satisfy the requirements of a *vrat* (a vow involving abstention from particular foods).

Continuities: the prominence of vegetarianism

When interviewed as young adults (in their final years at school or after leaving school), the 'Hindu children' again made frequent reference to vegetarianism as a practice with which they were familiar. In many cases they were currently, had once been, or intended to become, vegetarian, and they all knew Hindus who were strictly observant. They linked this variously with the association of the gods (especially Krishna) with animals (popular iconography shows him with a white cow and playing his flute); with being a Brahmin (i.e. a member of the priestly caste); with Morari Bapu, a famous performer-cum-preacher (see Nesbitt 1999b); and with the Bhagavad Gita (the much loved text of Krishna's battlefield 'sermon').

The young Hindus distinguished clearly between different degrees of vegetarianism, whether or not they were vegetarian themselves. One, for example, ate fish but not meat. Many took for granted a correlation between the strictness of a Hindu's diet and how religious that person was. In this regard eggs were singled out: thus a young Gujarati man commented on the inconsistency of his (Pushtimargi) family who 'say they are more religious' when in fact 'they eat eggs. If my gran was alive and she knew that they ate eggs, all hell would break loose.'

Indeed, those who had contact with *sampradayas* were aware of the stringent dietary code of, for example, a Swaminarayan aunt who was 'very, very strict: she doesn't eat onions, she doesn't eat garlic' and of a Pushtimargi grandmother:

> We wouldn't bring [meat] in the house, no eggs in the house . . . If I went wholly religious like my gran is, carrots, onions, garlic, they'd all be out of the door.

Beef

At each phase of the research the young Hindus distinguished most consistently between beef and all other meat. Respect for the cow – and so avoidance of beef – figured prominently. Whether or not they were vegetarian, or thought positively of vegetarianism, they all linked their religion with avoiding beef and adhered to this prohibition more or less assiduously themselves. Where they differed from each other was in how vague or certain they were of the reasons and in how strongly they felt about the issue. Comments ranged from 'something to do with religion' to expressions of affection and respect for the cow as one's 'second mother':

> The cow is treated as a holy animal in the Hindu religion. The reason for this is . . . seeing that the cow provides milk to children it is seen as being the second mother, Gaumata [literally 'cow-mother'] . . . so eating beef is like killing your own mother. (Punjabi man)

The strength of some speakers' feelings was unmistakable in reporting instances where their sentiments had been affronted. This was usually at school – one 20 year-old recalled:

> We had a cow's eye in one of our lectures and were told to dissect it. I wouldn't do that because . . . I believe that a cow for us is a mother and I wouldn't even dream of it.

Since the cow is sacred, a Punjabi woman's had felt upset by hearing 'you silly cow' used as an insult. A Gujarati woman remembered an incident when:

> I had a black eye . . . and then our year head said, 'Oh put a bit of steak on it and she'll be OK'.

Only two of the young people mentioned eating beef themselves, notwithstanding Gillespie's observation that 'many youngsters transgress religious taboos in consuming "fast" foods, Hindus by eating beef-burgers . . . ' (1995: 202). Another said that his parents ate beef but that he avoided beef because of the offence it would cause to his Sikh friends. (Many non-vegetarian Sikhs avoid beef, although this is not a specifically religious taboo for Sikhs.)

Periodic fasting

Those who ate meat also accepted the practice of abstaining from it at certain times. These were times when they were observing a *vrat* or religious vow which involved refraining from either all or certain foods for a specified period. One explained a *vrat* as:

> any sort of *sadhana* [spiritual exercise] that you undertake as your personal thing for God [although] most people do some sort of fasting . . . because that's what people find easiest to accomplish.

Observance included weekly *vrats* (Monday, Tuesday, Saturday were most often mentioned) and the annual *vrats* of Jaya Parvati (among Gujaratis) and Karva Chauth (among Punjabis). The Punjabis spoke of abstinence on a particular day of the week and associated Tuesday fasting with the goddess [Mata]:

> Tuesdays is one which springs to mind, because all of us do not eat meat and eggs on a Tuesday. It is associated with the Mata, the day when holy offerings are given to Mata.

One young Gujarati woman spoke of avoiding meat for a period of time both following her grandmother's death and coinciding with the lunar month of Shravan (i.e. roughly August).

> After someone dies in the family we have to do vegetarian for five weeks after her death – no meat, fish or anything like that. And so because it was almost

Shravan anyway so we decided we'd keep strict vegetarian diet for that month
and [Dad] read the Ramayan [*Ramayana*] that month.

Like the non-observance of birthdays, mentioned in chapter 2, abstention from meat for a period after a relative's death is a widespread practice
(Firth 1997). The young Hindus' familiarity with these periodic restrictions emerged prominently as a continuity with the earlier data. (Readers
interested in pursuing the subject of *vrat* further should read McGee
1991.)

However, while familiarity with the phenomenon of *vrat* was general,
young Hindus' opinion about its value differed. One young Gujarati man
understood fasting as a discipline prescribed by Brahmin astrologers to
offset malign planetary influence, from Shani (Saturn) for example.
Others readily observed regular *vrats* in order to precipitate a favourable
outcome. Thus one 17 year-old, desperate to cure his skin disorder, will-
ingly fasted on Thursdays on the orders of 'some monk or something'; and
a Punjabi brother and sister elected to keep the very exacting 'Ganesh
Chauth *vrat*' in the belief that it would help them succeed academically.

Although the young people engaged in periodic abstinence as a means
of improving their lot, some at least also enjoyed the associated practice.
A 16 year-old Gujarati girl had been observing Jaya Parvati (a summer-
time *vrat* involving all night vigil – usually spent watching Bollywood
movies) for four years and thought it was 'wonderful'. A young Punjabi
woman 'really liked' keeping the Karva Chauth *vrat*

because it's where you see all the ladies come in the temple dressed up as brides
again. It's really good to see them – they all look so pretty.

Over and above the colour and excitement she was

glad because I don't think that any other religions have things like that . . . It does
feel fulfilling in that sense that you deprive yourself of something in order to gain
something else . . . It's a way of remembering God as well.

Their acceptance of these periodic restrictions resulted, not so much
from ethical or health-oriented considerations, but from a feeling that the
traditional requirements would sooner or later be efficacious.

Some of the young people were observing more *vrats* than they had
nine years previously, others were observing fewer. One Gujarati man
had ceased to fast on Saturdays because his grandfather was no longer
there ('if you've got someone to do it with it's easier'). A 20 year-old
Gujarati woman's reduction in the number of *vrats* that she observed
accorded with her critical stance and with Sathya Sai Baba's lack of
emphasis on the practice. A 20 year-old Gujarati man too was critical,
pointing to the fact that 'if you are starving . . . and all you think about is
food' this defeats the object of 'giving to God'. In his view one's mental

discipline must conform with outward practice: otherwise this would be counter-productive.

Interestingly, parental opposition was high among discouragements to keeping *vrats*. Parents were opposed because of the potential detriment to health and education. A Punjabi brother and sister described the obstacles to keeping the Ganesh Chauth *vrat*, which included the sister's uncomprehending biology teacher's lack of sympathy for her refusal to dissect a rat during the *vrat* (since contact with animal flesh is to be avoided on *vrat* days), and their father's annoyance at her needlessly jeopardising her studies by missing her meals.

Like their parents, some of the young people perceived a link between fasting and poor health, and this predisposed some of them to question the advisability of the practice. It was parents' anxieties that also led to some who had become vegetarian returning to being non-vegetarian. Others may have been influenced by peer pressure to eat meat. That is what one 17 year-old's comment on the difficulties of observing his Saturday *vrat* suggest:

> I can't eat meat on a Saturday and it's really hard . . . if I go with my friends somewhere like to town or to a cinema, and they'll go down McDonald's and I can't eat.

Becoming vegetarian or non-vegetarian

During the nine years that separated my interviews, the young people's dietary attitudes and behaviour had been fluid, with both temporary and more long-term changes – both to being vegetarian and back to eating meat – as well as with regard to the observance of *vrats*. Where change had occurred – in some individuals' cases in both directions – it was among those who had been brought up initially as non-vegetarians.

Also clear is the diversity of trends from one generation to the next in the family: while some maintained a similar diet to their parents, whether this was vegetarian or non-vegetarian, other young people ate meat whereas parents did not. The reverse also occurred.

Vegetarian relatives were often mentioned, but only a few young people suggested that their own switch to vegetarianism had been a direct result of a relative's influence. At least as decisive was contact with spiritual teachers (*sants, babas,* gurus and *matas*). The 17 year-old Gujarati was the sole example of someone who had given up meat temporarily for health reasons. However, as the advice, which was intended to cure his embarrassing skin disorder, had come from a 'holy man', one could also see this case as evidence of the influence exercised by spiritual leaders over some young people.

Long-term contact with a *sampradaya* (guru-led movement) probably played a part as well in encouraging non-vegetarians to become vegetarian (Nesbitt 1999). One Punjabi woman's grandparents were Radhasoamis (see Juergensmeyer 1982) and, in line with the Radhasoami emphasis on vegetarianism, they had told her 'You're eating a chicken so you'll come back as a chicken'. Here belief in karma and rebirth is intrinsic to dietary restraint. In the case of a Gujarati woman her family's Pushtimarg principles, as consistently practised by her beloved grandmother, are likely to have contributed.

However, when questioned, the young woman suggested a more complex range of factors:

> All the grandkids made a pact one Christmas to say, 'That's it. We're all giving up meat'. [I] just sort of sat there and said 'I don't like the taste of this any more' . . . I think it was more of a dare . . . a new year' resolution . . . and then the morals came into it as we grew up . . . we shouldn't eat it because it's not in our religion and it's not fair on the animals.

It was this last issue of animal rights that had made one Punjabi woman decide to give up meat. She was vegetarian for a year 'having gone through sixth form in my school where we were given a lot of information on vivisection and animal rights and I just made the choice to be a vegetarian'. Her case was unusual for, although the issue was keenly supported by those who had always been vegetarian, it had not caused other non-vegetarians to abandon meat-eating. Some felt sorry for animals, and said they would not kill them, but nevertheless ate meat. Even among the lifelong vegetarians a 20 year-old Gujarati woman's passionate concern for animal rights was unusual:

> Animals have got as many rights as we have . . . I love animals and I think they're one thing that help us get things into perspective in life . . . If humans like to see themselves as superior . . . then with that comes a duty to protect anything under the food chain as well.

None was an activist – nor did they speak out about the factory farming of cattle for milk or the socio-economic injustice of western animal-centred food production (Karian 1994).

So too with spirituality. Both vegetarians and non-vegetarians linked vegetarianism with spirituality, but not as a reason for having actually given up meat. Indeed, the Gujarati woman who spoke up most eloquently for animals was alone in articulating a strong linkage between spiritual practice and what people ate and when. Her upbringing in a family of devotees of Sathya Sai Baba, which involved weekly Education in Human Values at the supplementary classes (Bal Vikas), had taught her about *ahimsa* (non-violence). She knew that there was support in the Bhagavad Gita for the relationship between a food's *guna* (quality) and its consumer's disposition. The ancient certainty that meat is *tamasik* ('dark'), and so induces sluggishness, resonated with her male counterpart's view – based on his fitness training – that 'heavy meats like steaks, lamb's liver slow the brain down because there is so much cholesterol entering the body'.

Clearly young British Hindus differ in their outlook and their lifestyle decisions, as do their parents, but patterns do emerge. Regarding diet the young people were used to pragmatic compromise out of respect for those whose dietary principles were stricter than their own. So several meet-eaters mentioned being vegetarian at home.

In addition to accepting that meat could only be eaten in certain company and contexts, some assumed that they would not be eating meat at every stage of their lives. Several expressed their expectations of personal change at a later stage in their lives, and this included diet, by becoming vegetarian in the future. One Punjabi woman had observed close relatives giving up meat:

> They suddenly get to a stage where they just feel repulsed by eating meat, and hopefully I'll get to that day soon.

This anticipation of change in due course included the expectation of observing more *vrats*. At the same time a number of young people affirmed that it was one's mental attitude to diet – and to periodic fasting – which was of more significance than the behaviour which one espoused.

Hierarchies of food

One area of both resemblance and difference between contemporary Hindu vegetarianism and westerners' vegetarianism is the widespread perception of a hierarchy of food (see Twigg 1979: 17) plotted in the lists below. In each list the foods at the top are the first to be given up whereas those lower down are avoided by only the 'most strict' vegetarians who subsist on the foods in the bottom line.

A. Gradation of food evident among young Hindus
   beef
   red meat
   chicken
   fish
   eggs
   onions, garlic, reddish foods/foods proscribed for individual *vrats*
   vegetables, grains, fruits and dairy produce

B. Gradation of food evident among westerners
   beef
   red meat

chicken
fish
eggs
dairy produce
vegetables, grains, fruits

Whereas the Hindu hierarchy is based on such principles as the sacredness of the cow – and of all living creatures – and the principle of *ahimsa*, as well as the division of foods according to their *guna* (quality) and beliefs about purity and pollution (especially evident among my interviewees from Pushtimargi families), the western sequence is a reversal of a traditional European ranking of foods according to their assumed nutritional value. This reversal is traditionally given expression in the Orthodox church by the progressive fasting during Lent and Holy Week, of which some pupils, for example many Greek Cypriots, will be aware. In western vegetarian thinking this is a hierarchy of the violence involved. Thus for vegans, unlike Indian vegetarians, dairy produce along with honey and the wearing of silk and leather are taboo because of the cruelty involved in obtaining them. It was only during the 1990s that beef conspicuously entered a separate category for the British public, and this was not out of reverence for the cow but because of fears of contracting the fatal Variant Creutzfeldt-Jakob disease as a result of eating the meat of cattle affected by Bovine Spongiform Encephalopathy (BSE).

Being Hindu and being vegetarian: 'menu pluralism'

What is clear is that any easy correlation between being Hindu or being vegetarian is misleading, and that the influences and decisions expressed by individuals' attitudes and practice are complex. They overlap with those of their non-Hindu peers, and cannot be summed up as a matter of simply conversion, ideology, fashion or tradition.

The young people did not feel bound to be vegetarian – or to appear to be – nor did they express a sense of guilt at falling short. Stricter dietary discipline is simply a future possibility, an accepted feature of other Hindus' behaviour, which both they and outsiders regard as markers of their community's identity. Possibly Hindu assumptions about life being a series of stages *(ashramas)* for which different lifestyles are appropriate are finding expression here.

Although Brahmin caste and vegetarian diet were occasionally linked by the young people there was no evidence at all for the association of changing one's diet with upward caste mobility. This phenomenon among Hindus in India was described by Srinivas, who gave it the name Sanskritisation (1967). Sansktitisation referred to the fact that, as being vegetarian was popularly associated with being of a higher (Brahmin) caste, families would conspicuously adopt this food behaviour in order to lose the stigma of being identified with their own lower caste. Nor does the Coventry data strongly support Gillespie's findings of young people tending to profess dislike for Indian food and to eat non-vegetarian western fast foods.

Several young Hindus differentiated between their reasons for being vegetarian, which they saw combining and interacting in their own case. One Gujarati man understood Hindus' vegetarianism as a corollary of belief in God (entailing a belief 'in kindness to all creatures'). This he distinguished from 'being vegetarian simply because it's a phase or a fad [with] no philosophical content'. Thus, like Twigg and other western writers quoted earlier, he contrasts two supposedly incompatible, cultur-ally specific motivations. Where he differs is on whether it is the Hindus' or the westerners' stance that has a committed philosophical or moral content.

The observance of *vrats* by some of the young Hindus fits Roger Ballard's 'kismetic' dimension of religion. In other words *vrats* are exam-ples of 'behavioural strategies which are used to . . . turn adversity in its tracks' (1999: 17). On the other hand, the more continuous practice of vegetarianism fits his 'panthic' or 'dharmic' categories to the extent that it is a response to 'the teachings of a specific spiritual master' (1999: 15) or is understood to be intrinsic to 'the divinely established set of rules to which all activities . . . should ideally conform' (1999: 21).

Although family belief in the sanctity of the cow, or exposure to such *sants* as Morari Bapu, is specific to the young Hindus, both school curricula and the media circulate information regarding health, ethics and cultural practice and no group's behaviour should be looked at as isolated from the rest. As Dwyer *et al.* pointed out:

> In more rapidly changing societies . . . the exercise of choice between menus becomes a possibility, in that individuals may be in a position to reflect and actively to choose between principles of selection. In this sense, such societies are characterised by menu pluralism. (1974: 288)

The Coventry research suggests that young Hindus are caught in the interplay of influences at work on society as a whole. So, young Hindus' attitudes towards vegetarianism may combine a traditional family norm with the contemporary western concern with animal rights and the language of 'conversion' may be as appropriate to Hindus who become vegetarian as to any other vegetarians. Motivations such as health and animal rights are further reinforced for some young Hindus by their aware-ness of the family's, *sampradaya*'s, or wider Hindu community's vegetarian principles and practice.

Given that young Hindus in Britain are exposed to the same influences at school and through the media as their peers, and the fact that aspects of Hindu tradition are widely circulated via religious education in schools and the media, there is little justification for examining changes in the dietary behaviour of one group in isolation from another. Stereotyping is definitely out. At the same time, as Raj suggests, food does provide a medium and a metaphor for exploring the flexibility in young people's understanding of Hinduism (2003: 101).

Tendencies to equate 'religion' or 'faith tradition' with particular behaviour homogenise the way in which we perceive communities. Chapter 3 continues the drive against stereotyping by sharing data from research among families who identified themselves as Christian.

The Diversity of Experience within a Faith Tradition

Researching 'Christian children'

It is easy to assume that families from a particular faith have more in common than may be the case – that they all celebrate major festivals on the same day, for example, or in the same way, or that they have similar expectations of life after death. This chapter challenges tendencies to regard Christians as more homogeneous than they are.

In most schools in Europe and North America more pupils and members of staff identify themselves – to some extent at least – with Christianity than with any other faith. Despite widespread variations, overall more of those who are actively involved in a faith community are Christian than Muslim, Hindu, Jewish or of any other faith. But the diversity of that Christian belonging remains largely invisible, apart from the historic sectarian divides, for example between Protestants and Roman Catholics in Northern Ireland.

The ethnographic basis of the present chapter is a study of the lives of 50 young people aged eight to 13 from Coventry, who identified themselves as 'Christian' (Jackson and Nesbitt 1992; Nesbitt 1993a, b; Nesbitt and Jackson 1992). (Christians' criteria of what makes someone a Christian vary, and include being born to Christian parents, being baptised or 'accepting Christ as your Lord and Saviour': the young people's views reflected this spectrum.)

All these young people regularly attended worship or youth activities related to a church, and they were associated with one or more of twelve denominations, most of which were listed by the local Council of Churches. Had the time available for the research included, additionally, children who did not participate regularly in a church-based activity, or whose church was regarded as heterodox by churches within the Council of Churches for Britain and Ireland, the resultant picture would have been even more diverse.

The research involved participant observation during collective worship in schools, and during church services, Sunday school classes (by various names) and other youth groups. Semi-structured interviews were conducted with at least one church leader or member whose concern was passing on the Christian faith to young people. Fifty young people were interviewed in their schools and of these 13 were interviewed subsequently on more than one occasion in their homes. The open-ended nature of many questions allowed each child to share his or her experiences, perceptions and opinions in detail.

Differences in religious socialisation (nurture), belief and ritual will be set in the context of the young people's ethnic and denominational diversity, and the relationship of these will be clarified. The issues that emerge include language, the calendar, baptism and the role of the family's country of origin in the young people's religious heritage and in the values and assumptions that they encounter.

Denominational diversity

Children who were selected for interview came from the following denominations: Roman Catholic, Church of England, Methodist, Baptist, United Reformed Church (URC), Salvation Army, Pentecostal (including Elim, the First United Church of Jesus Christ Apostolic and the New Testament Church of God), a New Church (the Coventry Christian Fellowship, an independent congregation – see Stringer 1999: 138–67 for a similar congregation), Greek Orthodox, and Ukrainian Catholic (a Uniate or Eastern Rite church i.e. a church which acknowledges the Pope's primacy but which adheres to Orthodox practice in most aspects such as its liturgy and calendar). The Church of England encompasses a spectrum of 'churchmanship' – of differing theological emphasis and of style in worship, and the interviewees reflected this (see Parsons 1989). In practice, it transpired that many children were associated with more than one denomination, or strand within it. Examples included Ukrainian Catholics attending Roman Catholic schools, the Greek Orthodox, Salvation Army and URC children attending a Church of England Aided secondary school; a Roman Catholic girl who went to a Protestant-led youth group which met in a Baptist church, the Punjabi Christians whose families attended both the local Church of England and Baptist church, and so on.

Ethnic diversity

With the exception of a Ukrainian girl, all the young Christians saw themselves as British, and most as English. Individual interviewees described themselves as also being Jamaican, Greek Cypriot, Ukrainian, Punjabi, Spanish, Greek and Pakistani, and these ethnic markers are included with the anonymised quotations. Two described themselves as not only Christian but also Jewish (their mothers were Jewish converts to Christianity), and one each as half-Spanish, -Greek, -Croatian and half-Chinese.

In some cases ethnicity and denomination were closely related. In addition to the (exclusively) 'English' children in the particular Methodist, Baptist, URC, Quaker and Salvation Army congregations, most of the Church of England interviewees defined themselves as (simply) 'English' and there was a high correlation between being Irish and being Roman Catholic (see Hornsby-Smith 1986 and 1989). Similarly, all the Jamaican interviewees attended the First United Church of Jesus Christ Apostolic or the New Testament Church of God (the single largest African Caribbean denomination [Toulis 1997: 25]). All the congregation of the church of St Wolodomyr the Great, the Uniate (Eastern rite) Catholic church, are Ukrainian. Most of the congregation at the Church of the Holy Transfiguration (Greek Orthodox church) are Greek Cypriot. (The smaller number of Greeks are associated with the nearby university.) The result is that for many children the culture of home and church are mutually reinforcing. For example, both at home and in church, Ukrainian Catholics celebrate Christmas on 7 January.

However, the degree of cultural reinforcement between home, church and school varies markedly from one community to another. To take the example of the Greek Orthodox and the Ukrainian Catholics: families observe Easter and its related days in accordance with the Julian calendar which predates the Gregorian one that is used internationally as a secular calendar, as well as by the western churches. As a result, except in years when Easter day coincides according to both calendars, young Orthodox and Ukrainian Catholics' Easter holidays are out of sync with family and church celebration. The Ukrainian Catholics of the UK, moreover, like some Orthodox churches, follow this older calendar for Christmas as well (hence the date of 7 January). This means that Christmas usually falls during the first week of the school term and so limits the celebration possible. At the same time this sense of exclusion intensifies awareness of belonging to a religious minority.

Both Ukrainian and Cypriot families encourage their children to attend language classes (in Ukrainian and Greek respectively) on Saturdays (cf. Constantinides 1977: 284–6 and Kotsoni 1990 on the UK Cypriot community's language classes). In both St Wolodomyr's and the Church of the Holy Transfiguration the service (liturgy) is in what is (for the children especially) a largely inaccessible language, although the Orthodox congregation hear key parts (e.g. the Gospel reading) in English as well as the Greek language of two thousand years ago.

The degree of religious and cultural homogeneity – as between home, school and church – is greater in the Irish Catholic community, and is markedly weaker in the Punjabi Christian community. In Coventry the Irish constitute the largest ethnic minority (Census 2001 2004). Irish settlement began in the mid nineteenth century and there are now 16 Roman Catholic churches in Coventry, 19 Roman Catholic primary schools and three Roman Catholic comprehensives (secondary schools). Home, church and school share a common language, many assumptions and the same religious calendar. To take two examples: the priests are mostly Irish and St Patrick's Day, commemorating Ireland's patron saint, is celebrated in school.

By contrast with this mutual reinforcement, the 60 or so Punjabi Christian families use their mother-tongue, Punjabi, in the home, and the most senior relatives understand Urdu, but neither their churches nor their Church of England school provides tuition for their children in either language, nor are parents concerned to perpetuate them. (Only Sikh Punjabis tend to promote literacy in the language, with Muslim and Hindu Punjabis encouraging their children to learn – in the Muslim case – Arabic and Urdu and – in the Hindu case – Hindi [see Nesbitt 1995b].) Moreover, the history of Christian conversions in nineteenth- and twentieth-century Punjab has left Punjabi Christians open to worshipping in several Christian denominations: in Coventry they attend Roman Catholic, Church of England, Baptist and Pentecostal churches. In the Anglican church the sermon is usually translated into Urdu or Punjabi for the benefit of older Punjabi members of the congregation, but the dominant language is English. Only in the weekly Bible studies, which are held in relatives' homes of a weekday evening, do the children hear singing, prayer and bible reading in Punjabi and Urdu, and the sound of tabla and harmonium. (This is the portable keyboard instrument which is more widely used in the UK for Hindu and Sikh devotional music, and which was introduced to India by Christian missionaries.)

The experience of Punjabi Christians demonstrates the way in which messages of the Christian child's home, school and church may be particularly at variance on the issue of 'other faiths' (Nesbitt and Jackson 1992). For example, one evening a visiting Pakistani evangelist led the Punjabi Christian Bible study group which one interviewee and her family attended. Coming as he did from a country in which Christians suffer discrimination and sporadic violence, he proceeded to interpret many biblical passages in strongly anti-Muslim terms. By contrast the child's Church of England secondary school presented world religions sympathetically in her religious education lessons. Her class had recently visited a mosque and had completed a work sheet on Muslim worship.

Neither church nor school reinforces, understands or necessarily knows of South Asian parents' concerns, such as the arranging of appropriate marriages or about the sinfulness of visiting, or accepting *prashad* (blessed food), in the places of worship that their close relatives attend.

When they move house Punjabi parishioners may request the vicar to bless the house, and when a family member dies the vicar is expected to come to the house to lead the prayers before the cortège sets out. Thus the religious practice of the home marks a departure from the English norms of the church, whereas in the case of Greek Cypriot, Ukrainian and Irish families the relevant churches provide the underpinning for domestic religious practice.

Festivals, fasting and feasting

Chapter 4 will suggest ways in which (to varying degrees for pupils from different communities) Christmas at home and school overlap, with school reinforcing a dominant, homogenised celebration. But Easter too points up diversity, whilst maintaining a common focus upon the central message of the 'rising' or 'resurrection' of Jesus Christ, victorious over ignominious death on the cross.

For the Greek Orthodox and Ukrainian children Easter often falls in term time because the date of Orthodox (and Uniate Catholic) Easter is usually later – by one, four or five weeks – than the date of Easter by the Gregorian calendar, which follows the reckoning of the Western churches. According to the Western churches' calendar Easter Sunday falls on the first Sunday after the first full moon after 21 March. The Orthodox Easter, however, falls on the first Sunday after the first full moon after the Spring equinox as calculated by the older Julian calendar (which is currently 13 days behind the Gregorian calendar). Additionally, Orthodox Easter has to fall after the Jewish Passover.

Greek Cypriot children described the build up to Easter in the UK. On 'Great Friday' (the Friday preceding Easter day), during the evening liturgy, girls move round the wooden *epitaphios* (a covered wooden stand, decorated with flowers and holding an embroidered 'icon' of Jesus' crucified body). The *epitaphios* signifies the sepulchre in which Jesus' body was laid. The girls sprinkle petals and perfumed water on to this.

Children referred particularly to the graduated fasting during the previous weeks of Lent:

> We're not allowed to eat meat on Wednesdays and Fridays because Christ died on a Friday. When we fast 40 days before Christmas and 50 days before Easter I don't actually go straight into the fasting . . . My mum fasts right from the beginning but my brother and my sister and me, first of all we don't eat meat. The last few days I have to give up oil, milk and dairy products, because you have to have tea without milk and bread without butter, and there's not a lot you can eat.[1]

Saturday, marking the resurrection event, brought a dramatic change. To quote the same boy, during congregational worship on Saturday morning:

They bang their chairs, stamp their feet. At night we're supposed to go round the church [i.e. outside] singing 'Christos aneste', which means God has risen. They hold an icon up and go under [it].

After you come back (at about 2 a.m. from the midnight service) it's the first time you're allowed to eat meat and eggs, and we first come home and have a feast. We break open the eggs. They're hard-boiled in food colouring – red. Mum gets a big pot and lots of eggs. We eat them for weeks and weeks afterwards. We always save the hardest for competitions to see whose doesn't break. The more colouring they've got on them the harder they are.

He continued:

When we've had enough sleep (i.e. on Easter Sunday morning) there's no church and it feels strange. We go to my gran's house, all my uncle and cousins, and we have a big meal. We play cards and eat . . . mince pies. It's good because we can have milk, because we haven't been having milk or butter or anything like that.

A friend of his referred to enjoying '*flaona*', a specially baked Cypriot cheese cake. Eggs are a common motif across the churches: hard boiled and dyed (for the Greeks and Cypriots), uncooked and elaborately decorated (for the Ukrainians). A Greek Catholic boy described how at Easter in Athens:

We paint the red eggs. When it's Easter night when the bell goes at 12 o'clock at night, you just crash the eggs, not break them, you see whose will break first. Most of the times at home we come back and there's sort of lots of fireworks going off.

In the Ukrainian church (on Saturday) the priest blessed with holy water the baskets which members of the congregation had carefully prepared. Each basket contained the food for Easter breakfast – *paska* (a rich yellow bread decorated with plaited dough), butter, often studded with cloves in the shape of a cross, cottage cheese, hard boiled egg, sausage, and – most colourfully – *pysanky* (brightly decorated eggs) plus some horseradish and salt (see Ukrainian Women's Association of Canada 1987).[2]

From infancy many Ukrainian children in the UK learn how to decorate fragile, uncooked white hens' eggs with designs. Diagrams and photographs of intricately patterned eggs are readily available from the Ukrainian Association of Great Britain which has many local branches.[3] The traditional method is similar to batik. It requires beeswax, a candle, fresh white eggs, jars of liquid yellow, orange, red, green and blue colour, made by boiling crepe paper in water, and a *kistka* for each child. The *kistka* consists of a wooden, pen-like shaft to which is fixed a small piece of hollow pointed metal. First the eggs are cleaned with white vinegar or lighter fluid to remove the natural grease. Each child heats the metal tip of the *kistka* in the candle flame, plunges it into the beeswax, and proceeds to cover with molten wax those parts of the egg which are to remain white.

The egg is then lowered into the yellow dye for about five minutes. Next wax is applied to all parts of the egg that are to remain yellow, and so on with each colour in turn. Then each child holds his or her blackened, wax-coated egg close enough to the candle flame to melt off the wax and reveal the design in all its glowing colours. Children experience the suspense of seeing if their egg will crack, the delight at the brilliant colours appearing as the wax melts off, or the grief at an egg cracking or breaking (Barratt 1994b).

For 'English' Christians the traditions varied from family to family and from one congregation to another. An English URC girl reported her family's annual Easter egg hunt:

> We have clues . . . Our mum and dad do them . . . every clue we had something little. At the end we have our Easter egg.

In the local Methodist Central Hall each Easter girls distributed daffodils to the congregation as they filed up to fix daffodils in a wooden cross, which had been packed with moist oasis. This cross was then hung up on the outside wall as a reminder to passers by of Easter. The youngest children in the Sunday school decorated an Easter tree with chicks and bows. In marking Easter in this way the church is incorporating a German tradition, which was suggested one year by nationally produced Sunday school materials. Easter gardens have a longer history in the British Isles. Some of the Irish and English young people were familiar with creating a small garden in a box or bowl by planting a few Spring flowering plants (like primroses) around a small cave made from stones. In their churches were larger versions of this.

In the Roman Catholic church on Easter Saturday night, new members were baptised and candles were lit from the imposing paschal candle.

Doctrinal diversity

Culture rather than doctrine underpins many of these different practices. Much of what the young people articulated showed theological unity and also a tension between religious teaching and secular convention. All the children spoke of 'Jesus and God', and there were strong resemblances between what they had to say. For example, on the subject of Christmas, a 13 year-old Cypriot, Greek Orthodox boy explained:

> Christmas for the English Christians has changed into a time of just receiving presents and giving presents. I think it's more of a time when Christ was born.

Similarly a nine year-old English Baptist girl stressed the importance of :

> Believing Jesus was born on Christmas day (and not just to think of opening presents) and saying 'Happy Birthday, Jesus'.

At the same time differences in emphasis and understanding were also evident. These clustered around the Holy Spirit, life after death, saints, baptism and holy communion.

Holy Spirit

The charismatic movement which swept through many denominations in the twentieth century probably had much to do with individual Christians' experience of the activity of the Holy Spirit. (Here 'charismatic' refers to personal experience of the outpouring of the 'gifts of the Holy Spirit' as described in the Biblical book entitled the Acts of the Apostles, which reports Jesus' disciples' experience at the feast of Pentecost following his resurrection.) Whether young people spoke about the Holy Spirit, and in what terms, corresponded to denominational teaching that they had received and to this trans-denominational charismatic experience in which members of some congregations (including Baptists and the Church of England) had been involved. Having a personal experience of the inrush of the Holy Spirit was central to the teaching of some churches – this was true of the Pentecostal churches and the New Church. The words of a New Church 13 year-old girl conveying the joy of the experience of 'speaking in tongues' are quoted in chapter 9.

Some of the most explicit references to the Holy Spirit came from three Jamaican Pentecostal children who talked matter-of-factly about 'being filled' (see Toulis 1997: 157–61). Their use of the term 'Ghost' for 'Spirit' echoes traditional usage and the language of the seventeenth-century translation of the Bible, the Authorised Version, which their churches still use, whereas in other English-speaking denominations twentieth-century translations are generally used. One 11 year-old boy explained that, to be a Christian, 'you have to believe in being filled with the Holy Ghost'. These young people recognised that speaking and singing in tongues were evidence of 'being filled'. They knew which members of their congregations were 'filled'.

> If you watch the people, the way they worship, you can tell Jesus is there, the Holy Ghost is there. (11 year-old Jamaican Pentecostal boy)

For the majority of the young Christian interviewees the Holy Spirit (or Holy Ghost) was a hazier idea, sometimes associated with 'ghosts'. Some associated the Holy Spirit with their church's teaching on the sacraments. To quote an 11 year-old Irish Roman Catholic boy:

> Most of the sacraments have got the Holy Spirit involved. Like at baptism the

Holy Spirit comes, at communion it comes and helps you, and it's the same at confirmation.

The father of a Greek Orthodox interviewee explained:

We believe that Christ is sitting at God's right side and the Holy Spirit is on earth. It's the Holy Spirit that gives the gifts now: it's the Holy Spirit that's in the church now – in the liturgy, the holy mysteries, the bread and wine, the body and blood of Christ. It's the Holy Spirit which changes the bread and wine into the body and blood.

A nine year-old Baptist girl spoke of the Holy Spirit in neither charismatic nor sacramental language when she explained:

I don't believe in ghosts, only the Holy Ghost. He's just with you all the time, or she's with you all the time, and looks after you and gives you some advice from God.

Although the young people's churches shared a formal belief in God as Trinity, i.e. as Father, Son (Jesus Christ) and Holy Spirit, most interviewees made no reference to the Holy Spirit when they were speaking about God. Those who did so demonstrate both a diversity and a degree of cross-denominational unity on a central aspect of Christian doctrine and experience.

Saints

Belief in saints differentiated the responses of the Greek Orthodox and, to a lesser extent, the Catholics, from those of the other young people. Some Protestant interviewees could name a few saints such as the British patron saints – St George, St David, St Andrew and St Patrick – because they had learned about them in school 'assembly' or Girl Guides. Roman Catholic children spoke about a few more, but it was only the Greek Cypriot Greek Orthodox interviewees who spoke at length about saints – about their name days (see chapter 1), about how they had visited monasteries associated with particular saints and about the miracles that they continue to perform. 'They're always where their icons are,' said one boy. To quote from a 13 year-old boy:

When I was three months old I had a hole in my neck and my mum and dad prayed to this saint, Agios Xenophos, and it healed up. So they – I – celebrate his saint's day.

Life after death

On the subject of what awaits people after physical death, views were very diverse. Of the 50 Christian interviewees ten had considered reincarnation positively, although not all still held this belief (see Nesbitt 1993c). Four Roman Catholics incorporated rebirth in their belief system:

> Probably like our souls go up to heaven and then we just wait to get in. But God's making a new soul for whatever we're going to be when we come back down . . . They do it about seven times. After that their soul would rest in heaven.
> (11 year-old Irish Catholic boy)

This accommodation of afterlife in heaven and rebirth on earth was one of the ways in which some children thought through beliefs that they encountered in the family, in church, and in religious education. Purgatory, or at least the possibility of a 'second chance', fitted more easily with ideas of rebirth than did some denominations' images of quick, and permanent, transit to heaven or hell. The majority (40) envisaged what happens after death only in terms of heaven and hell: heaven is 'where you have happiness and no sadness' (eight year-old Ukrainian Catholic girl) and 'where God will be' (13 year-old Jamaican Pentecostal boy), whereas hell is where 'they're not very happy and they have to do hard work like slaves' (13 year-old English Salvation Army girl) or 'you'd be burning all the time' (13 year-old Jamaican Pentecostal boy).

Two Quaker girls' suggestions showed different approaches – one pragmatic, the other speculating about the continuity of emotion:

> Sometimes they [the deceased] go to hospital to get used. (eight year-old)

> If you've lived one emotion really strongly in your life, maybe that emotion carries on, like you love everybody and are really full of love, then the spirit of love can carry on. (14 year-old Quaker girl)

What most sharply divided the young people was the theological issue of whether a person's 'faith' or 'works' are decisive. Those who had reflected on the possibility of being born again as a baby, and most of those who thought only in terms of heaven, or of heaven and hell, related this to the behaviour of the deceased before death. However, for the young people from each of the Pentecostal churches and the New Church, as well as a 'charismatic' Evangelical Church of England congregation, the decisive criterion for admission to heaven is whether the individual has confessed the Christian faith (e.g. 'asked Jesus into their life') and prayed for forgiveness. As a 13 year-old Pakistani Pentecostal boy explained:

> Everyone goes to meet God and they get judged. If they're Christian and if they believe in God, in Jesus, they go to heaven, don't they? And if they're not, they go to hell.

Baptism

Diversity along denominational lines showed most clearly in children's accounts of baptism and holy communion (see Jackson and Nesbitt 1992).

As regards the former, differences which the young people's experience illustrated centred on infant and adult baptism. Some children emphasised the importance of individual choice.

> The reason why as a church we don't believe in children being baptised is because you're making the decision for them and there's not much point because a lot of children who are baptised as a baby change their minds entirely and they don't live by anything they've been baptised by. (13 year-old New Church girl)

Children in churches with this approach conveyed the emotional nature of baptism. An 11 year-old Baptist girl described how 'My sister got baptised when she was 14, my mum was there and she gave her a towel, and my sister cried because she was so happy'.

A 13 year-old Punjabi Church of England boy, whose relatives go to both Church of England and Baptist churches, reported strong feelings on the subject of infant baptism as opposed to believer's baptism.

> The vicar was saying something about baptism and some people got angry because he was saying no one should take a second baptism. They say they didn't understand when they were little. He said, 'Your parents were Christians', and they said, 'Children shouldn't be baptised because they don't understand it when they're small.'

For one Jamaican Pentecostal boy the need for a second baptism could be of life and death importance. He described how a dying woman, already baptised in another church, was brought from hospital to be baptised in the First United Church of Jesus Christ Apostolic 'in Jesus' name'. Baptism in the view of 'Jesus name' churches must be in the name of Jesus only (i.e. not 'in the name of the Father, the Son and the Holy Spirit' – the Trinitarian formula), as this was how baptisms reported in the New Testament were performed (e.g. Acts 19: 5).

The Orthodox and Catholic interviewees took for granted the need for 'christening' (their word for baptism), as an infant if possible:

> They can be christened at any time you want as soon as they're born. Usually they leave it till the baby's about 40 days old, so you can handle them. (13 year-old Greek Cypriot Orthodox boy)

An 11 year-old Irish Catholic boy explained that being 'christened by Father' (i.e. the priest) was the way to become Christian.

The diversity of christening/baptism events, as well as the age at which they occur, comes out clearly from the children's accounts of what actually happens. In the Pentecostal congregations, the New Church and the Baptist church 'full water immersion' was required (see Toulis 1997: 146–9 for details of procedure at a New Testament Church of God baptism). An eight year-old girl, who belonged to a New Church, admitted to being too frightened to be baptised because I don't want other people watching. All the people stand round the pool and they're all watching you. Two men push them under the water and bring them back up. All your clothes stick to you. when you come up from the water they all clap.

A nine year-old Baptist girl contrasted the solemn atmosphere of baptisms that were conducted by her minister and the 'lack of reverence' when a New Church borrowed the premises and, amid shouts of invitation, people went up to be baptised in their ordinary clothes, apparently on impulse.

A nine year-old Church of England boy described, by contrast, an infant baptism:

All their relatives and people that they want to be godfathers and godmothers stand around in a circle, and the vicar or whoever's doing it will take the baby and dip his finger in the water and put a cross on the forehead. And then each person has to make a different vow or promise and then they get a candle – the mother and father – to remind you that Jesus was a baby, and he was the light of the world. And it says on it – there's like a blue candle holder – it says, 'You can only enter the kingdom of heaven like a child.'

Not only do Christians differ on infant baptism versus believers' baptism but also on whether baptism need involve total immersion. For the most part the interviewees described total immersion only in the case of believers' baptism. However, in describing her son's baptism as an infant the mother of a Greek Cypriot Orthodox boy said:

They bring it [i.e. the font] out when you're christened. It's got a base, two handles. The right way is the way he was christened, which is all of you three times, like Jesus was – everything completely up to your hair, right down. [The priest] dips you in the water three times and out. He has a way of holding [the child's] nose. I was scared in case he drowned, and he dips him quickly in and out three times.

As in a Roman Catholic christening, the Orthodox baby too is anointed with holy oil and, in the Orthodox case, this signifies confirmation. Also three locks of the child's hair are cut by the priest.

This is an expression of gratitude from the child, who having received an abundance of blessing through the sacraments of Baptism and Confirmation and having nothing to give God in return, offers part of its hair, which is symbolic of strength. (Coniaris 1981: 38)

Another denominational division, which parallels the division over infant baptism versus believer's baptism, concerns whether babies should be baptised or should instead be welcomed at a service of dedication. As the Baptist church stands unequivocally for the baptism of individuals who are deemed old enough to make a personal decision, babies and young children are not christened but are received into the congregation at a service of dedication or welcome:

> They first ask the mother and father if they're believing parents and R [the minister] takes the baby . . . he walks up and down the church and shows them to the family. He says, 'If you promise to be a loving friend to whatever her name is, will you stand?' and everyone stands. Then, at the end, he says, 'Will everyone sit?' and we have another song – 'Christ who welcomed little children . . . ' (9 year-old Baptist girl)

Salvationists, as a 13 year-old Junior Soldier described, have a dedication service:

> We're dedicated as a baby. The army sings a song about dedication and the parents go up to the platform and sit down and the Major stands up and the parents stand up as well, holding the baby. And they give the baby to the Major and he says a prayer.

In the Salvation Army, however, dedication is followed not by baptism but by becoming a Junior Soldier. Among Quakers the baby is informally welcomed into the Meeting and young people may opt later to apply for membership of the Religious Society of Friends – there are no longer 'birthright Friends'. The young people's accounts show the centuries-old debate between the supporters of infant and believer's baptism continuing, with children taking up their church's position, and only the URC officially accepting both (Husselbee and Thomas n.d.).

Holy Communion

The young people's commentary showed attitudes to Holy Communion also differing strongly along denominational lines. They used different names for the rite ('mass', 'Lord's supper' and 'holy communion), and their accounts indicated that frequency, content, and the prevailing mood during 'celebration' – as well as the prerequisites essential for full participation – varied by denomination. Prerequisites included: 'baptism' in the experience of the Jamaican boy from First United Church of Jesus Christ Apostolic, and of the Greek Orthodox children who had received the bread and wine ever since their baptism as babies; 'they have to be 18' (English Methodist girl); and 'you have to go to these confirmation classes' (Punjabi Church of England girl). Some spoke as if there were no prior requirements: 'Anyone can have it', according to an English 11 year-old URC girl and a 13 year-old New Church girl. The 13 year-old English Salvationist said that what distinguished her church from others was: 'We don't believe that you have to take bread and wine to be part of God'. A 12 year-old Catholic, half-Ukrainian girl distinguished between Roman Catholic practices and Ukrainian (Eastern Rite) practices:

In the Ukrainian church we believe in everything. We drink Jesus' blood and eat Jesus' body. In the English church we only eat Jesus' body and the priest drinks Jesus' blood.

For the Jamaican Pentecostals foot washing was part of the Lord's Supper since Jesus had washed his disciples' feet at the 'last supper' on the eve of his crucifixion (Toulis 1997: 151). The Ukrainian Catholic and Greek Orthodox communicants each received a spoonful of wine mixed with crumbled bread from the chalice. Bread that was unleavened (i.e. yeastless, consistent with the bread eaten at Jewish Pesach) was central to other churches – for example, a specially made wafer for the Church of England and Roman Catholic worshippers. In some churches the 'wine' is non-alcoholic because of a historic emphasis on teetotalism. In the British Free Churches (including the Baptist and Methodist) each communicant drinks from a separate glass. Childen described feeling scared at their first communion, aged seven (Catholics); helping the priest to officiate (two boys – one Orthodox, one Roman Catholic); and 'just getting a blessing' while older people received the bread and wine (Baptist girl).

Being a Christian in school

Being a Christian is not just an out of school matter. The Coventry study showed how children sometimes feel under pressure when the values of their churches and families clash with those of their peers – or of their teachers. In this respect too children's experience varies, in part according to the emphases of their denominations and families.

Two English girls – a nine year-old Baptist and a 13 year-old member of a New Church – referred to the fact that Christians should not swear. The latter spoke at length of the painful experience of being taunted for not succumbing to peer pressure to use bad language.

A profound religious experience can affect children's relationships with their peers. An 11 year-old Baptist girl reported that after 'asking Jesus into my life' at an Easter convention (Spring Harvest) she found it easier to talk to a school friend who had also asked Jesus into her life than to relate to her best friend, who had not had this experience.

A nine year-old Church of England boy related how he was victimised when other pupils discovered that he was a choirboy. A 14 year-old Quaker girl was acutely aware of supporting values, such as pacifism, which were at variance with those of many of her teachers and fellow pupils.

Clearly, for a minority of pupils at least, belonging to a Christian family and holding distinctive principles and having religious experiences can lead to a sense of isolation, and even to bullying. Belonging to a family which is also in an ethnic, and so cultural, minority may intensify the sense of being unusual. Religion may be bound up with strong views on 'other faiths' and communities and it may involve powerful emotion, individual and collective.

Implications for religious education

Intrafaith diversity (the variation within faith communities) is clearly pertinent to the concerns of teachers as pastoral carers and as religious educationists, but risks being submerged by perceptions of the differences between faiths. At the same time as seeking to appreciate individuals' experiences, commonalities both within faith communities and between them must be kept in sight.

Alertness for religious discrimination (including bullying) must not be eclipsed by focusing on 'racial' prejudice. For religious education teachers especially this is a salutary reminder as it is during religious education lessons that a pupil's distinctively Christian experience may come to the notice of their peers.

Awareness of the diversity of young Christians' experience has implications too for how Christian tradition is to be portrayed in religious education. The Warwick RE Project presents the tradition through the lives of young people from culturally and ethnically as well as theologically disparate churches in the UK (Barratt 1994 a, b, c; Barratt and Price 1996, Robson 1995). Increasingly curriculum materials aim at less Eurocentric representation – one example being McConnell (n.d.). The challenge for teachers is of balancing unity and diversity while arousing and maintaining the interest of pupils whose attitudes range from antipathy to all religion, through apathy to strong commitment to particular Christian or other expressions of faith.

Locally diverse forms of Christian community can be included by organising visits – to a Greek Orthodox church, for example. In some instances pupils' encounter with an unfamiliar form of the Christian tradition may awaken their interest. A deliberately inclusive approach to Christians' diversity – in line with global studies such as Chidester (2000) – will (no less than a multifaith approach) contribute to intercultural understanding.

Notes

1   Details of Orthodox fasting practice, the reasons for it and recipes for allowed foods can be seen on www.vegsource.com/lenten.htm (accessed 19 March 2004).
2   Details of the Ukrainian Easter basket's contents can be found at www.brama. com/art/easter.html (accessed 19 March 2004).
3   See www.learnpysanky.com (accessed 19 March 2004).

Festivals – Schools' Involvement in 'Tradition'

Education and changing festivals

Previous chapters have selected clusters of data from the field studies in Coventry in order to unsettle ways in which we perceive, and so portray, aspects of our pupils' experience. With the subject of festivals we move into an aspect of culture which is one of its shop fronts – as tourist literature for holiday destinations quickly makes clear – and an aspect to which schools (in the UK at least) contribute.

This chapter examines three festivals: Christmas, Divali and Vaisakhi – Christian, Hindu and Sikh, respectively. Changes underway in how they are celebrated are surveyed before noting the ways in which schools contribute to defining, perpetuating and raising public awareness of festivals. Schools affect – as well as represent – 'tradition', a situation which repays attention.

Schools not only teach about festivals in, for example, the religious education curriculum, but also extend the reach of festivals. In schools in England and Wales this occurs through 'assemblies' (what the law terms 'acts of collective worship') and through extra curricular cultural events, such as evening programmes of dance, drama and musical items. Festivals and associated foods crop up in school as expressions of religious tradition to a greater extent than many other aspects of culture. Indeed the emphasis on festivals starts in nurseries and playgroups for pre-school age children. Teachers and play group leaders' efforts are supported by features in professional magazines such as *Child Education, Early Educator, Education 3–13, Nursery World,* and *Practical Pre-Schooler.*

Amongst festivals Christmas remains the established mainstay and climax of the autumn term (at least in primary schools). Outside schools the continuing denominational and cultural diversity of Christians' observance of Christmas, and the impact of a 'secular' Christmas on Sikh and Hindu families, illustrate other processes that are underway.

While (Western) Christmas – like Easter – gives shape to the school year, because schools close for the annual public holidays, the Hindu festival of

Divali has, of recent decades, also achieved increasingly widespread recognition in the calendar of UK schools. Indeed some London schools have included Diwali in their annual holidays (Raj 2003: 146). This chapter will, however, give most space to continuities and changes in marking the Sikh festival of Vaisakhi, a festival that is still not widely known in the UK, and about which much less has been written than about Christmas or Divali.

Festivals have long interested anthropologists and social historians. To take some examples: Mc Kim Marriott reported his participatory observation in a North Indian village's riotous celebration of Holi, the Spring festival of colours (1966). Robert Jackson documented a quieter version of Holi in Coventry which climaxed in Gujarati families' circumambulation of an impressive bonfire outside their temple (1976). In her discussion of 'nationalism, syncretism and commercialisation' Marion Bowman tracked the ways in which (in Malaysia at least) the Muslim festival of Hari Raya Aidilfitri (Eid al Fitr) has taken on commercial aspects of secular Christmases (1994). Adam Kuper (1993) and Mary Searle-Chatterjee (1993) searched out the implications of the British Christmas for the family and for the construction of other social relations (e.g. through the exchange of Christmas cards) and, as a social historian, Connelly looked at how Christmas has become 'the festival of the children' (1999). What has largely escaped scholarly attention is the role of schools in the generally unquestioned relationship between education, celebration and 'culture'.

One critical approach which can be applied to schools' treatment of festivals has been the antiracists' dismissal of cultural programmes involving 'saris, samosas and steelband' as tokenistic, expressions of a divisive multiculturalism (Hall 2002: 21), a view shared by one London Hindu Punjabi teacher whom Raj interviewed (2003: 147).

A different sort of outcry by concerned individuals and organisations has been a sporadic protest on religious grounds to schools' endorsement of the (originally Pagan) celebration of Hallowe'en on 31 October. Some Christians express concern that it may encourage an interest in the occult (Homan 1991). But understanding of the multiple changes and continuities, as schools accommodate some aspects of certain festivals, requires a more textured account based on local case studies.

Writing on the basis of research conducted in London in the 1980s, Penny Logan drew religious educationists' attention to the highpoint of many Gujarati children's year, the nine-night Norta or Navaratri festival (which commences just one lunar month before Divali) (1988). Norta is the Gujarati name for the festival whereas Navaratri, from the Sanskrit words meaning 'nine nights', is the name by which it is most widely known. Logan mentioned the interaction between teachers' questions and pupils' response: 'the questions of an interested outsider and the opportunity to vocalise their experience may stimulate further questions in a child's mind'.

Marie Gillespie's study of 'television, ethnicity and cultural change' in Southall focused upon secondary school pupils from Punjabi (Sikh and Hindu) families (1995). She noted ways in which they incorporated aspects of Christmas and she reported on their creative subversion of a Divali concert in school. The present chapter will also raise issues which emerge from a broader survey of the intersection of festival celebration and school, and will consider the involvement of young people from one cultural or religious background in the festivals that have arisen in another tradition.

Christmas in families and schools

The research among young people from 13 local Coventry congregations who identified themselves as Christian revealed a high degree of shared or overlappping experience. They described shopping and putting up decorations at home. Some mentioned nativity scenes at home and in churches. Many took part in Christmas plays at church and in carol-singing. Christmas provided the theme for their Sunday school classes and there were parties organised by the teachers of these as well as at school. At home Father Christmas's visit, family get-togethers and 'a normal turkey dinner' with Christmas pudding were usual, although, as one eight year-old girl confided, 'I'm a bit tired of Christmas cake at Christmas'. As noted in chapter 3, children from a range of denominational and cultural backgrounds distinguished the religious meaning of Christmas as 'Jesus' birthday' from its current commercialisation.

The research also showed a marked diversity in the ways that Christmas was marked and in attitude towards the festival. For example, on 19 December, or the Saturday nearest to this date, the Ukrainian Catholic children celebrate St Nicholas's day and a man dressed to represent St Nicholas (Svjatyj Mykolaj) distributes their gifts. If they did not have to be in school on 7 January (the date of Christmas by the older Julian calendar which the UK's Ukrainian Catholics follow) it was on this day that they enjoyed their Christmas dinner of 12 meatless dishes, such as beetroot borsch, plus *cotletta* (meatballs) (see Ukrainian Women's Association of Canada 1987).[1] But, to quote one 12 year-old girl:

> We're allowed to miss [school] when it's a special occasion to do with another religion, but Mum hardly ever lets me take Ukrainian Christmas off.

In a rather different minority a boy from a Pentecostal Jamaican congregation explained that:

> I don't think that Christmas is true because . . . God didn't ask people to call it Christmas. It isn't in the Bible . . . it doesn't say in the Bible [that] he was born on the 25th December.

His condemnation is continuous with widespread Protestant suspicion of Christmas celebrations as both Pagan and Papist in pre-Victorian Britain and is of a piece with New Churches' (see chapter 3) which 'resolutely refuse . . . to acknowledge any festivals' (Stringer 1999: 196).

At the same time, Coventry-based research among young Sikhs and Hindus found that they too shared the secular features of Christmas with committed and nominal Christians and with the religiously unaligned. They sent greeting cards, decorated their homes and exchanged wrapped presents (cf. Baumann 1994: 106). In the words of one 12 year-old girl:

> We celebrate lightly, we don't do it religiously as Christ and all that. It's like a gathering and my cousins come down and give each other presents. We have a dinner and watch TV.
>   Christmas day we open all our toys and on Boxing Day we can mess about. I like messing about. (9 year-old boy)

Gillespie too encouraged her students (Punjabi Sikhs and Hindus) to write Christmas diaries. In these they similarly reported giving cards and eating and watching television with their families – though the delicacies might be vegetarian (1995: 103–6).

But some Hindu families do more than 'celebrate lightly' insofar as they incorporate an unambiguously religious element. While Gillespie reports a Hindu family in Southall 'put[ting] up the lights around a God they believe in' (1995: 104), an American scholar of Hinduism, J. Y. Fenton, reports that 'Many Hindus in America have told me that they perform puja [i.e. Hindu-style worship] for Jesus at Christmas time' (1991: 271). For devotees of Sathya Sai Baba in Coventry (who are all from Gujarati Hindu families) Christmas includes singing *bhajans* (devotional songs) in front of a swinging cradle holding an image of the baby Jesus. This devotion is patterned on Gujarati Hindu celebration of the birthdays of Rama and Krishna, on the days known as Ramanavami and Janmashthami respectively. At Christmas time Sathya Sai Baba's devotees also sing carols to residents in a home for the elderly (in accordance with Baba's exhortation to acts of service (*seva*).

As far as Christmas in schools is concerned, research in Coventry had no difficulty in finding that primary schools' preparations for Christmas included telling children the story of Jesus' birth in Bethlehem, how to make decorations to hang in their homes and greeting cards to give to their parents. In most schools there were rehearsals for an end of term event to which parents were invited. Pupils also made Christingles out of an orange, a red ribbon, a pin, silver foil, four cocktail sticks, sweets or raisins.[2] Preparation for Christmas continues to dominate the autumn term, even in schools with a majority of pupils from non-Christian South Asian families, although some have responded to demographic change since Alibhai's account of a 99 per cent Asian first school in Southall (1987).

The presence of significant percentages of Hindu, Sikh and Muslim pupils in some schools, and teachers' growing awareness of a need to introduce all children to cultural diversity, helped to mould some of the events observed in Coventry schools. By no means all the plays were nativity plays, and one school's presentation included, together with Christmas, a brief presentation of Divali and Hannukah (an affirmation of society's faith traditions, rather than a response to local expectation, as no Jewish pupils attended the school). By and large, however, schools' overwhelming emphasis on Christmas, and the lengthy preparations for special events continued the experience of previous generations of British schoolchildren and promoted assumptions about Christmas's place in the Christian tradition and in British culture that are shared by church leaders, church-goers and Sunday school organisers.

Divali

Since the 1970s Divali (the late autumn Hindu 'festival of lights') has also become established in the calendar of many schools and in the religious education syllabus. Divali (the name, like the alternative Dipavali, means a row of wick lights) falls on the day of the 'dark night', i.e. new moon, in the Hindu lunar month which approximates to late October/early November. Unlike many of the more locally-specific Hindu festivals, which are celebrated only in one state of India or in a smaller locality, Divali is pan-Indian. At the same time the festival's regional variations are innumerable in terms of the associated stories, the number of celebratory days and their significance, and the types of sweetmeats and savouries intrinsic to the celebrations.

Widespread features of Divali in India are the cleaning and decorating of houses, often with traditional designs outside the doorway – and an abundance of flickering oil lights and fairy electric bulbs. Fireworks explode chaotically in the streets. Hindus hope that Lakshmi (the goddess of wealth) will pay a visit, and recall how a door or a window used to be left open, even if fears for security now rule this out. Many people spend the night gambling. They remember too the story of how Rama, king of the North Indian town of Ayodhya, returned on this night with his wife Sita from his 14 year exile further south.

In the UK diaspora – as in India, Kenya, Canada, the United States, Australia, The Netherlands and elsewhere – Divali marks the climax to approximately a month of celebrations. Some 70 per cent of UK Hindus are Gujarati, and Gujarati families celebrate Norta (Navaratri) with enthusiasm for its nine days. All generations gather for vibrant evenings of circle and stick dances in temple premises and hired halls. The hub of the dances is a hexagonal shrine, portraying the Goddess in her various forms. The amplification and quickening beat of the music (played and sung by members of the community) leave no doubt of tradition's responsiveness to changing fashions.

For Hindu families that are rooted in Bengal this same period is suffused with memories of Durga Puja in and around Calcutta. Those with first-hand experience recall the images of the goddess and their public immersion in the river after nine days of worship. In other parts of North India these are the days on which the Ramlila is performed in public spaces, re-enacting the epic story of Rama's exile and return. In the UK, Punjabi Hindu families may visit their local temple more frequently during these days to worship the Goddess – this is especially true of the eighth day, on which young girls are given a red *chunni* (scarf) and other small items after a special meal. But many young people will be unaware of the significance of this or indeed of the tenth day, Dasahra, which marks Lord Rama's defeat of the demon king, Ravana, who had abducted Sita to Sri Lanka. About eight days later, ten days before Divali, Punjabi Hindu (and some Sikh) women keep the day-long fast of Karva Chauth (as mentioned in chapter 2).

For Hindu children in the UK, Divali night primarily means fireworks. Sikhs' gurdwaras as well as Hindu *mandir*s have ever louder firework displays. Gillespie (1995: 106] overemphasises the innovatory aspect of firework displays, although it is likely that, without the proximity of Guy Fawkes Day, Divali would have lost its fireworks on transplantation to the UK, much as Holi lost its anarchic throwing of colours.

For Gujarati Hindus this is also the day of Lakshmi Puja, worship of the Goddess of prosperity. Businessmen gather in the temple for the ritual blessing of their account books and computers (*Indiaweekly* 1999). On the next day, Annakut, spectacularly bountiful offerings of food are set out in the temple in front of the shrines of the deities. Some Sikhs too (among those who belong to the Ramgarhia community – see chapter 7) honour their newly cleaned tools in the presence of a picture of Vishvakarma, God represented as builder of the universe (Kalsi 1992: 119). For many Hindu families the final event of the festive season is (also the day after Divali) Bhai Bij (the Gujarati name) or Bhaia Duj (the Punjabi name), the day when married women cook a special meal for their brothers.

Some UK Hindu parents accept as part of Divali's annual content that they will be coming into their child's primary school to 'share Divali' by dressing pupils in Indian clothes, reading a story from the city library's multicultural book shelves or distributing sweets. Whether these are Indian *mithai* or 'ordinary' sweets will depend on how the parent gauges the children's likely reaction.

In schools Divali's main focus is on the story of Rama and Sita, and the storytelling and dramatic performances combine the narrative of Dasahra (Ravana's defeat) with the triumphal return of Rama to reclaim his kingdom. By concentrating on the story of Rama and Sita, teachers help to shape what Divali stands for. For example the telling of the story collapses into one festival narrative and dramatic reenactments that in North India are central to Dasahra, nearly three weeks before Divali. Focus upon Rama and Sita may displace other elements – notably the emphasis on Lakshmi/wealth.

However, the story which Madhur Jaffrey recalled from her childhood in Delhi assumes increasing prominence as it takes root in the religious education syllabus (1985: 80–4). This tells how a destitute washer woman gained great wealth from Lakshmi on Divali night as a result of her canniness when she was offered a reward for her honesty in restoring the queen's necklace.

As a result of schools' retelling of the stories, Hindu pupils have come, like their peers, to pronounce the names of Rama, Sita, Lakshmana and Ravana in the epic caste of the Divali story from the *Ramayana* as their (usually monoglot native-English speaking) teachers do, rather than as relatives do who have grown up with these characters. This means that, for example, young British Hindus too may turn the middle 'a' of Lakshmana and Ravana into a long, accentuated syllable. (For speakers of North Indian languages the final, third 'a' is inaudible and the second 'a' in Lakshman(a) and Ravan(a) is 'short', so that the syllables 'man(a)' and 'van(a)' rhyme with the English word 'won': Lakshmana and Ravana are pronounced more as 'Luckshmun' and 'Rahvun' respectively.)

At the same time as fostering Anglicised pronunciations, schools are forging young people's mental associations between individuals (their Hindu peers) and certain activities (e.g. eating Indian foods and dancing Indian dances).

The involvement of Sikhs in Divali (as a popular annual celebration) is left more ambiguous – with religious education materials including the explanation that Sikhs celebrate Divali because it was on this festival night that their sixth Guru, Hargobind, obtained the release of many fellow prisoners from Gwalior gaol where he had been imprisoned by the Moghul authorities. In fact Sikhs' new Nanakshahi calendar, designed by a Canadian Sikh and authorised for use from 2003, lists Divali under the name of Bandi Chhor Divas – literally Releaser of Prisoners Day – so emphasising its distinctness from Hindu tradition.

Vaisakhi – the 'traditional' festival

By comparison with Divali (let alone Christmas) the Sikhs' mid-April new year festival of Vaisakhi is a newcomer to UK school calendars. Vaisakhi is often explained as being the 'birthday of the Khalsa' (the nucleus of fully committed Sikhs – see McLeod 2003). Even its name remains unfamiliar to many outside the Sikh community, despite its inclusion in many religious education syllabuses, and in publications that cater for this (Babraa 1989; Cole and Sambhi 1986). But a Coventry-based study of young Sikhs' experience of Vaisakhi showed some of the ways in which, amongst other transformations, the festival is becoming enmeshed through some schools with a more generalised culture, and how changes in its perpetuation within the Sikh community have children particularly in mind.

Vaisakhi is also spelled in the roman alphabet as Baisakhi, following regional differences of pronunciation and spelling in Punjabi. By the Nanakshahi calendar it now falls on 14 April. In previous years it has fallen on 12 and 13 April. At this time of year rural Punjabis mark the Spring harvest, and for Sikhs worldwide it marks the day when the tenth Guru, Gobind Singh, called together his followers and initiated into a new brotherhood, the Khalsa, five men (now known as the *panj piare* or five beloved ones) who were bold enough to risk their lives for him. It was on this occasion that (according to tradition) the Guru announced a uniform of five tangible markers of allegiance to the Guru, markers now referred to as the five Ks because each has an initial K in Punjabi. (Historical enquiry suggests that in fact the five Ks may have been formulated as part of a much more gradual process [McLeod 1995: 81].)

In gurdwaras Vaisakhi morning is marked by ceremonial initiations into the Khalsa (starting before dawn) and the more public ritual cleansing of the orange pennant and orange-clad flagpole (the *nishan sahib*). Candidates for initiation receive *amrit* in the form of sweetened water which is administered in a private ceremony by five respected Sikhs who are known to maintain the Khalsa discipline. These men, who are also known as the *panj piare,* prepare the water by stirring it as they recite scriptural verses, and sprinkle it on each candidate's tongue, eyes and head. The candidates undertake to adhere from now on to the rules of the Khalsa including keeping their hair uncut.

Sikhs' ceremonial cleansing of the *nishan sahib* entails lowering the flagstaff – even from the roof if that is where it is mounted. Members of the congregation reverently remove the cloth wrapping, wash the pole in dilute yoghurt, and rinse and dry it before reclothing it in fresh cloth, including the pennant at the top which bears the *khanda* logo that is composed of three swords and a quoit. The recitation of Ardas (the congregational prayer) takes place outside.

Vaisakhi day is the culmination of a 48-hour continuous reading of the scriptures – the prelude to all major Sikh festivals. This reading is followed by rousing renditions of sacred hymns (*shabad kirtan*) by visiting groups of *ragis* (musicians). They perform to larger than usual congregations.

Adaptation of the festival to the UK include developments which hold good for other Sikh festivals too – notably the transfer of congregational celebration to the following Sunday, and the opportunity for a 'children's programme' in the presence of adults. Fieldwork in Coventry over a two and a half month period found Vaisakhi (a) taking on an educational function for young British Sikhs and (b) becoming part of some schools' multicultural provision.

Vaisakhi: provision for children

The events described above carry over to the UK context the central features of Vaisakhi celebrations in India. At the same time, with an evident concern for involving their children, organisers of youth activities in the gurdwaras seek to inform children and hold their interest and other Sikh organisations arrange events in a range of venues.

The build-up to Vaisakhi begins several weeks earlier in the Punjabi language classes that are held in schools and gurdwaras. Paralleling practice in other faith traditions (Jackson and Nesbitt 1993) the festival provides these classes with content. In early March in the fieldwork year children were preparing the big picture of the seminal event in 1699 that was to decorate one of the floats in the Vaisakhi procession.

Towards the end of a class in one gurdwara on 12 April a cake, covered in newspaper, was brought in. Then there were cries of '*Bole sonihal Sat Sri Akal*' (the Sikh cry of 'Blessed is whoever says "timeless truth is Lord")' as five teenage lads entered wearing turbans and an orange *kurta* (long shirt) over their ordinary trousers. Each also wore a sword about three feet long. The cake (made without eggs) was an oblong sponge with 'Vaisakhi' on it in brown Roman capitals. These *panj piare* stood in a row behind it while everyone said *Ardas*, and, when they reached the names of the original (Vaisakhi 1699) *panj piare*, they enunciated these very clearly. Next the five boys representing the *panj piare* cut the cake with a *kirpan* (sword), all hands together, before it was sliced for distribution. This gesture was clearly reminiscent of the ritual touching of the *karah prashad* (sweet wheat-flour pudding distributed in the gurdwara prayer hall) with the *kirpan* when *Ardas* is said. Like the birthday cake mentioned in chapter 1, the Vaisakhi cake contained no eggs.

Away from the gurdwaras, too, Vaisakhi celebrations include events that are organised by Sikh organizations with children particularly in mind. The 'Vaisakhi Festival' held in a large sports hall during the Coventry fieldwork consisted of races, sports for older participants, as well as an exhibition of Punjabi coins, pictures and books plus tapes and records of Punjabi songs, books and posters. Activities for children included colouring in outlines of *bhangra* dancers, playing Punjabi snakes and ladders, trying to assemble a Punjabi family jigsaw and to trace their family history on maps of Punjab. Souvenir brochures contained reproductions of winning pencil drawings of Vaisakhi by children under nine, winning essays on Vaisakhi in Punjabi and English by older competitors plus photographs of all the winning entrants.

Incorporating Vaisakhi in the wider community

Field notes recorded how at 3.45 p.m. on Sunday 12 April, the unusually long *kirtan* was drawing to a close in the Guru Nanak Parkash Gurdwara with a speaker urging people to explain the meaning of Vaisakhi if the procession led to questions. Outside in the car park, a lorry was being decorated with tinsel to serve as a float and Sikhs were gathering as police in luminous jerkins moved about. The Guru Granth Sahib was borne on a man's head to the lorry for installation in it on a *palki* (the appropriate wooden stand). At 4.30 p.m. the procession formed, with a band initially playing Beatles tunes, followed by two rows of *panj piare* dressed in yellow with swords pointing heavenward. Behind them came the float bearing the Guru Granth Sahib accompanied by an attendant (*granthi*). Men and women, all with their heads covered, followed behind singing. After them came the local radio car, recording the occasion, the Warwick Corps of Drums and then floats from two gurdwaras carrying children. The back of one gurdwara's float was covered with the picture of the first Vaisakhi which they had produced in their class.

   The Vaisakhi celebrations provided an opportunity for disseminating information about the Sikh tradition to the local non-Sikh population through handouts during the procession and via the radio coverage and newspaper reporting. The festival's significance in the eyes of the city council as an occasion for building harmonious race relations was evident from the presence of a councillor who addressed the gathering. Further civic recognition was symbolised by illuminations (incorporating Sikh words and English translations of these on disks attached to the lamp posts) and by a switching on ceremony. Moreover, the *Coventry Evening Telegraph* carried an illustrated report of the previous day's procession. Readers were informed that: 'Vaisakhi celebrates the creation of the Order of the Khalsa by the 10th and last guru [sic] Gobind Singh in 1699.' Three of the five Ks were listed and the procession was described briefly. Thus, this article provided background information (for a largely non-Sikh readership) while accommodating Vaisakhi in mainstream British awareness.

Vaisakhi in schools

Vaisakhi also featured in some local schools: in a primary school in the north of Coventry a peripatetic Punjabi language teacher gave her pupils their weekly lesson. Here, in the setting of a secular institution, a Sikh was passing on culturally specific information to young Sikhs about the meaning of the Khalsa and of Vaisakhi. She drew on a familiar parallel to help them to understand the excitement in rural Punjab:

> Like on Thursday here they're happy because they have wages, there they're happy with harvest. They give gifts and wear new clothes.

In another primary school the theme of one April morning's collective worship (to which parents were invited) was also Vaisakhi. Display boards exhibited pupils' drawings of the five Ks and the word 'Baisakhi' was surrounded by relevant pictures in felt tip. After greeting all present in Urdu, Gujarati and English, a group of children stood and read from individual cards about Vaisakhi before they all sang to keyboard, recorder and harmonium accompaniment:

> Thank you Lord for Baisakhi day . . . right where we are.
> Thank you Lord for the crops we've reaped . . .
> Thank you Lord for all your gifts . . .
> Thank you Lord for Baisakhi day . . .
> Thank you Lord for this new year . . .

Next a girl read about the 'birth of the Khalsa' and slides of Guru Gobind Singh appeared on the overhead projector as children stood in turn to read the story of Vaisakhi day 1699 from their sheets and to read out information about the five Ks and the principles that: 'There is one God', 'Never lie' and 'All people are equal'. A boy received a star for swimming, a girl received an Easter egg from the kitchen staff for helping. Then a ticket was drawn in a guide dog appeal.

A secondary school held an evening Spring Celebration which the programme described as a celebration of Id, Vaisakhi and Easter. Two pupils opened the programme by proclaiming a Sikh greeting and accompanying themselves on harmonium and *tabla* as they sang in praise of the tenth Guru. This was followed by items of music, dance and drama including *bhangra*, of the more traditional type, and a 'family *bhangra* disco'.

In the foyer of another secondary school, pieces of work produced in the school's Punjabi classes were prominently displayed: pictures and emblems of the Sikh community, an explanation of 'Baisakhi', and the prayers and Ks constituting Khalsa discipline.

More widespread than these Vaisakhi-related activities in schools in a city with a substantial Sikh population is the inclusion of Vaisakhi in religious education lessons. Pupils and teachers draw largely on curriculum books and audio-visual material focusing on the *amrit* ceremony, the *nishan sahib* and processions (e.g. Cole and Sambhi 1986).

Vaisakhi and cultural change

This overview of Vaisakhi over a two and a half month period in Coventry reveals changes that are occurring within the *Panth* (Sikh community), in part through local schools, as well as in relation to the wider society, the people of Coventry. Vaisakhi in Coventry illustrates the capacity of a festival both for perpetuation of the sacred (through *amrit chhakana*, the private rite of initiation into the Khalsa) and for mass dissemination (through the procession and local radio and press coverage). Concern to retain Sikh children's allegiance to their tradition and to steep them in its lore had motivated new departures. Meanwhile, through the Vaisakhi festival, teachers and the city library service seek to promote a well-informed plural society.

Vaisakhi also emerges as an exemplar of the diversity of processes interacting in the nurture of children from a faith community and in the education of young people in schools. Festivals have long provided channels of cultural transmission through ritual, story, fairs and the expressive arts (Marriott n.d.). In diaspora situations, minorities pass on and reinforce significant history and behavioural codes more formally by teaching which is often centred upon major festivals (Jackson and Nesbitt 1993; Nesbitt 1991b). The festival provides children with the stimulus of highly visual liturgy centred on the renewal of the *nishan sahib* and with the solidarity of a massed procession in which they can participate fully. Moreover, an enjoyable event – the sports day – and education through drawing and essay competitions and quizzes, are organised specifically for the children. In parallel with this the festival organisers look outwards to the local non-Sikh community and incorporate non-traditional details such as the local band in the procession.

Meanwhile, despite innovations, Vaisakhi remains a centrally religious occasion in a way that Christmas is not. Like Christmas (celebrated on the day of such pre-Christian European mid-winter festivals as Saturnalia) Vaisakhi is celebrated to coincide with a day of rejoicing (in this case a Hindu Spring harvest festival) whose origins predate the emergence of the faith tradition concerned. But the day's importance in the genesis of the Sikh community has eclipsed earlier modes of celebration.

In this understanding of Vaisakhi, Sikh children emerge as one of several 'constituencies'. In Coventry, as far as the private ceremony of *amrit chhakana* is concerned, Vaisakhi conforms to the French sociologist Emile Durkheim's understanding of festivals as being for insiders of the group concerned. By contrast, the procession – involving local bands, a councillor and ceremonial switching on of street illuminations – was clearly 'public ritual'. Bystanders (in fact there were very few) were anticipated, addressed and provided with handouts. Children, in this analysis, are both insiders and outsiders, a part of the family but (unlike the older members of the community), in need of explanation and encouragement, much of it in English.

Such events can be understood, from different perspectives, as variously elders' attempt to present a traditional festival attractively for children, as perpetuation of a Sikh emphasis (from the time of Guru Angad) on physical fitness and contests (Khushwant Singh rep. 1977: 52), or as an instance of Mark Orans's 'rank concession syndrome' whereby an aspect of majority culture is appropriated to signal an ethnically specific event (1965). The library service had organised the exhibition, an example of institutional recognition of the need to build minority children's esteem for their cultural heritage.

By affirming and accommodating an annual celebration the city council is integrating a minority faith community. Together, the locally conspicuous Vaisakhi festival, the Sikh pupils in schools and a prevailing educational philosophy of multiculturalism and social inclusion, result in educational initiatives – especially 'Vaisakhi assemblies'. Contextualised by the format of school 'assembly' Vaisakhi is validated by the educational establishment. Meanwhile Vaisakhi provides a basis for moral injunctions (e.g. 'never lie'). The song 'Thank you Lord' suggests careful melding of the Sikh calendar and an originally Christian hymn form. Schools take on some responsibility for disseminating information about Sikh history and the Khalsa code of discipline, thereby promoting understanding between pupils of different backgrounds and contributing to the nurture of Sikhs in their faith tradition.

Both the preservation of 'traditional' *bhangra* as a staged event and the fusion of *bhangra* with western disco music illustrate processes of change in the diaspora – processes in 'secular' Punjabi culture not paralleled in the 'religious' domain. At the same time the incorporation of praise of the Guru in a school cultural programme illustrates the practical applications of a local educational policy's inclusiveness. The mix of a *shabad* (hymn) with older-style and disco-style *bhangra* music in the school 'Spring Celebration' was strongly reminiscent of Christmas-tide events in schools, with their blend of religious song and partying.

In line with this, schools – some at least – are facilitating some teaching about Vaisakhi and the Sikh tradition in Punjabi classes. However, these involve only a small minority of pupils. The attention of all pupils (in some schools) is annually focused upon Vaisakhi through morning assembly, cultural programmes and displays of writing and artwork on this theme.

Festivals and community cohesion

Clearly, whether we look at children's experience in their families or in school, Christmas, Divali and Vaisakhi exemplify changes that are underway in a society which is demographically and historically weighted towards Christianity.

Certainly, as far as Christmas is concerned, families from many religious and cultural backgrounds participate in secular aspects of the festivities. This increasingly shared practice provides an example of what the social anthropologist Gerd Baumann calls 'syncretization by convergence' (1994). In other words two faith communities have absorbed practices which were previously characteristic of a third (and in this case socially dominant) tradition. The cake and cake-cutting in the Sikh Sunday class are another example of convergence.

Reflection on her Sikh and Hindu students' accounts of Christmas led Gillespie to agree with Baumann's analysis (1992) that 'through Christmas rituals . . . youth and their parents negotiate their subtly differing relation-ships to surrounding "others"' (Gillespie 1995: 104). Baumann had critiqued the way in which Durkheim 'read' ritual (Baumann 1992). Anthropologists have assumed since Durkheim that 'ritual is best under-stood as an act internal to the category or group that celebrates it or celebrates itself through it' (Baumann 1992: 98). However, on the basis of his own data from Southall, Baumann argues that rituals also implicate 'others' and can even be addressed to them. These 'others' include other Punjabis and their white peers with whom they discuss what they did at Christmas. This takes further the British Hindu Punjabi actress and author Meera Syal's suggestion that 'joining in with the festivities is more a case of good manners than a gesture of solidarity' (1997).

Less comfortably, in her eloquent denunciation of 'A White Christmas', Yasmin Alibhai vehemently exposes 'the central power relationship where Christian social rites dominate' 'behind the goodwill and expansiveness' (1987: 16) and sees the injustices of colonialism continuing. She (and other South Asian critics whom she quotes) are particularly incensed that teachers excessively emphasise Christmas for much of the Autumn term in schools with pupils who are almost all Muslim, Hindu and Sikh fami-lies. Their protests raise questions about what schools are doing, what they should be doing, and how aware those involved in festival-related activi-ties in schools are of the issues. The point is that cultural evenings and religious education, assemblies – to which parents and governors are often invited – and nativity plays do not stop at acknowledging elements in some families' calendars and kitchens. Rather, such activities in UK schools also perpetuate culture, embedding it in the consciousness both of members of faith communities and of those outside them. In so doing schools trans-form 'tradition' and create new fusions.

Schools' Christmas activities (along with the media, advertising and local illuminations and carol singing) contribute to the formation of each pupil's experience – but in different ways. In some cases domestic and community practice (whether religious or more secular) is reinforced. In the cases of children from some Ukrainian Catholic and Cypriot Greek Orthodox families, their home tradition is further jeopardised or weakened through schools' tendency to present a homogenised dominant version of tradition. In all cases schools themselves (teachers, dinner ladies, parents) are involved in the fashioning of 'tradition'. The popularity of the Christingle is an illustration of this – the introduction to children and their families not of a tradition long embedded in the UK but of a 'custom [which] started in Moravia (part of Slovakia) 250 years ago' and which is promoted by the Children's Society.[3]

In its presentation of a homogenised version of tradition the school reinforces television, the principal source of information for many South Asians (who seldom if ever visit a white Christian home – least of all at Christmas) (Gillespie 1995: 102). Moreover it is television, as Christmas's principal activity, which brings a shared experience to members of all communities.

Meanwhile Divali's inclusion in assemblies and cultural events raises the question of how the extended Christmas season is being multiculturalised and how the school year, and underlying Christian year, affect minorities' festivals. Schools' adoption and adaptation of Divali illustrates processes of incorporation and cultural hybridisation (as well as homogenisation) that are underway in many schools. Will Vaisakhi fuse with Easter and Spring festivals in pupils' consciousness? Already Hannukah (which is technically classified by Jews as a minor festival) now has in Britain a much higher profile than other 'minor' Jewish festivals. By contrast Raksha Bandhan, the widely observed Hindu festival that celebrates the tie between brothers and sisters, which has been brought to teachers' attention by Wayne et al. (1996), escapes attention because of falling in the summer holidays.

In the context of minority festivals' inclusion in school, pupils come to identify peers from particular groups with particular practices. But teachers are usually unaware of their role in this: the ways in which 'information' may contribute to stereotyping, to individuals' identity formation – the realisation that 'you celebrate Divali if you're a Hindu' (Nesbitt 1998c: 105).

At the same time as 'othering' individuals as 'Hindu' it is probable that schools' attention to festivals blurs insider/outsider distinctions and gives rise to some Christians' outcry against Divali in schools. In some years local UK newspaper reports register a local parent's protest at a school celebrating Divali. Letters to the editor suggest that there is only a thin line between affirming culture, on the one hand, and nurturing into religion (or at least of being suspected of doing so), on the other. This correspondence also raises the issue of whether pupils are – or are encouraged to be – 'insiders', as well as whether 'Divali' is 'devil worship' (Garala and Nesbitt 1987).

Such parental unease about the domestication of Divali in the autumn term's calendar echoes Alibhai's objection to Christmas (1987), which is shared by many Jewish and Muslim parents. But it also merges with the more vocal Christian resistance to Hallowe'en (Homan 1991) as non-Christian, anti-Christian and a legitimation (and affirmation) of the occult, with all its dangers for the impressionable young.

Schools' integration of such festivals as Vaisakhi and Divali into curriculum and extra-curricular activity illustrates the way in which education is open to becoming a means of legitimation of minority practices. This becomes apparent in the enthusiasm of faith community spokespeople to have defining dates included in the Shap calendar of world religions.[4] But this legitimation comes at the potential cost (from the perspective of some 'insiders' to faith traditions) of being blended into a multifaith calendar of mid winter and Spring celebration.

As a cultural feature, straddling home and school, a festival is a significant point in the mutation of 'tradition'. Christmas, Divali, Vaisakhi – and Chinese New Year, Id and Hanukkah – call for ongoing attention from reflective educationists as well as offering an invitation to social anthropologists.

Notes

1   Recipes are also available on line at http://www.infoukes.com/culture/traditions/ christmas/sviat_vechir.html (accessed 1 January 2004).

2   For details of Christingles see www.request.org.uk/main/festivals/christmas/ christingle/christingle01.htm (accessed 1 December 2003).

3   http://www.request.org.uk/main/festivals/christmas/christingle/christingle01.htm (accessed 1 December 2003).

4   The Shap Calendar of Religious Festivals is available from The Shap Working Party, PO Box 38580, London SW1P 3XF, UK, www.shap.org. Tel: 00 44 [0]20 7898 1494; fax: 00 44 [0]20 7898 1493.

5

Belief and Practice – God and Holy Water

Belief and *bhakti*

With its focus on festivals, and on Vaisakhi in particular, the previous chapter suggested ways in which UK schools contribute to families' experience of festivals – and so to cultural change. The concern in the present chapter is the mismatch between richly diverse assumptions and behaviour in a faith community and the simple statements of 'belief' and 'practice' which religious education in UK schools and religious studies in some higher education courses present.

One issue is language: what word(s) in Indic languages does the English word 'God' translate? A second issue is the limitations of a Christian paradigm of 'religion' for understanding Sikh (and other) pupils' lives. In particular we will look at young Sikhs' use of the word 'God' and at their understandings of what *amrit* (holy water) is and how it is used. More detailed discussions can be found in Nesbitt and Jackson (1995) and Nesbitt (1997 and 2000).

It is easy to conceptualise religions as combinations of belief and practice, with the emphasis on belief as prior to practice, or as providing its basis. Doing so is consistent with the paradigm that religious education syllabuses and curriculum materials generally maintain, and perpetuates a particularly western/Christian understanding. It lends itself to reproducing what adherents should believe and should do (according to the promoters of orthodoxy) without acknowledging adherents' actual values, hunches, hopes and fears and how they express these in behaviour. There is also the question of whether 'practice' is one's behaviour as a whole, or that part which is consciously 'religious' or which is characteristic (or even distinctive) of how 'believers' (are supposed to) behave.

Because Sikhs memorise and repeat Guru Nanak's sacred 'root formula', the *mul mantar,* it is easy to regard this as a 'creed'. Its opening '*ik oankar*' (the Gurmukhi numerical symbol for 'one' followed by the word '*oankar*') readily translates as 'there is one God'. (Gurmukhi is the script of the Sikhs' scriptures and also of modern Punjabi.) This translation fits comfortably with Jewish, Christian and Muslim belief. Arguably, the alternative rendering of a contemporary Sikh scholar, Nikky-Guninder Kaur Singh, that 'one reality is' (N.-G. K. Singh 1995: 1) is closer to the Guru's mystical insight. But it is further from a 'belief' that young Sikhs are likely to articulate, and from the Judaeo-Christian and Islamic world-view.

There are several words in Punjabi which are translated by writers on Sikhism as God – Vahiguru, Akal Purakh, Satguru, Paramatma, Rabb among others – and these all have different connotations. Vahiguru, for example, first appears not as an equivalent for 'God' but as an exclamation of wonder at the Guru (McLeod 1995: 216). The Guru Granth Sahib includes many more, drawn from Islam (e.g. Khuda, Allah) and from the Hindu tradition (e.g. Ram, Hari).

For Sikh devotees it is not so much the recital of statements of belief as the internalisation of the Nam (divine name and essence) through remembrance and repetition (*simaran* and *japan*) which is vital. It needs to be borne in mind, however, that it is probably the case that many Sikhs, for much of their lives, will not be maintaining this devotional practice. But in the case of the devout Sikh this reiteration occurs through frequently repeating 'Vahiguru' and 'Satnam' ('whose name is truth'), and through daily reading, reciting, singing and hearing passages of Scripture. Their immersion is physical, mental and spiritual; it is holistic rather than being a (primarily) cognitive, verbal assertion. The experience is one of *bhakti* (faith, loving devotion, *bhagati* in Punjabi) as expressed in practice, whereas the English word 'belief' often has more cerebral and more prescriptive and exclusive connotations.

Adults' use of the word 'God'

Before reporting young UK Sikhs' use and understanding of the term 'God' it is important to note the usage of Sikh adults with whom they had contact. In speaking about God, including their teaching of Sikh children (in English) during the fieldwork period, they used the word consistently with Sikh teaching as represented in both Sikh literature and school curriculum materials. Their statements included:

God helped me a lot.
There is some supernatural power which I give the name of God.
God is one; he doesn't like nationalism.
Only God's name and good action can uplift the soul.

One teacher emphatically corrected children who said 'God' for Guru and stressed the oneness of God as indicated in the formula *ik oankar* by the use of a single digit rather than the word 'one', which is divisible into several letters. However, some inconsistency was also evident: one teacher explained: 'Guru Nanak is God: God is one but, like humans are different colours, Hindus have Krishan [variant of Krishna], Sikhs have Guru Nanak.' Moreover, in her exercise book, one child attending the Punjabi class in her primary school had written in a list of Gurmukhi words and their English meanings, 'Guru is a God' – and this had been ticked.

Speakers varied in referring to God as either 'he' or 'they'. Since the plural pronoun conforms to the convention in Indian languages of using a plural to show respect – as with French '*vous*' and, originally, the English 'you' – this should not be taken to indicate polytheistic belief.

Sikh children's use of the word 'God'

Unsurprisingly, given the adults' fluid usage, the young Sikhs' usage did not conform straightforwardly to the religious education curriculum books' clearcut statement that Sikhs believe in one God. An earlier publication (Nesbitt 2000: 1) recalls the occasion when, while marking a class's examination scripts, I realised that it was the non-Sikh pupils who had written that Sikhs believe in one God while the Sikh pupils had written that Sikhs believe in ten gods.

During their initial interview in the Coventry-based study the eight to 13 year-old interviewees were shown the *ik oankar* symbol and were then asked what it meant. In almost every case they enunciated the words '*ik oankar*' and translated these as 'one God'. In subsequent conversation the children frequently mentioned God as interacting with them, either benevolently or to punish. They spoke of respecting and loving God, of thanking, turning to and listening to God, and of God as loving, helping and forgiving them. Young Sikhs accepted that God's intervention could, as the following account shows, be particular and with visible result:

> My mum had It [*amrit*, holy water] once from India. No one drunk it and a few weeks later it was vanished and my mum goes, 'God's probably going [i.e. saying], "You're not going to drink it so I'll take it away from you".'

The young people frequently spoke of God's activity in their lives in connection with prayer (see chapter 9). God, according to one child, speaks to people 'in your mind', telling them, for instance, not to be naughty, and an eight year-old girl revealed that:

> When I am asleep, when I pray [to] God, I have a feeling that God comes into me . . . He says like, 'What's the matter?' in my ear . . . When I was stuck on my mathematics . . . he helped me and he gave me B with a line under and that's a good score.

A ten year-old girl similarly connected 'God' with academic success when she explained: 'If you believe in God more you grow bigger and faster and your brain expands and you can memorise things.' God made rules and might punish people for bad deeds such as swearing. This, and God's role of rewarding good deeds, were mentioned particularly in connection with dying, as by this nine year-old girl: 'The body stays here but the soul of them goes up to God . . . and if they're so good and they love God really, really a lot God will keep them.'

'God' as a translation of 'Guru'

At the same time, reflecting the conceptual diversity which was apparent in their elders' English usage, the young people made it clear to varying degrees that 'God' was also a translation for 'Guru'. They directly equated 'God' and 'Guru' both when they were asked the meaning of 'Guru' and when they were asked for the meaning of 'God'. The assumed inter-changeability of the two words is also evident respectively from two young people's references to *gurpurbs* (anniversaries associated with the Gurus' lives, e.g. the annual celebration of the birth of Guru Nanak) as 'God's birthday', and from descriptions of incense burning and repetition of prayer ('*path*') in front of a 'photo of God'. Both adults and children refer to religious pictures (which they often have in the form of retailers' trade calendars) as 'photos'. Children's rationales for expected behaviour were based on the same equation.

Sikhs ain't allowed to smoke. Our Gods ain't smoking, that's why.

(This ten year-old boy's statement refers to Guru Gobind Singh's prohibition of tobacco.)

You have to have something on your head because most of the Gods had something on their head because they had long hair. (nine year-old girl)

There was a particularly strong equation of the first Guru, Nanak and the tenth Guru, Gobind Singh, with 'God'. I showed all the children a picture of Guru Nanak and asked what it portrayed. The following response is typical: 'the first God, Guru Nanak'. The religious educationist, Brian Gates, too had found a generation earlier, that, when he asked children to draw a picture of God, the 32 Sikhs' drawings 'were mostly in the form of Guru Nanak' (1976). 'God' also referred to Guru Gobind Singh – both as historical Guru and as the Guru alive today:

You put it [*kara*, i.e. steel bangle] on your wrist, it's to remind you of God, Guru Gobind Singh Ji. (nine year-old girl)

Many references to 'God' were to pictures of the Gurus. One girl explained how such pictures came to be painted:

> They pray to him, they pray, then God showed their picture and sometimes, like they draw it. They pray and a picture like God comes like in their mind and they see it. Then they try and draw him and put it on the wall.

God was understood as visible to those who have practised *nam simaran* (mindfulness of God's name, e.g. by reading scripture) in a sustained way, as emphasised by another young woman:

> They say God is everywhere . . . If you do *nam simaran* a lot you can see God. My mum was telling me once, she never used to do *path* or anything, then once in her mind she saw a light flashed . . . she saw sort of God picture . . .

An 11 year-old boy reflected at the greatest length on the relationship between the concept of Guru, for which he used the word 'messenger', and what he called 'the real God':

> We've got ten Gods plus the eleventh, the holy book, and that is really what I like about [my religion]. We've got eleven Gods and we know which one we can pray to – the one that is, the one who actually made us . . . Guru Nanak and the other ones are messengers from the real God. I don't know [who the real God is]. He . . . is with us and he tells Guru Nanak . . . what we should do when we are Sikhs. That's the same [God] for every religion. The person who's hearing your prayers is the one you pray to, so it's up to you. If you want to pray to the eleven Gods you can. If you don't want to you can pray to the real one. So it goes from us to Guru Nanak and Guru Nanak passes on to the real God.

Given that the scriptures are believed by Sikhs to be the living Guru, it is not surprising that some children equated God not only with the ten historic human Gurus but also with the Guru Granth Sahib, the 1430-page volume of hymns which is central to all corporate Sikh acts of worship.

The 11 year-old's thought develops even in the process of articulating it, with a hierarchy, or a line of communication between 'us' and the 'real God', emerging. Other subjects did not show this level of conceptual discrimination. Some did however, distinguish between 'God' and 'Guru' (much as some Christian children speak of 'God and Jesus'). So, referring to the *janam sakhi* story of Malik Bhago (a rich man whose invitation Guru Nanak rejected in preference for an honest, poor man's hospitality), a ten year-old boy explained that Guru Nanak squeezed blood from the rich man's *roti* (bread, *chapati*) 'by his magic from God because he was really good'.

'God' and 'Babaji' as equivalent terms

To understand what some young Sikhs said one needs to consider the word *'Baba'* or *'Babaji'*, a term which is also used for the Gurus including the Guru Granth Sahib. The word *Babaji* (the *ji* is honorific) is a respectful term for addressing and referring to elderly men and means (paternal) 'grandfather'. It is also the usual way in which devotees address or refer to a living spiritual leader or *sant*. Although this is not part of official Sikh belief, and it is condemned by many Sikhs, there is a tendency for *sants*, charismatic spiritual masters – some of whom are believed to have healing power – to be regarded as if they were not only preachers of the Gurus' teaching but as Guru themselves (Nesbitt 1985; Tatla 1992). A ten year-old boy, who had needed a cure for his asthma, recalled the following visit to a *sant*.

> We went to Wolverhampton once and we went to this God's place . . . [he gave my mum] water to drink every day . . . she went to God and he goes [i.e. says] that he [the boy] has to drink this and he can't eat egg or [non-vegetarian] stuff like that.

Coventry, like some other cities with large Sikh communities, not only has gurdwaras that are managed by elected committees, but also gurdwaras established by the followers of living *sants* whose authority is unquestioned in matters such as their running and organisation.

Further conversation showed that those young Sikhs who said *'Babaji'* did not simply use the same word *'Babaji'* for two distinguishable entities, God and a human *sant*, but that (a) they (and their parents) believed that the *sant* was indeed God in respect of supernatural powers, and that (b) *'Babaji'*, like 'Guru', refers to the scriptures.

Multiple usage of 'God' and 'Babaji' by individual children

Although not all these young Sikhs used the word 'God' in as many (from an outsider's standpoint) ways the excerpts below from an interview with a nine year-old boy, who was not a devotee of a living *Baba*, illustrate the not unusual conceptual span of individual usage.

1 My God was never borned [sic] and he never dies.
2 My God wasn't a Muslim.
3 If anybody prays to God all the time they get all powerful.
4 This man – he's a priest, God, right . . . he growed [i.e. grew] bigger and bigger . . . The God picked the baby up.
5 Under my God's bed . . . because my God ate all of it in his mouth.

Here in (1) God is understood as in *mul mantar* which declares the 'one reality' to be '*ajuni*', not taking birth, whereas in (2) 'God' is used for Guru Gobind Singh. In (3) 'God' may have been meant in a transcendent sense consonant with the *mul mantar*'s stress on oneness or could equally well have any or all of the senses evident in (2), (4) and (5). In (4) the boy is recounting the story of Vasudeva carrying his divine son Krishna which he had seen in the *Mahabharat* (Hindu epic) on television. In (5) he uses the term 'God's bed' for the stand (*palki*) on which the Guru Granth Sahib rests and suggests that he shares the belief that the Guru Granth Sahib (like Hindu deities) physically consumes food which is offered by devotees. This spectrum of usage —with the absence of (4) and the addition of 'living spiritual master' – can be paralleled in some individuals' usage of '*Babaji*'.

Understanding the young people's concept of God

Examination of the young Sikhs' apprehension of the sacred through their usage and understanding of 'God', 'Guru' and '*Babaji*' shows first their unanimity in taking for granted the existence of 'God', unlike many of their more secular peers. The relationship between 'God' as translation for '*oankar*' and 'God' as equivalent to 'Guru' or '*Baba*' is left unclear, with only the most articulate attempting to spell out the possibility of God as both one and many – or at least as ten or 11.

When considering the broad spectrum of use and understanding of the word 'God' it must be remembered first that interviews revealed that in every young person's home adults spoke Punjabi and in many homes English was used by none or only a minority of the adults. As a result Sikh children were hearing about cultural and spiritual matters in Punjabi in the home as well as in the gurdwara. When they used the English word 'God' it is reasonable to assume that they were translating concepts which they had absorbed not only through English but also through their mother-tongue. Such an explanation makes it easier to understand why it is that the Sikh children's most frequent use of God was not overtly monotheistic but as a translation of 'Guru', or of the even more inclusive Punjabi word '*Baba*'. 'God', a word drawn from a language other than their mother-tongue, has been given the encompassing conceptual content of the mother-tongue folk term '*Baba*', as well as of '*oankar*' and other words for divinity or transcendent reality which are translated as 'God' in books on Sikhism.

Thus bilingualism – including as it does code-switching – introduces a complicating factor to the American anthropologist, James P. Spradley's analysis of terms as 'analytic' or 'folk' terms (1980). Both insiders and outsiders (both Sikhs and their non-Sikh teachers) may share a term – in this case 'God'. What needs to be examined is – to use another American anthropologist Clifford Geertz's adjective (1983: 57; Jackson 1997a: 34) – the 'experience-near' concept which it expresses. This can only be clarified by searching for the Punjabi terms for which it is serving as synonym. There is in English no term encompassing an equivalent spectrum of meaning.

It is possible also that, when using the term 'God', Sikh children do invest it with something of the meaning that it has for a western, English-speaking society, shaped as this has been by the Judaeo-Christian tradition and European philosophy. When Sikh children hear the English word 'God' it is often from westerners – and in school – and it is possible, but by no means certain, that their understanding and usage of the word are also coloured by western culture without their realising this. Although the Coventry Sikh findings differ markedly from findings among their Christian peers an overlap is nonetheless clear. Many of the Sikhs' statements about God in the context of prayer, punishment and judgement resembled statements from their Christian peers.

Also discernible, in some statements, is the Hindu ethos which permeates the wider Indic context in which Sikhism arose and in which it continues to exist. Simultaneous emphasis on God's oneness and on a plurality of 'Gods' is unproblematic in the Hindu context. The children had watched episodes of the televised Hindu epic, *Mahabharat* [*Mahabharata*], with enthusiasm. When they referred to Hindu gods, whether distinguishing them from 'our Gods' or identifying them with 'my God', they conveyed an assumption of shared or cognate heritage.

Shifting the focus from 'God' to *amrit* will highlight the comparable conceptual breadth of this term too, and will exemplify the similar gap between practice, according to normative statements, and young British Sikhs' experience.

Amrit in curriculum books and Sikh literature

Curriculum books explain that *amrit* is the sweetened water that is stirred and then administered in the rite of initiation to the Khalsa. Butler (1993: 40–1) and Draycott (1996: 26–7) provide a double spread on 'taking amrit' or 'Amrit Sanskar'. Mention is also made of *amrit* as the sweetened water which is put on a new-born baby's tongue (Butler 1993: 38). Cole and Sambhi's dictionary definition summarises thus:

> Nectar. This is made from water into which sugar crystals (patashas) have been stirred with a double-edged sword, a khanda, while certain scriptural passages are recited. It is used in naming and initiation ceremonies. (1990: 37)

Only Dhanjal mentions the miraculous healing power of the *amrit* (sacred water) of the pool in what are now the precincts of Harmandir Sahib, the Golden temple in Amritsar (1993: 13 and 34).

Realistically, at least for younger pupils, curriculum books leave out of account the spiritual significance of the term in Sikh understanding (in scripture and commentary) which is included in Cole and Sambhi's definition of *amrit*:

> Guru Nanak stressed the concept of amrit as Nam or Shabad, the name or word of God, rather than something material: 'God's word is true and sweet, the stream of nectar; whoever drinks it is emancipated' (AG 1275). (1990: 37)

Similarly, in his interpretation of verses by Guru Nanak, Guru Ram Das and by their eminent follower, Bhai Gurdas, one commentator draws together the *amrit* of 'the Name of God in the heart of man and of 'communion and union with God' and the 'Mystery of Baptism' (Kapur Singh 1989: 180).

Kapur Singh also includes in his exposition the *amrit* of the ancient (Hindu) cosmic myth. *Amrit* (etymologically related through Greek and Latin respectively to English's 'ambrosia' and 'immortal') means undying. In Hindu literature it often refers to the 'elixir of life' (Patwant Singh 1988: 32) which the gods won by competing with the demons in churning the ocean of milk (Ions 1967: 48; O'Flaherty 1975: 270–80). A drop of this *amrit* is believed to have fallen to earth where Amritsar now stands, the Punjabi city dear to Sikhs for its Harmandir Sahib (Golden Temple).

In curriculum books the focus is on initiation in the *amrit* ceremony on Vaisakhi day; there is no mention of *amrit* as water that has been empowered by its proximity to the Guru Granth Sahib, to the *nishan sahib* (gurdwara flagpole bearing the *khanda* sign) or to a historic Guru or living Baba, and which then, in its turn, is used by individuals for empowerment and purification, as will be illustrated below. This omission itself accords with the influential *Sikh Code of Discipline*, the *Rahit Maryada*, which states that practices such as placing water near the Guru Granth Sahib during a reading are forbidden (McLeod 2003: 386)). Yet the young Coventrian Sikhs' references were to *amrit* in this sense more frequently than to *amrit* as the sweetened water of initiation in 1699 and in contemporary initiations.

Amrit in the young Sikhs' experience

'Holy water' and '*amrit*' were not the subject of prepared questions in the semi-structured interviews but many of the subjects used these terms unprompted in answer to questions on their daily routine, on the five Ks (external signs of Sikh commitment), or when recounting a visit to India, in addition to talking about the role of *amrit chhakana* (receiving initiation).

References were so frequent that during analysis of the data the transcripts were submitted to a computer search for mentions of '*amrit*' and 'water'. Of the 45 interviewees, 32 spoke about *amrit*, three without using the actual word. *Amrit* was the word for sacred or sacralising water most often employed by the subjects in English conversation, although followers of a locally based *sant*, Baba Ajit Singh, used the variant '*amritjal*'. The words '*jal*' and '*pani*' – both meaning 'water' – were used less frequently to refer to water in this devotional context.

The young Sikhs mentioned *amrit* or holy water in the following contexts: their daily routine (morning and evening); spiritual masters, i.e. *Baba*s (in particular in association with illness and examinations); procedures centred on the Guru Granth Sahib both in the gurdwara (being laid to rest in the evening) and in their home (being brought in for a special occasion); travelling in India; Guru Gobind Singh and Sikhs who maintain the discipline of the five Ks. Examination of the appearances of *amrit* in the Coventry data shows that most references would provide an answer to one of five underlying questions:

(1) What transforms water into *amrit*?
(2) Where do you get it from?
(3) Why do people use it?
(4) How is *amrit* used and treated?
(5) What is the effect of using it?

The transformation

The manner in which Coventry tap water becomes *amrit* (a medium of power) is mysterious but, when asked to do so, children who had referred to *amrit* indicated the following ways. First, as suggested by the prohibition in *Rahit Maryada*, water is believed to become *amrit* by standing under the Guru Granth Sahib. An 11 year-old girl explained:

> It (amrit) [is] . . . in a big thing [like] and there's water in it . . . and someone has to do the path [reading] and it's a holy book where they read out and all that. When it's all finished, all that goes into the water and that's why we call it amrit.

She did not mention whether the container was left open during the reading, a practice which suggests that any lid would act as a barrier to 'all that' going to the water. Nor is it clear to what 'all that' refers. Popular usage suggests that the utterance of the Gurbani (the Gurus' utterances which comprise the Guru Granth Sahib) releases an energy which is absorbed and subsequently mediated by the water rather as an audio-tape captures sound for subsequent transmission. To quote one Punjabi teacher: 'They leave it open, the jars, and when they say prayers three days, *akhand path* they call it, and all the prayer goes into it, so that makes the holy water.'

Second, *amrit* was mentioned in connection with a spiritual teacher (*Baba*). Subjects mentioned collecting the water from two Babajis. One girl explained: 'He [*Babaji*] [like] prays on the water to do whatever job the person say, that's how it's different.' Here the image is of a person of known spiritual power charging (in both senses of the word) a specific allocation of water to carry out a specific function. This can be compared with the instance of the godman Sathya Sai Baba cited in Jackson and Nesbitt (1993: 124).

A third way in which water is transformed into *amrit* was mentioned by another 12 year-old boy, referring to a practice unique in Coventry to the gurdwara which is presided over by Baba Ajit Singh:

> You know where the *nishan sahib* [Sikh pennant] is, there's a bucket of water to clean that up [i.e. the concrete base of the *nishan sahib*] every Sunday. They throw water to clean it up and then, when it comes down, everyone calls that holy water. They put it in bottles.

Fourth, there was a suggestion of a transforming effect on the water which is used for purifying the path of the Guru Granth Sahib when it is carried on the reader's head (e.g. to its night-time place of rest). A ten year-old girl said: 'You use ordinary water [to flick in front of the Guru Granth Sahib] but I think it's because it turns into *amritjal* [while you're doing that]. I don't know [how].'

Fifth, young people also mentioned holy water in connection with Sikh pilgrimage places in India. Their accounts suggest (as does some pilgrim cum tourist literature on Sikh historic religious sites) that through its asso- ciation with the place where a Guru or saintly person lived the water continues to be imbued with healing power. For example:

> When I went to the holy place where there's water coming out of the moun- tain and I had to stand in it and I had to have a deep breath and then go in and then when we had it then they allowed us to get bottles and fill them and at the temple the water was coming from.

In the traditional account of Guru Gobind Singh's initiation of the *panj piare* (the 'five beloved ones', his first followers to be initiated as Singhs), the Guru made *amrit* by stirring water, to which his wife had added sugar sweets. He used a *khanda* (two-edged sword) to stir the water, while repeating certain prayers. Present-day *panj piare* similarly sweeten the water at the early morning ceremony for initiating new members of the Khalsa (see chapter 4). However, children are unlikely to witness an *amrit* ceremony and so very few interviewees described water being transformed into *amrit* in such a rite.

What emerges clearly from the young Sikhs' accounts of transformation, taken as a whole, is the fact that, to quote Patwant Singh, *amrit* can mean 'water sanctified by the touch of the sacred' (1988: 32). The sanctification may involve one of the historical human Gurus or the scripture which is the living Guru, in the form of the volume (as when it is conveyed to someone's house or to its nightly resting place) or in the sense of the spoken content (as during a *path* or an initiation ceremony). In the latter case the *panj piare* represent the Guru just as the first *panj piare* did when Guru Gobind Singh himself, in turn, received initiation from them in 1699 and, moreover, all the words which they utter as they stir the sweetened water are from the Guru Granth Sahib or from a composition of Guru Gobind Singh.

In the case of water empowered or sacralised by contact with the base of the *nishan sahib* it has to be remembered that Sikhs treat the *nishan sahib* in a manner sometimes reminiscent of Hindus' treatment of a *murti* (image), when they annually bathe it in yoghurt and reclothe it. The power associated with it was evident from Sikhs' eagerness to touch those in physical contact with it at the ceremonial reclothing of the pole.

One characteristic attributed to the sacralised water is that, unlike most water – but like *Ganga jal* (Ganges water) in the experience of Hindus – *amrit* will not 'go green' (Nesbitt 1991: 25). In other words the water's new power is physically effective not only in countering disease but also in averting the growth of organisms in the water.

It is not surprising that children whose families attended gurdwaras established by the followers of a charismatic leader reported collecting *amrit* for domestic consumption from '*Babaji*'. In the case of Baba Ajit Singh both a reserve at the house where he stayed on visits to Coventry and water direct from rinsing the base of the *nishan sahib* were mentioned.

Reasons and methods for using *amrit* and its effects

The reasons which young Sikhs volunteered, and the effects that they mentioned, were all good and desirable in their eyes: empowerment, healing (e.g. to cure 'throat-ache' and 'asthma'), purification (of the area over which the Guru Granth Sahib is to be carried), academic success and protection from harm. The methods for obtaining these benefits were drinking the *amrit*, splashing or sprinkling it and – though less often – bathing in it, or in water to which *amrit* had been added.

An awareness of the transformative, empowering effect of the *amrit* with which Guru Gobind Singh initiated his Khalsa is clear in one ten year-old girl's account of the event in 1699:

> *Babaji* . . . turned them [five volunteers] all alive again and made them into *panj piare*, and then he made strong *amritjal* and he put something in it and then a bird

came, got a bit – it was just a little bird – and then when he had it there was an eagle. I think it was in a tree, and then the little bird went and killed it.

Accounts of the initiation of the *Khalsa* often include this story of the small birds which turned into fighters after drinking from the bowl of *amrit* which Guru Gobind Singh and his wife had prepared (see Macauliffe 1985: 94).

Regarding academic success, an 11 year-old recalled: 'Yes, my cousin went to the gurdwara and he prayed and drank it, and then he got I think it was three straight A's and he's gone to Sheffield University.' Regarding protection a nine year-old devotee of Baba Ajit Singh described an evening ritual:

What my mum does is she like gets some *amritjal* and fills a glass with *amritjal* and then she starts like splashing it on the house to keep it nice and safe. She does it outside as well . . . on the pavement . . . near the gate.

Her ten year-old sister volunteered the view that 'I think it's to keep robbers out – outside, because we've got a path outside and we do it there'. In relation to the fear of intruders the use of *amrit* can be understood as having the psychological effect of allaying fear, as suggested by the words of a Punjabi woman referred to in Nesbitt (1991: 25). Alternatively subjects may have regarded it as literally marking a boundary within which no harm could befall.

Most of the references to *amrit* above are to two applications, namely drinking and sprinkling. The young people spoke of both as daily occurrences in the home. Describing what happened in the morning, after prayer, an 11 year-old girl said:

Then you're supposed to drink *amrit* which is *pani* [water] you put round the house . . . it's just a small cup and everyone has a bit out of it . . .

They mentioned drinking *amrit* in the evening as well as in the morning. Thus a ten year-old girl who attended the Ramgarhia gurdwara said:

Afterwards [after bedtime prayers] we drink this sort of water. It's called *amrit*. First you put water, then you . . . get special water [at the gurdwara] and you put it into the water you've already got, and it's holy and you drink it after you've done your prayers. You pour some and you count five and you stop drinking. We only drink it five times.

'Splashing' is the translation of *chhitta*. One girl wrote in her diary: 'I have been woken up by *amrit* splashed on my face this is done so that the house is splashed with goodness.' Her sister elaborated:

When we get up my mum goes round the house with *amrit* which is – it's *pani* [water], it's water and it's kind of like blessed water and you're supposed to splash it round your house every morning . . . We've got two big bottles in the cupboard downstairs and you're supposed to splash it round with this long stick called *dhup* [incense] and it lets off smoke and this smoke is also blessed as well and it's supposed to bless your house every morning.

The children stressed hygiene and cleanliness as vital for anyone who was in contact with *amrit*. For example, reporting his father's daily routine, a 12 year-old boy said: 'First he'll have a bath, then he'll throw the holy water with his fingers, like spread it all round the shop and round the house.' Likewise a ten year-old girl mentioned: 'We've got to have a bath before we have it.'

Apart from bathing, or at least having clean hands before handling *amrit*, the followers of Baba Ajit Singh would recite the sacred formula '*Dhann Guru Nanak*' (Great is Guru Nanak) before drinking the holy water. Moreover, if those concerned are not already vegetarian, this daily drinking of *amrit* may be preceded by abstention from meat and eggs. As with holy water in Hindu tradition, children mentioned that the *amrit* is put in a clean container and that it may be added to tap water, thus increasing the quantity without diluting the efficacy and purity of the *amrit*.

Whereas unfamiliarity with scriptural language may impose a barrier between young diaspora Sikhs and the verbal content of worship, *amrit* retains its immediacy and accessibility. The children see, taste and feel it and experience the ensuing sense of well-being. As a non-verbal channel of empowerment it is as potent in the diaspora as in Punjab.

Reflection

In most published English-language accounts of the Sikh tradition for the lay reader there is no whiff of this complexity. 'God' and 'Guru' are clearly distinguished and '*Babaji*' does not figure, although the '*sant*' receives a brief mention in at least two curriculum books (Butler 1993; Dhanjal 1987). Many curriculum books contain Guru Nanak's *mul mantar* in Gurmukhi script with an English translation. The textbook presentation is of a unitary God, bereft by English translation of the intertextuality – the rich patina of cultural association – of the Gurus' many words for the divine, and conceptually distinct from the Gurus and from the concept of Guru.

The ethnographic inquiry into some young Coventrian Sikhs' understanding of 'God' shows the diversity of their religious worlds. Concerned Sikh elders might regard this scenario as evidence of widespread popular misconceptions fitting with a discredited Hindu paradigm and encouraged by (false) *Babas*. Meanwhile, to the psychologist the young people's – and their elders' – understandings of 'God' may exemplify stages in a Western/European model of conceptual development. While the development taking place in some individuals' thinking was apparent in the transcripts of their reflections, the range of adults' usage of the word 'God' and of their attitudes to *Babas* – from scornful rejection to self-sacrificial veneration – must also be taken into account. Certainly the findings vindicate the ethnographic method in uncovering the multi-faceted Sikh world inhabited by young Sikhs, and the points of contact and divergence between this and the text book image of their religious nurture. My contention is that teachers need to be critically alert to a tendency to the slipperiness of language, to the tendency of over-simple reduction of 'religion' to codified 'belief' and of overlooking the gap between normative statements and popular expression.

The Coventry research suggests that as far as the tapping of sacred and sacralising power is concerned, the diversity of popular Punjabi religion described by Harjot Singh Oberoi in nineteenth-century Punjab has survived, not however as a diversity of identity but as a multiplicity of symbolic meaning (1994). *Amrit* is not only the tenth Guru's water of baptism or the 'nectar of *Nam*', but is also water which is imbued with the potent purity of *Ganga jal* or which serves as a medium for the power of miracle-working saints. In its current meanings *amrit* demonstrates how the rich tradition of popular Punjabi religious belief and practice is now on offer in Sikh guise from Sikh practitioners. For many young British Sikhs it is an unproblematic feature of their tradition.

For religious educationists and teachers emergent issues from this chapter's discussion of fieldwork among young UK Sikhs are the gap between the normative and the operative – between the rhetoric and the reality of religions – and also between the representation of religions in the syllabus and the experience of pupils (and staff) in schools. One question is: what are the grounds for distinguishing 'belief' and 'superstition' – a question that is pursued further in chapter 6. The present chapter is offered to support the argument – not necessarily that the content of published curriculum materials should become more complex (or defy the best intentions of religious 'leaders'), but that ethnographic accounts can deepen and sharpen the 'religious literacy' of those teachers who are representing a faith (in this case 'Sikhism') and who are pastorally involved with members of the associated faith community. Awareness of the detail and dynamics of experience, and of its articulation, in one 'community' opens one up to the likelihood of similar diversity in other communities.

Tradition and Choice – What Young Hindus Believe

6

Late Modernity and Choice

To what extent do young people choose their beliefs? How do these relate to published accounts of adherents' beliefs? What distinguishes a belief from a superstition? With these questions in mind this chapter shifts from interviews with eight to 13 year olds who identified themselves as Sikhs to interviews with 16 to 23 year olds who identified themselves as Hindus. Choice is discussed with reference to three ideas (or 'beliefs') that recur as central themes in publications on 'Hinduism'. These are beliefs about 'God' (as one or many), about karma (the moral law of cause and effect) and about *dharma* (which is sometimes rendered in English as 'right conduct'). *Dharma* is the term used for an individual's responsibilities to the family, because of being, for example, a son or a daughter.

The fourth area to be discussed is *nazar* (the evil eye). This is not, any more than any other cross-cultural presuppositions or anxieties, one that figures in curriculum books on Hinduism, or on any other faith, and neither pupils nor their older relatives are likely to bring it to the notice of others. It concerns a globally widespread explanation of certain misfortunes in terms of the damaging effects of the 'evil eye' of hate, envy and fear. The young Hindus' views on *nazar* are included in order to question assumptions about what is privileged by the term 'belief' and what is written off as 'superstition', about the distinctions that are often drawn between 'religion' or 'faith tradition' and 'culture' and between 'faiths', and about the authority of anyone to arbitrate.

The processes that characterise society at the start of the twenty-first century are variously subsumed in the term 'modernity' (Giddens 1991: 5; Heelas 1996: 135), 'late modernity' (Giddens 1991: 29, Leganger-Krogstad 2001), high modernity (Giddens 1991: 27) and 'post-modernity' (Smith 1993). I understand 'late modernity' as subsuming these various modernities, which the respective authors elaborate by reference to increasing globalisation and de-centralisation and to the concomitant plurality, fluidity and provisionality in human experience

– not least religion. For Skeie (1995) religious plurality is a significant aspect of post-modernity, and pluralism is a significant reponse to it. In addition to scholarly attention, the religious aspects of late modernity frequently attract media coverage (e.g. Bunting 1998; Creedon 1998).

For analysts of our late modern society, choice is a recurrent theme: 'Choosing seems now to be our inexorable fate' (Melucci 1997: 62). Consider also:

> Every person growing up in this late modern world, then, faces a continuous challenge to make choices, to maintain commitments to specific practices, values, and persons, and to integrate these choices and commitments, together with emotions, volitions and experiences, into a more or less consistent personality. (Wardekker and Miedema 2001)

In both academic and popular writing it is this presupposition of choice as a dominant feature of late modernity which stamps the metaphors, usually food-related, for the religious and cultural diversity of the 'global village'. Images of supermarket, buffet, cafeteria, smorgasbord, cocktail abound, as was evident in the spate of journalistic outpourings that followed the sacking of the then England foorball team coach, Glen Hoddle, for publicly expressing his belief that disability could be attributed to karma (e.g. Nickolds 1999). This has certainly been true, too, of rhetoric in the public debate on the nature of multi-faith religious education.

Choice is a recurrent and crucial aspect of the experience of young British Hindus (currently in their teens and twenties), belonging as they do to a religious minority within a wider society that is variously termed 'secular' (Østberg 2003) and 'post-Christian' (Ota 1997).

As chapter 9 will explore further, some observers reflect on the resultant adaptation of members of such minorities in terms of all-out 'culture-clash' with individuals torn 'between two cultures' (e.g. Anwar 1976, 1998; Ghuman 1994). Their critics (influenced by Friedrich Barth) have taken aboard his understanding of ethnicity as 'situational' (e.g. Drury 1989) or have employed metaphor – in this case from linguistics – such as 'code-switching' (Ballard 1994; Nesbitt 2000). Whichever model is favoured, it seems that young British Hindus are faced with ongoing choices between alternative value systems and behaviours. The continuous matching of individual cultural expression to the culturally disparate arenas of their lives suggest that young British Hindus may well engage in frequent and unavoidable choice.

In talking of their beliefs and values do young Hindus mention or indicate that they have made choices? If so, between what systems? On what issues? Vegetarianism is one, as we have seen in chapter 3. Who or what have been decisive in the formation of beliefs that they articulate? Answers could include, for instance, parents or the media. Moreover, do these young people's choices suggest particular patterns – a preference for the 'scientific' viewpoint over the 'religious', for example, or a rejection of some traditional Hindu beliefs and practices as 'superstition'? Furthermore, do the young people apply or appeal to 'reason' in adopting their particular stances? Another important question is whether processes underway in young people's lives can appropriately be called 'choice', i.e. to what extent individuals are 'free' and their actions are 'undetermined'.

Areas of belief

God/gods

All the young people expressed a firm conviction of the existence of God. Without exception they believed in God and gods: the term 'god' covered 'photos' (pictures of deities and spiritual teachers) and an unseen, divine protector 'up there'. The young people used the word 'God' as well as Hindu terms such as (in the case of one male undergraduate) 'Bhagvan', Swami' (Lord), 'Antarayami' (inner director) and Brahma (God as creator). Most respondents slid from singular to plural and vice versa with no sense of contradiction. In the words of one female Gujarati employee: 'If an English person said to me, "I believe in God, do you believe?" . . . I would [say], "I believe in every god,"' and in the words of a female Punjabi employee: 'In my house any god's obviously welcome . . . God's God, there's one God out there, so that's what I believe in as well'. God's singularity or plurality was not a problem in the way that it is for many non-Hindus looking in on the tradition; cf. Kurtz (1992: 1–5) on his mental block when Hindu informants talked of 'individual' goddesses as being all 'one'. It is true that two young women stressed the plurality more than the others, who voiced the prevalent Hindu understanding that 'all gods are one' – and so Ganesh, Krishna etc. are 'forms' or 'facets', or are comparable to the ministers of a single government (the analogy for the one ultimate God).

Karma/ reincarnation

Almost as general as belief in God/gods, though relatively few used the term 'karma' unprompted, was a feeling (a belief?) that good deeds are rewarded and bad deeds are punished. One undergraduate was unusual in his ability to define the term karma as 'meaning the cycle of birth and death [and] also . . . the fruits of one's actions'. A sixth former (a Punjabi woman) admitted:

> I always bring that [i.e. karma] into nearly everything that happens to everybody else, that they must have done something wrong in their past life . . . sometimes

> when things happen and you just can't explain it, in our religion we actually have an explanation for it. A lot of people say 'Oh why did this happen to me, why? why?' and it's nice to be able to . . . say 'well they must have done something wrong in their past life and they are paying for it in this life.'

Incidentally, the reason that the word 'karma' has not been italicised is its currency in contemporary English. When UK-educated Hindus use the term they usually pronounce it, as English-speakers generally do, as if it was 'calmer'. In their families' Indian languages the pronunciation is rather different. For example, the Punjabi form 'karam' rhymes with the English word 'Durham'.

In most cases the young Hindus emphasised the likelihood of repercussions in this life rather than in a future existence. So a male sixth former said:

> I don't think of it as: if I do this well . . . I'll have a wicked life after I die. I think of it as treat others how you wish to be treated yourself . . . People who aren't nice to people haven't got any friends.

At the same time some of the young people appeared to accept that punishment or reward for action in a previous life could result in rebirth as a creature of a different species. In the words of a male undergraduate:

> I believe if you do nice things and help a lot of people well you can come back as a nice person or a nice animal . . . I think that if you do good things then you can come back as a nice say plant.

Some scepticism about reincarnation, especially regarding rebirth as an animal, was also voiced, with one female undergraduate feeling there was 'no real evidence', a male sixth former undecided between reincarnation and heaven and his sister, a university student, dismissing any notion of 'coming back as a dog' as 'silly'.

Dharma/responsibility

Some spoke of their duties and responsibilities as members of their families. Traditionally, certain expected roles are determined to a great extent by gender, by relative seniority and by relationship (Jackson and Nesbitt 1993: 43ff.). So a son's responsibilities would differ from a daughter's and an elder son's from a younger brother. Thus, when asked a general question about what he believed, another undergraduate articulated his duty as a son:

> My main one [belief] is taking care of my parents, that's my main one. That's the main belief that I really do believe in. I hope to carry it out the best I can.

Similarly, a female sixth former told me that 'I think that is important in the Indian families actually that the older children, and the parents, it is their duty to look after the younger ones.'

Nazar (evil eye), jadu (magic) and misfortune

Whereas assumptions in the three areas discussed above are the subject of formal teachings enshrined in scripture, exemplified in the ancient epics and wealth of stories about the gods (*purana*), and expounded by philosophers, the association of calamity with *nazar* ('the evil eye') is a 'folk belief' which is generally described as being an element of 'culture' rather than of 'religion'. All the young Hindus were aware of the fact that at least some members of their community attributed individuals' misfortunes to the fact that another community member had 'cursed' them or set an 'evil eye' on them. For both the young Punjabis and Gujaratis the key word was *nazar*. However, they differed in the amount of credence they gave to this belief. Both South Asians themselves and others disparagingly call this 'superstition' (e.g. Dosanjh and Ghuman 1996: 59) and it is – implicitly at least – written off as due to illiteracy or to low levels of education. In 2001 only 30 per cent of 342 13 to 35 year old Hindus said that they believed in magic (tantra, *jadu*, *nazar* etc.) (Santosh and Bhanot 2003: 25).

However, for millions of individuals from diverse ethnic and religious communities – including some Christian communities – a persuasive explanation of misfortune, especially of sudden unexpected catastrophe, is the agency of other people's jealousy. For example, Barbara Meyerhoff reports this belief and very similar practices among European Jews prior to their migration to America (1978: 153–4) and Alison Shaw alludes to *nazar* among Pakistani Muslims in Oxford (2000: 200–1). In the case of Hindus it is problematic to write off curses and spells as (simply) 'culture' and not religion, given the existence of 'exorcist' traditions and temples among British South Asians (see e.g. Geaves 1998b: 82 on 'black magic' in the context of devotion to Baba Balak Nath, a popular focus of reverence for many Punjabis). *Nazar* is especially feared in relation to babies and young children because their beauty may stir envy or 'tempt Providence', and any seeming praise may attract misfortune. This is also related to anxieties, widespread among South Asians in Britain, about resentful individuals performing *jadu* (spells involving tell-tale items such as hair or cloth) and the fear that such activity can result in disaster such as sickness. Steps are taken to avert the evil eye. For example, relatives apply a *kala tika*, i.e. a black mark, usually a small smudge on a baby's face. In order to counteract the effect of *nazar* they may burn chillis in the sink. This would happen if a baby were upset, apparently because someone had looked at it.

A male student realised that the best policy was to 'say nothing' about someone else's house, as either praise or criticism was liable to be construed as *nazar* and another explained:

If you keep saying to this girl that she is really sweet or good looking . . . the mum might say 'nazar lage' . . . you might be tempting fate . . . I reckon that if you keep going long enough saying things like that then you are tempting fate and the opposite could easily happen . . . It's like exam results . . . people come up to me and say 'oh you know you've done well' . . . and you say, 'Don't say that', because if you're saying that then probably the opposite will happen.

Whereas the Gujarati man quoted above suspended disbelief in *nazar* because of his parallel experience of the effect of tempting Providence in relation to examination results, a female sixth former (a science student) had established the 'logical reason behind it' that allowed her to go on believing in a 'superstition'. She explained what for her was the vindication of the practice of applying *kala tika*:

The *kala tika* idea, I saw it in the Ramayan [i.e. film of the *Ramayana* epic] when Sita was getting married they put a *kala tika* on her and then I asked my mum, 'that's what we believe in as well?' She said, 'Yes'. So you can see that's what the gods all used to believe in as well.

In both these cases the young people's comments provide evidence of doubt, and of reasoning involving parallel situations. It is to this matter of weighing up alternatives that we now turn, in relation to three prevailing worldviews: 'scientific', Christian and atheist.

Weighing up alternatives

Science

A scientific worldview had hardly impinged consciously upon views emerging from the young people's Hindu tradition. However, four men and two women did reflect on belief in creation by God versus belief in the Big Bang theory and the theory of evolution, and on divergent explanations for near-death experiences. In the cases of these six young people it had challenged traditional understandings without necessarily weakening them. So, on evolution one Punjabi sixth former recalled:

I remember my biology teacher stressing that Darwinism was true . . . over lots of generations we've evolved and it's nothing to do with God creating this or God creating that . . . I just said, 'You can't say that sir' . . . I don't so much believe in the Big Bang but I believe God created everything as it is . . . I think he is always changing things and doing things.

One of the young men saw a discrepancy between the Big Bang theory which has 'got some sort of method behind it which is believable' and 'God saying "Let there be light" . . . but, deep down inside, you always think that maybe God did say it "let there be light" and there was light . . . you don't know.' Another admitted that he didn't know if creation was a Big Bang, saying: 'I believe in God but I also have this thing about the science aspect of it, which is clashing'.

One male undergraduate accepted that scientists don't believe in God and he had adopted the view of his biology teacher who said 'science is the study of God's creation'. He went on:

> I definitely believe in God and that God created the world and everything, but having learnt physics and chemistry and having read a few things about . . . the origin of the universe, . . . people say that there was no God and that things just progressed as . . . obeying natural laws. But I think that God created things, and things like evolution happened by themselves. I mean God is there: it's just that he doesn't show himself overtly.

Alone among the interviewees he also pointed out that:

> The Hindu timescale is completely different from the timescale of scientists in the order of how things happened, when people appeared on earth and things like that . . . the *yuga* [age]'s huge, and Ram was born a whole yuga before Krishna, so that was several hundreds of thousands of years before, and scientists say that by that time you know civilisations weren't there and people weren't around, but that doesn't stop me from believing.

In vindication of Hindu views a student made the following points: the suggestion that the world resulted from a single atom is at least as unbelievable as that it was created by God; the 'Vedic scriptures . . . had information . . . before science'; and because of the transient nature of science: whatever you learn in science is refuted by what you learn at the next stage whereas the truths of religion 'have been there and have remained the same since time immemorial'. As the term 'Vedic science' suggests, for contemporary Hindus there is no essential clash between their faith tradition and new breakthroughs in scientific thinking; rather, Hinduism is seen to be 'ahead of the game' (a tendency exemplified by many Hindu writers, e.g. Prinja 1996: 41–3, 153–8, 178–80 and evident in Santosh and Bhanot 2003: 126).

A psychology student (brought up as a devotee of Sathya Sai Baba) referred to alternative explanations of near death experiences. Her studies had enabled her to focus in her reading and her dissertation on the subject of religious belief. She acknowledged that the scientific basis of the course had also challenged her religious belief:

> I think that there is an absolute truth, but I've got to say that studying it can make you turn quite negative towards any sort of an alternative to science . . . I don't think I could ever turn a non-believer, but then I've got to say being at university has made me question a bit more definite facts that I've been taught through my life.

She had come to realise that on matters of faith 'there's no way of proving it, so it is very personal, very subjective' and had found within her studies insights that appealed to her: she cited with relief Plato and Socrates 'talking with a dualist idea, where you can have a reality that you can't quite touch as well as . . . a physical and mental reality, and they both can exist in parallel universes.'

Christianity

Not only did the young Hindus engage with pervasive 'folk belief' and with the scientific paradigm, but they were constantly encountering aspects of another religious faith, Christianity. Unlike science, however, Christianity was at no point mentioned by the young Hindus as being at variance with their Hindu tradition and the Gujarati student of psychology declared that she believed as much in Christianity as in Hinduism. The Gujarati sixth former's quotation from Genesis in his musings on creation (quoted above) is one instance of the fusion of Hindu and Christian elements in their religious understanding. Another is the readiness with which 'Jesus' and 'the Jehovah's Witness God' were mentioned alongside Hindu deities when talking of God and gods. One young man (who when interviewed as a 12 year-old had likened the coconut used in *puja* to a Christingle) now drew from his knowledge of Christianity an endorsement for his own (ISKCON-based) certainty of a personal God:

> You should not only have impersonal contact, but also a personal contact with God . . . something which I know Christians firmly believe in.

His sister (a sixth former) had found mutual understanding among her contemporaries at school to be based on lived experience of faith rather than on identifying with the same faith. Of her 'best friend' she said: 'I think that's how we became friends because she has a very strong faith and so have I.' Moreover, as will be noted in chapter 10, individuals' reporting of 'religious experience' recurrently referred to being in a Christian place of worship.

Atheism

By contrast with Christianity, atheism – which they said they encountered in their peers – was totally rejected by all the young people. In the words of one female undergraduate: 'I think [like] religion gives you something to believe in . . . it gives you a purpose.' A male undergraduate expressed the view that 'I think it [atheism] is a sign of stubbornness, a sign of ignorance, a sign of not wanting to understand, a sign of thinking you are too clever and you think that you know everything', and he criticised the hypocrisy of declaring yourself an atheist and 'go[ing] to a church for any weddings'. When the young Hindus referred to acquaintances who were atheists these were in all cases peers or teachers of non-Asian background. They felt uneasy with the atheists' laughing at RE lessons – far more so than at hearing about other faiths. A male Gujarati undergraduate probably spoke for the others in articulating the distinction that he perceived between those who believe in God and those who reject any such dimension, rather than between believers of different faiths.

Tactical choice?

Some comments showed the speakers' internalisation and accommodation of secular interpretations of prayer. One male sixth former prefaced his account of offering money in the temple before his examinations with the words: 'I have a superstition'. An undergraduate quoted below rationalised his devotions as psychologically therapeutic:

> I say Hanuman Chalisa [forty verses in praise of the god Hanuman] once every morning . . . then I use the *mala* [prayer beads] . . . I say for each [bead] '*om namo shivai*' [invocation of Shiva] I do that twice . . . I find that it helps relax me . . . Before I start revision [it] just helps me understand a lot more of the work . . . it is more to do with mind over matter: if your mind is relaxed you will take a lot more in.

Young people showed evidence both of reasoning (or of assimilating the reasoning of others such as ISKCON exponents of the tradition), and of a will to retain their religious faith.

There was also evidence both of some tactical decision-making and of 'hedging their bets'. An undergraduate was unequivocal on the subject of religious and scientific accounts of creation, identifying:

> two level[s] of thinking . . . if I want to pass my examinations I have to say the things which my examiner wants . . . but if I was to . . . have a talk with my examiner . . . I would be sceptical . . . The religious view seems to be . . . more believable.

On the subject of praying a female undergraduate demonstrated her awareness of keeping her options open or of getting the benefit of the doubt. So, she explained that, as well as praying in a more traditionally Hindu way: 'just in case He's Christian' she framed her prayers in 'the normal Christian way of like "Dear God" and then I say "Amen" at the end'. However, to talk in terms of tactical choices is to disregard the conditioning or interacting factors in the young people's experience from earliest childhood which predisposed them to their present assumptions and attitudes.

Interacting factors

As explained in chapter 3, in relation to their dietary practices and assumptions, the young Hindus are affected by both the influences of society at large (e.g. mainstream television) and those of their smaller 'membership groups', their family, ethnic and faith community, *sampradaya* ('sectarian movement') and supplementary class. A male student's reasons for belief in *karma* illustrate this mutual reinforcement process:

> just because it's part of our teachings, part of our heritage, part of our scriptures which I wholeheartedly believe . . . you always hear someone saying that 'it's in our Shastras [ancient Hindu law codes], that . . . plus [Sathya Sai] Baba teaches about reincarnation as well.'

Home/family

Belief in the malign potency of *nazar* and *jadu* was solely attributed to hearing and seeing evidence of this in their family and neighbourhood. A trainee indicated how she had come to believe in the evil eye:

> They *nazar utar* [remove the effect of the evil eye] that means . . . they get someone's hair . . . and screw up the paper and you've got to sit with the little boy and then they go round seven times or three times round the head. Then they burn it . . . and if it smells that means nothing has happened to him, nobody has done anything, but if it doesn't smell that means somebody has definitely been looking at him . . . At my nephew's party, when he was two years old, they must have been saying things about him, outsiders, and he got really ill the next day. So we had to nazar utar, and **it was true**.

Another woman (a science student) showed the influence of her mother:

> They put a black dot on the forehead, don't they? It's like a *kanku* [vermilion powder], sort of black, it's meant to *nazar na lage* jae [avert the evil eye]. We all do it, my mum did it for us. Her mum had seen black magic in India and **I believe her**.

Similarly testimonies to reincarnation frequently referred to the immediate family – in this case to birth and subsequent comment on the new-born baby's resemblance to a deceased relative. To quote the same science student:

> I believe it in a sense, like one of my uncles passed away and then his son had a baby boy, and I felt like it was him . . . For every death there's a new life anyway.

Another female student recalled her 'nan' saying that someone may be 'reborn back into the same family'. Apparently corroborating this a male sixth former said that he was sure that at the moment someone died someone else was born 'and that was him again'. He illustrated his point:

'My little niece is only three years old now and my dad said, "Oh it's my mum, she's come back again"'. However, by adding 'They don't mean it but they just say it', the young man suggested that this was not a deeply held conviction.

In addition to what close relatives said, influences on young people's beliefs were mediated in the home in a variety of ways, including pictures and Asian films and television programmes, notably Zee TV. One sixth former recalled a picture that was intended to encourage vegetarianism:

> I still remember it vividly: there is a picture of a tiger at the top eating its prey, and at the top is a copy of that picture with the man eating meat.

The undergraduate who had emphasised his filial duty recollected:

> Sunrise radio they have programmes where they have Brahmin[s] on and they talk about that [caring for parents] and my mum will say, 'Listen to what they are saying' . . . and it just keeps on going in and in, and then you just realise.

As reported earlier, one female sixth former's continuing belief in *kala tika* had found support in the televised *Ramayana* (a combination of authorities – divine activity as recorded in ancient scripture combined with the most contemporary and persuasive of media).

When young people referred to the *Ramayana* and *Mahabharata* it was usually to screenplay or to stories as mediated by elders (such as concerned adults in *sampradayas*) or stories published in English. For instance, the Amar Chitra Katha comics are a popular resource. Young British Hindus have almost no direct contact with the text – even if they hear Morari Bapu's exposition of the *Ramayana* they are at a lingistic disadvantage (Nesbitt 1999b). In India too, over the centuries, only a minority (usually Brahmin men) have been able to read Sanskrit. For the most part the myth and morality of the tradition circulated in vernacular story-telling and expressive arts such as dance and drama. Marriott pointed to the likelihood that film (and so television/video) versions of the epics would gain a pan-Indian status at the expense of local variants (n.d.).

Mainstream television documentaries, too, were adduced by the young Hindus as confirming them in their view of reincarnation. In the words of a woman trainee:

> I've seen loads of films on reincarnation . . . on TV and we've seen some videos at school – religious studies . . . it was on TV three years ago and it is about two little girls . . . I believed before that but this made me more stronger.

Sampradaya

What some young Hindus said clearly indicates the influence of a guru-led grouping (*sampradaya*) in both the idiom and the theological content of their understanding. To take the example of reincarnation, one under-graduate (whose parents had been devotees of ISKCON during his childhood), was alone in linking reincarnation with both the concept of *mukti* (liberation from the cycle of rebirth) and Vaikunth (Vishnu's heaven):

> We believe in reincarnation but . . . that is not a jackpot prize. The jackpot prize is to receive . . . complete salvation which is being detached from all modes of life and receiving eternal life . . . in Vaikunth.

Moreover, he informed me that while studying the Big Bang theory in 'A' level science he had attended a conference in Birmingham organised by 'Hindu Temple Councils for Hindus in Leicester and Birmingham . . . and we had [ISKCON] devotees giving a lecture on the Big Bang theory'. He went on to outline 'the religious view' (i.e. ISKCON interpretation) that Lord Krishna's 'first son Brahma . . . a demigod . . . produced the world . . . with other demigods taking their roles.' Meanwhile, another undergraduate, a follower of Sathya Sai Baba, reported:

> Baba has said that scientists will never be able to prove that there is a God, and as far as I can see there is no way of proving there's a God apart from sheer belief.

Participation in ritual

In addition to *sampradaya*-specific, or at least *sampradaya*-reinforced inputs such as these, belief was fostered, enacted and strengthened through participation in family-centred ritual action. For example, when a parent or grandparent died the young Hindus' parents would feed the birds. Although they did not spell out rebirth in this regard, the idea that there was a strong sense of connectedness between the soul of the deceased and these living creatures (cf. Firth 1997: 111) is clear in what a female sixth former recalled:

> When my granddad died we like fed birds with rice and things for 13 days, and my dad was saying that was because the human soul stays near the family for 13 days before it actually leaves completely. So feeding the birds we're [like] feeding him.

One science student recounted his experience of the benefits of *puja* [worship involving offerings]:

> When you have a *puja* at home, where we have the brahmin come round when you buy a new house, get away evil spirits and that, I feel that's linked with the *puja* as well, the *arati* [climax in which a lighted wick is circled before the deity] . . . we did one here where we invited all our cousins down, and if you're going through a bad phase . . . we have a *katha* [reading and exposition of a narrative]

... where the brahmin comes and you go through a *vidhi* [rite] ... and he goes into each room, blesses each room to get rid of any evil spirits that were there before, or blesses the house basically so you have a good home life ... he sprays water in all directions ... I suppose psychologically you feel safer ... we hadn't lived here for that long, you feel a bit insecure but I think after that's done you feel a bit safer ... it just feels more like home.

Most movingly, another male undergraduate recounted how on his father's death:

What we call *pagri* [turban] is put on ... by my *tayaji* [father's elder brother]. . . . It was tied onto the top of my head, a pink colour ... All the prayers were said by a few religious priests there, then the turban was tied on my head. The point of that is to show that all responsibilities that my father had held would now go onto my shoulders ... his work commitments ... me and my mother and my younger brother and sisters ... It's a bit like a degree ceremony ... the whole temple was full of people ... Then I had to carry my father's picture, take it out of the temple.

Significantly, he was aware that this ritual was scripturally sanctioned, and he explicitly linked his experience with Lord Ram [Rama], the exemplar of *dharma*, when he explained that the turban-tying is:

derived directly from religious scriptures as one would see from the Ramayan ... Lord Ram, when his father passed away, was given responsibilities for the rest of the family. So the Ramayan is supposed to be the book to show how the ideal human should act.

Above all, in relation to a sense of divine presence, the young Hindus described the experience of praying (more frequently than ritual) as effective – both in achieving peace of mind and enabling them to cope with crisis (usually examinations). Chapter 9 reports some of these experiences.

Testing circumstances

Evident, too, from the young people's statements was the part which testing circumstances played in making beliefs their own. Not only did they repeatedly refer to prayer as a support at exam time, but several referred to the trauma of bereavement. Testing circumstances could also undermine practice, as one Gujarati student made clear by reporting that he had discontinued his daily prayer routine after his father's death. However, in the case of another male Gujarati undergraduate it was his experience of life with two disabled brothers (one very severely disabled), together with the family's resultant devotion to Sathya Sai Baba, that enabled him to speak with assurance of his more profoundly disabled brother's predicament:

Now we look at it more as a blessing for us . . . I mean he's probably the way he is because he did something in his previous births, that's how we look at it, so it's far easier to handle really.

Cumulative reflection

To regard this young man's faith in *karma* as 'choice' – using the smorgasbord image – may be to disregard the influence exerted by his family's Hindu tradition, by the teaching received from Sai devotees and his parents' coming to terms with tragedy. But perhaps, looked at more closely, the smorgasbord/buffet language of the analysts of late modernity should not be seen as superficial, trivial individual preference, since our selection of food illustrates continuities with individual nurture that is embedded in a cultural continuum. Certainly, in the young Hindus' case, their beliefs are conditioned and, to varying extents, resourced by their upbringing and family environment. When faced with conflicting possibilities, such as creation versus the Big Bang or the rationality/ irrationality of applying a black mark to avert downfall, they look both to the inadequacies of the alternative (e.g. the unbelievability of the Big Bang and to the transitory nature of scientific claims) and to 'evidence' for a religious belief – such as television documentaries on reincarnation. In other words, the young people's views, while recognisably continuous with tradition, suggest a process of cumulative reflection. For example, on the subject of *avatar* (God incarnating) a Punjabi woman undergraduate mused:

> In some ways God lets things happen just so that we can learn a lesson from it, but he's there for us if it gets out of hand . . . I don't believe that God himself would come incarnated as a person, I believe that God makes himself known through people and gives them the strength to find a solution . . . . I believe that God shows himself through Ram, but isn't God himself.

Reflection had led her to reject belief in *jadu* [magic]:

> The only way I've come across it is when my cousin was born and she's got Down's Syndrome and her parents are very much into all this *jadu* . . . so they've got lots of ceremonies done for her and she's got this thing around her neck, it's . . . got something in it that's supposed to protect her. And I think it causes more harm than good because people start believing in it for nothing . . . and it stops them taking responsibility for their own actions.

Young Hindus are reaching decisions based on pragmatism and becoming convinced that things work in certain ways through their observations. To give an instance:

> One day in our shop we had extremely low takings . . . My mum got worried, so she goes to our local priest [and] he goes, 'I know who cursed you, cursed

your shop because you're doing so well.' . . . He gave my mum some water and he blessed it. He goes 'Sprinkle some' with like grass . . . round the shop . . . The next day my mum sprinkles it and the takings shot up . . . and then he goes, 'Someone in your shop has dropped something which is doing this curse . . . so . . . you have to find this and bring it to me and I'll take the curse off . . . It's like a packet with rice and . . . *kankotri*, the red [powder]' . . . . About a month later my mum found a packet like that and she took it to him and things were all right again . . . We've had people trying to curse you by chucking meat in your garden.

In at least one case (the psychology student) awareness of the development of her own philosophy of life was infused with appreciation of her father's less questioning devotion as a devotee of Sathya Sai Baba. Her comparison of her own scientific conditioning with her father's capacity for unswerving total faith suggests a sense of loss as well as gain, reminiscent of Melucci's verdict:

The paradox of choice therefore creates a new kind of psychological pressure, and confronts us with new problems. Choosing among so many possibilities is a difficult undertaking and what we discard is always more than what we choose. There is an inescapable sense of loss which generates the main forms of contemporary suffering. (1997: 63)

Loaded terminology

In giving glimpses of this cumulative reflection, the research also challenges the distinctions easily drawn between 'faith/ religion' or 'beliefs' and 'superstition'. Young people expressed both certainty and scepticism with regard to both karma/ reincarnation (regarded as a pukka Hindu 'belief') and *nazar* (generally regarded as a 'superstition'). The one interviewee, quoted above, who could define karma went on to acknowledge that he did not think about karma when embarking on a course of action, but 'that is how I feel I should be thinking'. 'Feeling how I should be thinking' probably equates well with the experiential aspect of 'beliefs' for many individuals who have been nurtured in more credally-based religious systems.

Regarding both *nazar* and karma, some scepticism was expressed. At the same time, young scientists adduced as evidence for their view circumstances which would be unconvincing to non-theistic 'rationalists'. But of course if these are grounds for qualifying as a 'superstition', then so is the 'belief' that there is a God. If religious educators are to develop 'religious literacy' in pupils, this must include facilitating their thinking about why certain views are dignified as 'beliefs' and others as 'superstitions'. This will involve consideration of the role of 'authorities', scriptures and leaders as well as the pertinence of researchers' statistics.

Tradition and 'post-post tradition'

David Smith, a Sanskrit specialist, has challengingly flagged up the late modern character of the Hindu tradition (1993, 1999). He questions the assumed sequence of traditional–modern–post-modern, and (1993: 158) he criticises the sociologist, Anthony Giddens, for the statement that:

> In virtually all smaller pre-modern cultures there was only one main religious order . . . In larger traditional societies, where religious orders sometimes were more diversified, there was little pluralism in the modern sense . . . (Giddens 1991: 194)

Smith persuasively presents the view that the Hindu tradition has, over many centuries, been post-modern in the following respects: it is a 'supermarket' in so far as choice (e.g. between deities for particular worship or, indeed, between monotheism, pantheism, polytheism, atheism) reigns, and in its emphasis on consumption. Moreover simulation, spectacle and sensation are themes as prominent in Hindus' traditional dealing with divinity as they are in late or post-modernity.

This is a salutary reminder when looking at young Hindus' 'adaptation' to globalisation and the western metropolis. The tradition itself provides scope for accommodating apparent contradictions, as the Gujarati male undergraduate was well aware in relation to theology:

> There are different levels of Hinduism, and on the very basic [level] you talk about Gods and different goddesses, and then when you progress you realise that all the different Gods are in fact the same, and that's when you start to talk about the world being an illusion and that it's not reality. The real reality is that of being one with God . . . As you progress you have to end up changing how you think.

So far so good, but Giddens was talking of contradictory authorities rather than of the diversity on offer within a system, however pluriform and multi-centred. Arguably, it is not the diversity of religious beliefs and practices, but the contradiction between a dominant late modern paradigm of individualism and assumptions of a dharmic hierarchy of roles that will rock the boat of Hindu tradition, and so individuals' equilibrium, most forcefully (Ghuman 1999).

Although the responses on family responsibility and *dharma* quoted earlier do not indicate this tension, it may well be this – rather than such other areas of 'belief' as the existence of God – that will show most turbulence in future. As far as gods, karma and indeed *nazar* are concerned, the Coventry research suggests that young Hindus are comfortable with a range of dissimilar worldviews, whether their approach is one of encompassment – to use Baumann's term (1994) – by, for example, bringing the

'Christian God' into the personal pantheon; or of finding mutual endorsement (for example, ISKCON devotees and Christians preaching a personal relationship with God); or of compartmentalisation like one would-be medical student who said that she had never thought of the implications of Hindu belief for medicine or vice versa. It is possible that further research is needed to identify whether what we have observed as characteristically Hindu flexibility, and as yet further evidence of the ancient tradition's adaptability and its easiness with late modernity, is in fact second nature to minority youth more generally. Where values are concerned, this may well be a generation of 'jugglers' (Ota 1997). A further possibility is that this degree of flexibility and integration is characteristic of twenty-first century western urban young people, whatever their religious identity.

7

Caste, Hindus and Sikhs

Caste and schools

Barbara Easton's resolve to understand how her secondary school pupils in Wolverhampton felt about caste was mentioned in chapter 1. The present chapter focuses on this issue by looking at young British Sikhs' and Hindus' awareness of belonging to a caste, their assumptions about other castes and their views on the nature and significance of caste. What is under review – caste – is part of the lived experience of many millions of Hindus and Sikhs in India and elsewhere. These millions include young people, teachers, parents and others involved in the UK education system, as well as in North America and other parts of the diaspora.

As was the case in chapter 5, a key concern for educationists is the extent to which the portrayal of caste in the curriculum – in religious education, for example – corresponds with contemporary experience, especially that of colleagues and students. In presenting so vexed a subject, accuracy and sensitivity may pull the teacher in different directions. So too may sensitivity to the understandings of individuals from widely varying caste backgrounds.

In two important respects this chapter parts company with the two previous chapters. First, the spotlight is on both Hindus and Sikhs. There is a comparative element in the reporting of fieldwork observation among young Sikhs and their Hindu peers. (Those aged 16 years or more are referred to as 'men' and 'women', rather than as 'boys' and 'girls'.) Second, what is under scrutiny impacts on pupils' relationships and self-esteem in subtle and powerful ways. Caste is a subject that concerns not only religious educationists but all who are concerned with the welfare of South Asian pupils. The voices of Ravidasis in this chapter show how caste-based experience challenges simple attempts at classifying individuals as 'Hindu' or 'Sikh' and colours young people's perceptions of religious identity.

Caste in the curriculum

Caste appears as a topic in religious education syllabuses in the UK – for example in syllabuses on Hinduism for the General Certificate of Secondary Education which pupils take at the age of 16. Here the problems include (a) the lack of clarity for the reader in distinguishing between the past (and is it an ideal past or the actual past?) and the present. How, for example, are teachers and pupils to make useful connections between the fact that Hindus in the UK include many from *kshatriya* families and the fact that the duty of a *kshatriya* includes 'to take responsibility for shortcomings in their kingdom' (Das 2002: 82)? A second issue is that (b) some curriculum materials draw a distinction between Sikhs and Hindus with regard to caste which may be similarly misleading as far as contemporary Sikh and Hindu experience is concerned.

   To illustrate (a) Das provides a detailed account of *varna* (see below) (2002: 82–3, 104–5) in which he is careful to distinguish between 'the ideal varnasrama system' and 'actual practice and related issues of caste and untouchability' (82). But the reader who has no first-hand experience of Hindu communities will not know how conscious individual Hindus in India or the diaspora are of having the duties which he lists for each *varna*. There is little sense of how, if at all, this system connects with the sense that young British Hindus have of who they are or of what is expected of them. In less careful textbook accounts this is even more the case. For example, with no suggestion of the diversity of human behaviour or of the numerous changes that have occurred over many generations, or that his summary may sound bizarre to many Hindus – including many Brahmins, Whiting tells us that:

> Brahmins may eat only rice cooked by brahmins, but vegetables cooked by anyone. The lower classes may drink liquor but brahmins may never do so. (1991: 96)

As for (b): some writers simply indicate that Sikhism rejects caste while others suggest a tension between injunction and practice. So Draycott (1996: 44) stresses that 'The Gurus rejected treating anyone as inferior or superior on the grounds of caste.' Whiting states, 'Also forbidden is the caste structure, though this may be allowed in practice' (1991: 145) – this unnuanced interpretation will be questioned below. The distinction between 'condemnation' by the Gurus and continuing practice is more grounded in the contemporary UK reality by Piara Singh Sambhi who points out that:

> The sense of being a member of one of these groups may be stronger in Britain than in India. In one town there may be a Bhatra Sangat Gurdwara, Ramgarhia Sikh Gurdwara and Singh Sabha Gurdwara, each attended by a different section of the community. (1991: 206)

Gujaratis, Punjabis, Hindus, Sikhs and caste

These statements make for an interesting comparison with one from the *Religions in the UK Directory 2001–03* which was formulated in consultation with members of the Sikh community.

> Sikhism teaches that there are no distinctions between people and rejects the concept of caste (or *zat*), which therefore has no religious significance for Sikhs . . . Other terms which appear in the title of some Gurdwaras, such as Ramgarhia and Bhatra, are historically related to economic categories and are rooted in the history of the forbears of the families concerned. (Weller 2001: 559)

This statement predisposes the reader to expect that (if we use religious categories) for young Hindus caste will be less relevant than for young Sikhs, and (if we use regional or ethnic categories rather than religious ones) caste plays a more influential part in the lives of young Gujaratis than young Punjabis. This would be in line with Steven Vertovec's observation of Hindus in the UK:

> The overall salience of caste distinctions among Punjabis in Britain, and in India itself, is arguably less marked than those associated with other regional social structures . . . Among British Gujaratis, in contrast, there are many significant levels or spheres of differentiation. (Vertovec 1996: 79)

These statements attempt, even less than the statements in some curriculum books, to reflect the complexity of the social structure to which the word 'caste' refers. Interested readers would do well to consult two publications. In the first, Dermot Killingley provides a detailed and authoritative explanation of the relationship between the two underlying divisions of South Asian society to which 'caste' is applied (1991). In the second, Mary Searle-Chatterjee and Ursula Sharma bring together scholarly discussion of the ways in which 'caste' persists and changes (1994). Their clear contention is that caste is misunderstood if it is simply read in terms of a hierarchy based upon the polarities of purity and pollution.

The term 'caste' obscures the crucial distinction between a *varna* (the Sanskrit term for the four classes with which text books so often equate 'caste') and the *jati* (*zat* in Punjabi). The four *varnas* are Brahmin (priest, teacher, intellectual), Kshatriya (warrior, administrator), Vaishya (merchant, farmer) and Shudra (artisan, labourer). Many students learn that these are the 'four castes', without realising that 'caste' – if it is to be used at all – is more appropriately used to translate our second term, i.e. *jati* or *zat*.

Members of the thousands of *jatis* continue to position their *jati* within the ancient four-tier framework of *varna*. But members and outsiders do not always agree where a particular *jati* fits. For example, a Rajput may be in no doubt that he is a Khatri. At the same time a member of another *jati* may disagree with how the Rajput positions his caste. Khatri is the Punjabi form of Kshatriya, the second *varna*, which is often translated as the 'warrior caste', even though Khatris' centuries-old specialism has been book-keeping and business, not military service.

Membership of both a *varna* and a *jati* is hereditary. Both are associated in popular consciousness with occupations: the Brahmins as priests, the Rajputs as fighters, the Sonis as goldsmiths.

For centuries it has been expected that marriages will be arranged between members of the same *jati*, although it is not as simple as that, since families know the unwritten rules which restrict the number of marriageable clans within the *jati*. Moreover, the family's geographical roots are a factor, so that – according to time-honoured practice – a Soni from the Surat region of Gujarat would not marry a Soni from the Saurashtra region. Some *jatis/zats* do not fit into the four-tier *varna* hierarchy. Although often referred to as 'Shudra', these are the *dalit* castes (*dalit* means oppressed and refers to castes once known as 'untouchable'). In the UK the Punjabi castes associated with the Valmiki ánd Ravidasis temples (in Greater London and the West Midlands) are probably the most numerous of these (see Nesbitt 1991).[1]

In what follows, young Coventrian Sikhs and Hindus use both *varna* names, such as 'Brahmin' and 'Khatri', and *jati* names, such as 'Dhobi' or 'washerman', 'Lohana' – a Gujarati trading caste (Michaelson 1987) – and 'Jat', the farmer caste of Punjab (Pettigrew 1972). They did not use the terms *varna, jati* or *zat*. For that matter they used 'caste' for ethnic or religious community rather than for either their *varna* or their *jati*. For their *varna* (if they are Brahmins) or for their *jati* they instead used the word 'community', which translates the Hindi and Gujarati word '*samaj*'. The Gujaratis use '*samaj*' for the caste associations which organise events such as celebration of the annual festival of Navaratri (see chapter 4).

Two 19 year-old Gujarati men clarified their usage for me. The Prajapati (Prajapatis' *jati* is associated with carpentry and construction) explained:

> We don't use the word 'caste', we use the word 'community', and only recently did I become aware that what I was regarding as my community was my caste.

His Brahmin peer also pinpointed young people's different understandings of the word 'caste':

> There is two sort of definitions of caste. There is one where it is basically the important Gujaratis, the medium Gujaratis and the lower Gujarati – that sort of caste. [Or] do you mean caste as in 'English' [and] 'Gujarati'?

In what follows I shall use 'caste' for the young people's designations of themselves and others in terms of hereditary communities, whether they refer to themselves by *varna* or *jati* titles.

Exploring caste in the Midlands

Easton's students were from Wolverhampton families with roots in Punjab in North India. More particularly she had come to realise that they all identified themselves with one of two hereditary communities: the Jat (see Pettigrew 1972) and the Chamar (see Juergensmeyer 1982) castes. Two field studies at Warwick University have also involved young people from these same castes, although for the Chamar families I have used the term Ravidasi which does not have the negative connotations of 'Chamar'. This is because many adult members use this name for their caste (at least in a religious context).

Nesbitt (1991) provides a detailed report of the study of young Ravidasis and of their peers from another caste with a history of oppression in India, for whom I use the more honorific term 'Valmikis' (see Nesbitt 1990a and b, 1994; Leslie 2003). Like the title of their temple-cum-community centre the title 'Ravidasi' is a reminder of their links with the *bhagat* (saint-poet), Ravidas. During both periods of fieldwork the issue of caste (or of *zat biradari*, to use a Punjabi term) frequently surfaced, sometimes in relation to school. Three more studies involved Hindu families, both Punjabis and Gujaratis, from a wide range of castes. The young people and their relatives often referred to their own families and others' by caste names.

Young Hindus' conception of caste

Mary Searle-Chatterjee and Ursula Sharma suggest that caste is what people 'do' rather than what they are (1994). In India the ways in which people have 'done' caste have come down to observing an apartheid based on rules of purity and pollution. This has meant, as the quote from Whiting earlier in this chapter suggests, only receiving cooked food from, and eating together with, people from certain castes (*jati*), and only sanctioning marriages within their own *jati*. Caste membership was hereditary and closely bound up with caste-specific occupations. A Darzi man, for example, would be a tailor and a Soni man would be a goldsmith. These *jati* communities would all be economically interdependent.

Although the young Hindus and Sikhs in Coventry made numerous references to their 'community', none of them mentioned purity and pollution or excluding others from eating or worshipping with them. Older members of Valmiki and Ravidasi families, by contrast, recalled having had to sit apart from their higher caste class fellows during their schooling.

None of the young Hindus mentioned economic interdependence but they frequently equated their caste with an occupation, whether with 'fighter' (a young man from a Khatri family), 'farmer' (the Patels), 'carpenter (the Prajapati) or 'goldsmith' (the Sonis). They made this occupational connection, even though only the young people from Soni families had relatives who still carried on the traditional craft, and the young Sonis whom I interviewed were themselves going into careers in pharmacy rather than into their families' jewellery and watch businesses. However, young people did refer to the fact that caste membership was hereditary and also to the requirement (whether they regarded it as desirable or otherwise) for marrying within their own caste.

Only one young Hindu, a Gujarati from a Soni family, voiced the traditional respect for Brahmins, the priestly caste.

I know that Brahmins are classed as a very high class people . . . A lot of Brahmins go further into more depth in religion.

However, when speaking of their own *jati* or family name in relation to another, some of the Gujarati Hindus used words that suggest a vertical ranking.

Being Lohanas we're higher than Kumbhars. [Kumbhar means potter.] (Lohana woman)

Desais are basically Naiks as well . . . but we are just a touch lower. (Brahmin man)

People lower down in caste say they drink and smoke, but they say that because we are the highest caste we are not supposed to. (Brahmin woman, showing an awareness of the prohibition that Whiting set out – see above.)

We have, like, different levels of caste and ours is, [like], not the highest, but it is quite high. (Soni woman)

We are not the highest, but we are on a respected position on the scale. (Patel woman)

A farmer's not exactly bottom, but it's not . . . top. It's middle, and then you have Brahmin and business men on top. (Patel man)

Young Hindus' attitudes to the caste system

In all these cases the speakers were quoting what their elders had told them, whilst rejecting – or at least distancing themselves from – this hierarchy. So a Punjabi man of Rajput *jati* explained:

[A Rana] is a Thakur . . . My mum was telling me in India they are quite a high caste . . . but I'm not really too bothered.

A 19 year-old Gujarati Brahmin man provided an overview of the system, which he strongly condemned as 'racism':

You collect these points [for doing bad things] and obviously the more points you get the crapper life you get next time round. If you get maximum points for being a total, total bad person, then you come out in the next life something like an ant. And if you are really, really good, then you become someone in a higher caste . . . Naik, Desai: above that you've got priests and then you've got the whole caste system. Then, right at the bottom, you start going into animals . . . and you come down to an ant as lowest.

Here he is envisaging a continuous scale, encompassing both the animal kingdom and human – or at least Indian – society, with karma (as cosmic moral law of cause and effect) as the determining criterion for individual placements.

Young Hindus' attitudes to the caste system ranged from outright rejection to an almost uncritical acceptance. Condemnation was voiced by members of very disparate castes: a Punjabi Valmiki woman, a Punjabi Ravidasi man, a Gujarati Patidar woman, and a Gujarati Brahmin man, who stated:

I don't like saying like, 'I'm above someone else and you're above me'. It's wrong . . . It is basically just like racism.

The Patidar woman expressed the view that the caste system 'is the main downfall of Hinduism really', and the Valmiki woman declared:

I don't believe in the caste system. We are all equal because it is labelling someone for what they used to do in past life.

It was a Prajapati male, whose views on social issues were traditionalist and conservative, who suggested that the present character of the caste system fell short of an earlier ideal, explaining.

How the caste system was supposed to work, in that some people were meant to do some jobs, others were meant to do different jobs. It's not that this person does this job and he is hence lower than this person. All people were supposed to be equal, doing different jobs.

This envisages the caste system as a social harmony of people in differentiated but equally valued hereditary occupations as per Das's account of *varnashramadharma* (2002: 105). He is critical not of the hereditary principle, but of caste-based discrimination against some people on the grounds that their caste is 'lower'. Another young man's emphasis was that one's position in the caste system should be (or that it used to be) determined by one's conduct, not by heredity. But in practice both these young men seemed at ease with caste (even in its fallen state), and were ready to marry within their *jati*.

Caste, friendship, marriage

Over and over again young Hindus declared that, whatever its implications for marriage, caste was immaterial to friendship. For one young man, a Gujarati from a Patidar family, caste provided a subject for jokes:

> I had a friend who is a Brahmin . . . I only found out at the end of my schooldays . . . I goes, 'Well, I can't talk to you then' . . . We just joke around about it.

Presented like this, caste among young British Hindus emerges as carrying no ill feelings and causing no actual discrimination, even though they have a hierarchical image of it. It is the subject of marriage which throws caste into higher relief.

A Gujarati Soni man articulated the irrelevance to caste to friendship (as distinct from marriage) in this way:

> We have friends of different castes – Dhobi as well . . . One of my dad's friends, he's like a brother to me . . . It's just when it comes to that marriage point . . .

It was on the subject of marriage partners, as opposed to friends, that these young people recognised caste as being a traditionally decisive criterion of acceptability. Indeed many accepted this for themselves, with reasons that ranged from a Gujarati Patidar woman's 'because I've been brought up expecting that' and 'It's not like a complete change, because I suppose if you marry into a higher caste just the way that they behave and everything is going to be different', to the more reluctant:

> The only reason why I'd get married to say a Gujarati Naik . . . would be . . . 'cos my parents go [i.e. say], 'You shouldn't marry this, you shouldn't marry that', and it would just be like shameful to them. (Gujarati Brahmin)

A minority totally rejected their family's expectation or preference that they would marry within their caste. These young people included 'low' caste Punjabis – a Ravidasi man and a Valmiki woman – as well as 'higher' caste Gujaratis, a Patidar and an Oshwal woman.

Some of the young people told stories of their contemporaries, including relatives, who had married out – whether into another caste (e.g. a Kumbhar with a Lohana, a Patidar with a Mistri), or into a community of both a different caste and another religion, or into a community differentiated by both religion and ethnicity (a Punjabi Valmiki with a Gujarati Muslim). In each of these cases the couple had met with initial objections, which in some cases had meant an ongoing rejection from their own families.

Some of the young people were their parents' eldest child. As a result they had a sense of responsibility as regards the likely impact of their own behaviour on the freedom of their younger siblings and cousins. For these young people the likely cost of rejection by their families and of bringing shame upon their parents was not a price worth risking for the uncertain gain of flouting the family's expectations that their marriage would be arranged with someone from their own caste.

By contrast some others (both men and women, and both Gujarati and Punjabi) were prepared to risk marrying across caste boundaries. In some families there had already been a precedent which had won some level of acceptance. In fact one Gujarati Soni woman had already, with her family's full approval, married a Vaniya (i.e. a member of a traditionally trading *jati*) whose brother had married her cousin.

She had heard no adverse comment, regarded such marriages now as commonplace, and believed the difference between the Sonis and Vaniyas as nothing more than 'seeing a different set of people at occasions' such as weddings. Widely held was the view that attitudes to inter-caste marriages were softening, and that caste restrictions on the selection of spouses would fade away in due course.

Attitude to their own caste

Some young people expressed pride in their own caste, or at least satisfaction with it. For example, the Khatri man was happy that Lord Krishna was a Khatri (i.e. a Kshatriya or warrior) like him. His sister's experience had confirmed the impression that:

> When we do meet a lot of Khatri families they are very nice families, and you want to know them. And I am not saying that lower caste families are no good, or higher caste families are no good. But it is amazing how many Khatri families we know and they are very nice people.

Strikingly different was one Gujarati Lohana's assessment of his own caste:

> I'm ashamed of being a Lohana because I've never met so many back-stabbing people in all my life . . . How come all the other Hindus . . . all the different castes can go to a hall and celebrate all together and yet the Lohanas have to be different?

The young Gujaratis make frequent reference to their 'community' or *samaj* (caste association). Some commend the institution: 'I suppose it [*samaj*] is a good thing because it keeps us in contact . . . because they usually organise a trip in the summer'. Others castigate their *samaj* as gossiping and interfering. In this respect a Gujarati Patidar (Patel) woman speaks for others:

> It is just gossip, gossip, gossip that it all boils down to . . . If something happens in the family, then the parents just get it from the community.

Another criticism was the elders' unwillingness to share control of the samaj with younger people.

Young Sikhs' articulation of ranking

When a ten year-old Sikh girl, who had never lived in India, was asked which pupils in her school attended the optional Punjabi language classes she immediately – and, from the researcher's point of view, unexpectedly – provided a breakdown of the class along the lines of their family's caste. Given this readiness to think in terms of caste it should have been no surprise that one of the factors in being – in their words —- a 'proper Sikh' was which caste an individual belonged to. On one occasion a Punjabi Jat girl was shown a picture of the *panj piare* (five traditionally accoutred male Sikhs) in a procession, and was asked what sort of people they must be. Instead of replying, as anticipated, that they were Sikhs who kept the rules (i.e. observed the discipline that is required of Sikhs who belong to the Khalsa, the nucleus of initiated Sikhs), she responded without hesitation that 'of course' they would be Jats.

None of the young Gujarati Hindus said anything that suggested that membership of a particular caste made anyone more Hindu or less Hindu, and none of the Gujarati Hindus referred to being a 'proper' Hindu, on the basis of caste or anything else. Perhaps parallel was one devout Gujarati Soni woman's suggestion that the Brahmin friend was (because she was a Brahmin) better suited than she was to speak publicly about Hinduism. The young Sikhs, whatever their caste, distinguished Sikhs from 'proper Sikhs' and in some instances they associated caste membership with this distinction. A 13 year-old Jat girl explained:

> We're Jats, they're top of the caste. We don't usually believe in caste, but we're Jats and there's Ramgarhie, Chuhre. [see below for an explanation of these terms]

According to another Jat girl:

> If there's a Jat and a Tarkhan, a Tarkhan is a carpenter and a Jat is a farmer. The Tarkhan is the Indian and the Jat is the Sikh.

This summary neatly, though misleadingly, links *zat* with occupation, national origin and faith tradition. By using derogatory terms such as 'Chuhre', the plural of Chuhra, for Valmikis and 'Tarkhan' for Ramgarhia, and by referring to occupations that characterised those castes, young UK Sikhs demonstrated the way in which a sense of a caste hierarchy is perpetuated through the use of disparaging labels and a folk memory of presumed ancestral employment. This practice is consistent with the stereotypes of three Sikh castes which older Sikhs volunteered in Nottingham (Nesbitt 1980).

Young Jat Sikhs' differentiation between themselves and members of 'lower' *zat*s also alluded to the land of Punjab – to its soil. Traditionally this has been owned and worked by Jat farmers. Members of other *zat*s were landless, a state of affairs which was entrenched by the terms of the Land Alienation Act which the British passed in 1900 (Khushwant Singh 1977: 154–6). Ramgarhie (Tarkhans) were artisans whom the Jats employed (Saberwal 1976; McLeod 2000: 216–36). On top of this, Jats regard the Ramgarhias ('Tarkhans') as having come to the UK from Africa, rather than directly from Punjab (see Bhachu 1985). This perception is based on the fact that by far the majority of Sikhs who settled in East Africa, and so the vast majority of the Sikhs who migrated to the UK from Tanzania, Uganda and Kenya in the 1960s and 1970s, were Ramgarhia.

By contrast, none of the young Hindus distinguished between *jati*s either on the basis of land ownership (or landlessness) or on the basis of having closer links with either India or Africa. They did, however, readily speak of their own *jati* in terms of its ancestral occupation, but less frequently of another's *jati* in such terms.

Valmiki and Ravidasi voices

The young Valmikis and Ravidasis echoed the higher caste Sikhs' caste-related ranking of 'Sikhs' and 'proper Sikhs'. For instance, one Ravidasi (i.e. Chamar) boy reported:

> There's three castes. The first one is – I've forgotten. The second is Jat and the third is Chamar. And the first one are true Sikhs, like they carry the Ks at all times . . . They say their prayers. I'm not one of those. I'm not high caste.

Similarly, a Ravidasi girl who identified herself as Hindu clearly distinguished between her own community and 'true Hindus', by saying 'We are more free than they are.'

The adjective that these two young people used for other Sikhs and Hindus, i.e. 'true', is value laden. This may carry connotations of greater restriction rather than of superiority, although the Ravidasi boy's statement suggests a clear sense of hierarchy. However, 'Shukra' (also from this caste) stresses that 'I have yet to come across a *dalit* [i.e. member of a formerly Untouchable caste] 'who thinks that people are born superior and inferior' (1994).

Together with their awareness of caste as a vertical hierarchy went the experience of suffering prejudice or at least of fearing it. For example, one young Ravidasi expressed her fear that, at school, children from other castes might have been nasty if she had said what her caste was when they asked her. Her brother recalled their father warning him against making friends with Jats. He went on to say that when a Jat had invited the family to dinner, 'my dad said because they're Jat we shouldn't really go down their house, because he's afraid that one day they might say, "We don't want to know you."' His sister expressed the opinion that 'Pure Hindus – like the higher castes of Hinduism, like Brahmins' would have 'judged' her, if they had known her caste.

It was only Ravidasis and Valmikis who mentioned during their interviews that their parents had taught them to say that they were 'Hindu Punjabi' or that they did not believe in caste if anyone asked them what their caste was. One Ravidasi family avoided using the family name. To quote the daughter:

All I know is . . . apparently our surname indicates that we are one of the lowest castes, but I don't use it. None of my family does.

This identification as 'Hindu Punjabis' shows how a 'faith' label can be used to distance oneself from the caste prejudice of (higher caste) Sikhs, rather than implying any sense of actually belonging to the (higher caste) 'HP' community of, for example, Raj's London-based study (2003).

Growing awareness

Aged eight to 13 both the Sikhs and the Hindus identified other children by their caste. The longitudinal study of young Hindus indicated that during their teens young people learn more of the implications of caste membership. Importantly, they learn that they are expected to marry within their caste – or at least that this has been family practice until recently. This may also be the time when they discover what their caste is – as happened with the Ravidasi woman, when her parents informed her at the age of 16.

School also contributes to this awareness: both Valmiki and Ravidasi interviewees mentioned being asked by their peers what their caste was. Religious education provided information about Hinduism in general and about the caste system in particular. This same Ravidasi woman referred to religious education as a source of her knowledge about caste. The influence of social studies is discernible in her explanation of caste as part of a more general social phenomenon:

There is always someone in a religion who believes they are higher than others. Like in the olden times it was the priests above all the lowly peasants.

It was their involvement in marriages, and preparations for their own, that had made the young women, especially, aware of their families' and community's expectations. Their awareness included the realisation that any social deviation on their part could have an adverse effect on their younger siblings and cousins. For instance, there might be more resistance to their living away from home as students, or more difficulty in finding them spouses from appropriately respectable families when their turn came to get married.

In conclusion

The fact that the hymns of Ravidas, the Chamar saint, were included in the sacred text by Guru Arjan Dev, the Sikhs' fifth Guru, shows the lack of importance that the Gurus attached to caste status. They rejected it as a vertical stratification. Unequivocally Guru Nanak and his successors affirmed that in the hereafter name and caste (they used the word *jati*) count for nothing (see McLeod 1976: 85 for examples). One institution established by the Gurus challenges the practice of separate cooking and eating arrangements for the higher and lower castes. This is the *langar* – the gurdwara canteen which is open to all. The Khalsa, too, subverts caste division. As partakers of the sacred *amrit* (holy water) of initiation all *amrit-dhari* Sikhs belong to the family of Guru Gobind Singh's wife. They shed the surnames that indicate their caste.

But the Gurus did not overthrow caste in the sense of horizontal linkages binding society together – they did not, for example, advocate that marriages should be arranged out of caste. To call them social revolutionaries can be misleading for those readers who are unfamiliar with the society concerned.[2] Structurally Punjabi society has continued to preserve caste endogamy – marriages are seldom sanctioned between, say, a Ramgarhia and a Jat. Parents are still less prepared to sanction the union of a Chamar (Ravidasi) or a Chuhra (Valmiki) with a Jat. The fact that caste divisions persist among Punjabis in the UK owes something to British rule in India. Nineteenth- and twentieth-century census takers in British India required people to enter their caste. Lawmakers reinforced the distinction between landless and land-owning castes with the Land Alienation Act of 1900. By encouraging Punjabis of the Ramgarhia caste (carpenters, blacksmiths, masons and brick-layers) to move to East Africa as indentured labourers, the British laid the basis for further distinction between castes. Ramgarhias moved to the UK (in the 1960s and 1970s) with the self-confidence which they had developed as a middle tier in the black–brown–white social hierarchy of colonial society. Ramgarhias perceived Jats and others who migrated to Britain direct from Punjab as lacking a certain sophistication. Unsurprisingly, gurdwaras were established in the UK by committees which corresponded to different castes. Nesbitt (1980) explores this further in relation to not only Jats and Ramgarhias but also the Bhatra caste in Nottingham (see also Nesbitt 1981).

The Coventry fieldwork in the 1990s showed that gurdwara congregations did not conform strictly to caste membership. Many of the young Jats were attending Punjabi classes in the Ramgarhia gurdwara. Other factors affected their parents' gravitation to a particular gurdwara. Nevertheless, Jats and Ramgarhias did not frequent the Ravidasi gurdwara. In the context of the twentieth-century history of their castes it is not surprising that young people grow up with caste-based stereotypes and assumptions about each other. Anjali Purewal argued, on the basis of earlier research in Bedford, that the very absence of caste in wider British society, e.g. in the workplace, and the economic parity between castes encouraged the higher caste Jats to assert their superiority by reference to their traditionally dominant status.

What matters for educationists is that they recognise caste as a reality, albeit a shifting one, in the lives of young people of South Asian background. (This chapter will not venture into the implications of caste for South Asian Christian and Muslim families in the UK. Arundhati Roy's *God of Small Things* leaves no doubt of the coexistence of Christian identity and caste-consciousness. For the relevance of caste as a social reality among UK Muslims see Shaw 2000: 111–36.) For the teacher the persistence of caste-based prejudice means sensitivity to possibilities of name-calling in the playground or of anguish and animosity in the higher classes of the secondary school if relationships between the sexes cross the invisible lines.

For the teacher of religious education it means taking a more analytical look at the ways in which the curriculum portrays caste in the contexts of both Hindu and Sikh tradition. Pupils need to be assisted in unpicking the difference between preaching and practice. This means examining the relationship between the Gurus' teaching that birthright status is irrelevant to *mukti* (liberation from the cycle of birth and rebirth) and the accepted convention of marriages being restricted to members of the same *zat*. Are these necessarily contradictory? Are they consistent? Summaries such as Whiting's (quoted above) which refer to the Gurus (or Sikhism) forbidding or abolishing or reforming the caste system (or structure) are inaccurate in as much as the Gurus did not speak in terms of 'structure' and 'system'. As such summaries do not distinguish between vertical hierarchy and horizontal linkages the reader is likely to assume that the Gurus would have called for marriages to take place between members of different *zat*s.

The issue of caste also calls into question the boundaries that are so often drawn by both insiders and outsiders between Hindus and Sikhs. Clearly, in terms of self-identification, the Valmikis and Ravidasis do not conveniently fit into this framework, unlike the Punjabi Jats who identify themselves unequivocally as Sikh and, for example, the Punjabi Brahmins who are, with very few exceptions, equally sure of their Hindu identity.

Tackling caste in the classroom is a sensitive matter. In a BBC Radio programme in 2003 a member of the Valmiki community and a Professor of Indian history condemned the perpetuation of caste in British religious education lessons (BBC 2003b).[3] Conversely, on another occasion, a Chamar condemned accounts of Hinduism which do not deal with the iniquities of caste. By this he meant 'classical' conceptions or practices of *varnashramadharma* as well as contemporary manifestations. Meanwhile material from the International Society of Krishna Consciousness carefully reflects the complexities and fluidity of caste, and argues that 'caste is quite different from *Varnashrama-dharma*, for the latter simultaneously promotes spiritual equality whilst acknowledging material diversity' (Das 2002: 105).

The presence of South Asian pupils in class increases the sensitivity of any attempt at representing caste, especially given the authority (see chapter 10) with which some young people regard what they learn in school. It also makes the effort all the more important.

Notes

1   On the Valmiki community see Nesbitt (1990a and 1994). Nesbitt (1990a and 1991) refers to both communities.

2   See e.g. R. N. Singh 2003; www.sikhnet/sikhs.htm (accessed 2 December 2003).

3   Following this broadcast Caste Watch UK has been set up by members of the Valmiki and Ravidasi communities in order to monitor, publicise, and so reduce the incidence of cases of caste-based prejudice and discrimination in the UK.

British, Asian and Hindu – Multiple Identities

8

Between two cultures?

A lot of people who don't have a bilingual or bicultural existence . . . say, 'There must be a conflict there.' It's much more complex. (Chadha and Bhachu 1996)

It is easy to think of the identity of young people – our pupils and students – from minority communities in terms of a clash of cultures, and this view is supported by a body of scholarship as well as by the media. However, the Coventry studies of young Hindus show that identity formation is not so simple, nor is it so negative as the language of 'clash' and 'conflict' suggests, although pain is certainly evident in some young people's narratives. What these convey strongly is the way in which one's identity is forged in part through encounter, and the importance of particular contexts – including the educational environment – for particular formulations of who one is. Whatever our role – whether as teachers, students, friends or fleeting contacts – we contribute to each other's narratives of who we are.

British-born or -raised members of ethnic minorities continue to be presented as 'between two cultures' or the 'half-way generation' (Anwar, 1976; Taylor, 1976; Watson, 1977; Taylor and Hegarty, 1985; Ghuman, 1994, 1999, 2003). Alternatively they are described as 'bicultural' (Ghuman, 1991; Dosanjh and Ghuman, 1996: 24, Drury, 1989). Either way, a binary model is adopted, and this has been challenged by other scholars and by members of the communities concerned. For example, Avtar Brah exposes the fallacies implicit in the 'two-culture' model (1996: 40ff.). She points out that the model suggests that both British and Asian culture are unitary, when in fact they are infinitely varied and complex, and that it disavows the possibility of cultural interaction and fusion. Similarly Aloneftis's study of Greek Cypriots in London resulted in a critique of the 'two-culture' model (1990). Steeped in his observation of South Asians in Britain, Roger Ballard commends substituting for culture clash the metaphors of code switching – on the analogy of bilinguals' incorporation of elements of one language in the structure of another – and cultural navigation (which, however, suggests avoidance rather than integration) (1994: 29–33). Similarly, the earliest of the Coventry-based studies found the concept of multiple cultural competence more appropriate than binary models are for understanding the experience of British Hindu children (Jackson and Nesbitt 1993: 174–8), and the Norwegian educationist, Sissel Østberg, refined this into her model of integrated plural identity (2003).

The American anthropologist Kathleen Hall conducted a study of Sikh teenagers at 'Grange Hill High School' in Leeds (2002). Hall interrogates her data in the light of Homi Bhabha's concept of 'translation' (1994), 'a process that enables the creation of new hybrid forms of cultural identity' (Hall 2002: 192). With regard to the tensions involved in their being British and being Sikh, Hall argues that:

> Second generation British Sikhs are negotiating these intersecting fields of power and meaning. Through their struggles they will continue to challenge and slowly and subtly reshape the radicalised and reified boundaries of 'both'. (2002: 192)

It is with this understanding that, instead of uncritically adopting a binary model, the present chapter will examine young British Hindus' identity along the three axes of Britishness, Asianness and their religion. Regarding religion, a press report on the National Hindu Students Forum traces the growing importance of Hindu identity for young Hindus and the inadequacy of 'Asian', 'British' and 'Indian' to describe this group (Chauhan 1997). Similarly, Alison Shaw reports young British Muslims' primary identification of themselves with Islam (1994) and Jessica Jacobson found that young British Pakistanis distinguish their own primarily Islamic identity from their parents' regionally defined identity as Pakistanis (1997).

In so doing they assert the primacy of the 'true teachings' of Islam over ethnic interpretations and subcontinental cultural norms, and affirm solidarity and unity transculturally and transnationally with other Muslims. Gardner and Shukur had noted the parallel tendency among Bengali Muslims in Britain (1994: 161–4) and Husain and O'Brian similarly find religious identity superseding ethnic and national allegiances (2001). With these findings in mind the following discussion explores whether being Hindu parallels being Muslim as a preferred primary identity, and if so whether the contributory factors are the same.

Central to this examination of respondents' expressions of their own identity is consideration of the nature of the process of identity formulation and articulation. This process of ongoing self-narration, which often involves experiences of school and higher education, is the subject of the next section.

Narratives of encounter

In the Coventry study it was autobiographical anecdotes which gave meaning to the young Hindus' identification of themselves with such terms as 'British', 'Hindu' and 'Asian'. Frequently, during the interviews, individuals recounted incidents as a way of articulating their identity. Integral to these narratives of identity were their encounters with other people. From these they had learned how they were identified by another person and they had become aware of differences between one social group or category and another (Tajfel 1981). In applying 'British', 'Asian', 'Hindu', 'foreigner', 'black' and other terms to themselves these young Hindus recounted conversations with a school-teacher or with contemporaries at school, as well as with university friends and lecturers, and with colleagues. They referred to encounters in India, as well as to racist confrontation in Britain and they compared their identity with their Indian- or African-born parents' sense of identity.

In some of these narratives of encounter the young person wholly or partially accepted an identity which had been ascribed by someone else. This could be an authority figure – a primary school teacher, a parent or a university lecturer. For example, while recognising that her father would dislike and reject the label 'black', a Punjabi social sciences student explained:

> I've been taught through my course that 'black' means Asians and Africans . . . Apparently that's the politically correct term.

Here the tutor seems to be echoing Tariq Modood's political justification of 'black' as uniting diverse powerless communities in an effective anti-racist movement (1988), rather than appreciating the divided reactions of South Asians to a term which is disparaging – not least in South Asian languages such as Punjabi (Baumann 1996: 161–72).

One source might reinforce another: this same young woman commented, 'My aunt tends to use [the term 'black'] a lot because she works for the Equal Opportunities Commission, so I pick it up from her as well.'

Some young people told of encounters with their peers at school which had pointed up aspects of their own identity. To quote another young Punjabi woman:

> There was [sic] some kids that came from different countries where they couldn't speak English . . . they were more Indian and I was more English.

Racist confrontation, a more unsettling type of encounter, had also precipitated conviction about identity. A Gujarati undergraduate recalled:

> People say, 'Oh go back to your own country, go back to where you come from, you Paki this . . . ' I'm not a Paki, I'm a British citizen. I'm a Hindu, I'm a British citizen. 'How can you be British if you're a Hindu?' Why can't I be? I was born here.

So, unmistakably, encounters – each unique – were part and parcel of individuals' narrative of identity. The frequency of encounter in the narratives is consistent with Henri Tajfel's insights into how the individual derives from the group 'a place in society' (1981). Encounter with others, he suggested, involves comparisons which enable individuals to distinguish their group's identity from that of another group.

An integrative understanding of these narratives of identity, which differentiate one respondent from another and differ at various points in the individual's life, is provided by Paul Ricoeur's insight that identity is not in opposition to either diversity or plurality (1988; Meijer 1995: 98). In Ricoeur's view personal identity is a history – or story – and, as such, it is an interpretation. Similarly, writing about modernity, Anthony Giddens described self-identity as 'the reflexive project of the self, which consists in the sustaining of coherent, yet continuously revised, biographical narratives' (1991: 5). Likewise Kehily (1995) described identity as 'self-narration' and quoted Weeks:

> Identity may well be a historical fiction, a controlling myth, a limiting burden. But it is at the same time a necessary means of weaving our way through a hazard-strewn world and a complex web of social relations (1987).

This understanding of identity was foreshadowed four decades previously by the psychologist, Erik Erikson, when he wrote of identity in terms of a process – a process which both interacts and integrates (see Friederichs and Gupta 1995).

Like other narratives, the narrative of self-identity has an affective quality and one's choice of words, tone of voice, facial expression and body language are all significant data. Emotion is noticeable, in even brief quotations from the research data: uncertainty, anger, pride infuses the young people's articulations of their identity. The word 'feel' recurred:

> Up until maybe about two years ago I never really felt that I belonged in Asian community . . . all the Asian music . . . I was always very western. (Punjabi woman student)

> I feel I'm Indian, I feel I'm a British person. (Punjabi woman trainee)

Feeling was conveyed too by demeanour, tone of voice and turn of phrase as in a male Gujarati student's equation of 'we', 'Hindus', 'your own culture' and 'your own race':

> What gave me great satisfaction . . . is when we, when Hindus destroyed the

temple at . . . Ayodhya . . . You do what you have to do to defend your own culture and your own race. (male Gujarati student)

(Ayodhya is a town which Hindus regard as the birthplace of Lord Rama. In the 1990s it came to media attention because of a dispute between Hindus and Muslims which climaxed in December 1992 when Hindus demolished an unused mosque on the site of his birth.)

Certain affective motifs are evident in respondents' narratives, among them the experience or fear of being regarded as 'foreigners'. In the words of another male Gujarati student:

I describe myself as British but I think I'm not British and I'm not Indian. If I go to India they consider me as a foreigner and here I think I'm considered as a foreigner because I'm not English . . . basically you don't fit anywhere.

This resonates with the experience probably two decades earlier of a fictional (semi-autobiographical) Punjabi Hindu girl, 'Meena', the central character in Meera Syal's novel *Anita and Me*:

I knew I was a freak of some kind . . . living in the grey area between all categories felt increasingly like home. (1996: 149–50)

Foreignness was tied to particular situations but, through narrations of the type below, the feeling is revived and relived.

My housemates talk a lot about 'foreigners', foreigners in the way that they're visiting this country, not British citizens. And I tend to see myself as British in that sense, that they are talking about someone else rather than about me. Or like if we've got a visiting lecturer who we can't understand what she's saying, they'll just be sitting there going 'bloody foreigners' . . . I do sometimes feel . . . 'I'm a foreigner as well', . . . if they're saying something about Asians or blacks then I feel very much a foreigner, but if it's something to do with another country, then I'll feel British. (female Punjabi student)

I am Hindu, that's what I am, I'm Asian, I'm British - a British citizen but I wouldn't class myself as English. Yesterday we had a run in with two people . . . and they were like 'Get out of here, you foreigners' . . . and I get out of my car and I say . . . 'We are not foreigners, what the hell do you think you are saying?' (female Gujarati student)

I work with a lady and she was asking us . . . 'Are you British?' She wouldn't understand, she doesn't really know about religion and that, 'Are you British? Are you definitely British people?' and it's really hard explaining, because I say to her 'Well we are British because we were born here, but we are also our religion. We can't change that' . . . But they said, 'Well what are your Mum and Dad then?' So I said, 'I don't know, they were born in India' . . . They said to me 'Why do you call yourself British?' 'Well', I said, 'Well I am British as well, I am born here'. I can't help myself, I'm Hindu as well at the same time. (female Punjabi trainee)

The category of 'foreigner' is unstated in the third of these excerpts and foregrounded in the other two. 'Foreigner' conveys rejection, otherness and dislocation. These experiences of encounter, interpreted and remembered, become incorporated in the ongoing narrative of identity.

Plural identities

Some respondents' accounts of their identity – for example, the male Gujarati student quoted above – appear to support the 'between two cultures' model. Young people spoke of being 'half and half', but in one case this expressed a Ravidasi's problematic relationship to Sikhism and Hinduism (see below), and in another to the influence of an English 'father'. Although this form of duality doesn't necessarily imply 'between two cultures' in J. H. Taylor's sense, they described themselves as 'neither nor' as well as 'both and' ('I wear English clothes and Indian clothes . . . I watch a lot of Hindi films and I watch a lot of English films'). The identities some articulated were multiple rather than dual:

> I'm a Gujarati Lohana and a Vaishnav as well . . . I've got about six sub-cultures that I belong to.

Here 'Lohana' is the speaker's caste – see chapter 7 – and 'Vaishnav' refers to her *sampradaya*, i.e. religious grouping – see chapter 3). On occasions they spoke of themselves in comparative terms ('When I was in India . . . I thought I was more British than I was Asian') and they distinguished where they were 'from' (England) from what they were (for example, 'British Indian', 'British-born Indian').

However, to characterise these young people's identity as simply bicultural is to misrepresent the shifting, complex individual narratives. What is clear, nonetheless, from their reflections on their identity and from their narratives of encounter, is that certain identifications – 'British', 'Asian' and 'Hindu' - emerge more strongly than others. What they mean by these terms is examined in the light of Jacobson's analysis of their Muslim contemporaries' self-identification as British, Asian and Muslim (1996).

Being British

As illustrated above, some of the young people's assertions of being British arose from narratives of racist confrontation. Born and raised in Britain, respondents knew they had rights equal to those of other British citizens.

In parallel with the experience of British Bengali and Pakistani Muslims on visits to Bangladesh and Pakistan, their realisation of their cultural

Britishness surfaced on visits to India (Gardner and Shukur 1994: 158; Jacobson 1997: 247). To quote a Punjabi male student:

> In India I probably felt more British there than I've ever felt before. I was missing it so much . . . I do take England as being my home.

As a Punjabi male sixth former pointed out, in Britain they were most likely to be aware of what differentiated them from others. Their awareness, during visits to India, of how British they were resulted from a combination of homesickness and people's attitudes to them as 'foreigners'.

Despite the fact that parents who came to Britain as young adults sometimes describe themselves as British, in the view of the young people whom I interviewed, their own British identity distinguished them from their parents as well as from earlier generations of their families, all born in India or an African country:

> My mum and dad don't call themselves British, and that is because we are born here. (Punjabi woman trainee)

> I class them [parents] as African Asians, but I don't class myself as an African Asian. (Gujarati woman student)

Such comments suggest their perception that in their families Britishness was no deeper than their own generation. Moreover, Britishness would not necessarily be their own lifelong identity. One Punjabi distinguished aspects of identity which could be altered, rather like a passport, from those which were constant. The former depended on, for example, one's country of birth or residence, the latter on hereditary membership of a group.

> Hindu Punjabi is really me, because I can just go to another country and become a different citizen, and then I wouldn't be British any more . . . If I lived in Belgium I'd belong to Belgium . . . but I'd always be Hindu Punjabi.

This relative temporariness of Britishness, as compared with other aspects of their identity, resonates with Ambekar's view (1997: 40) and the view reported by Short and Carrington:

> When the children were asked if one could stop being British a not insignificant number said it was possible 'if you went and lived in another country and learned their ways'. (1995: 236)

Even without focusing upon South Asian communities in Britain, Cohen has shown that British identity is 'fuzzy' – 'historically changing, often vague and to a degree, malleable' (1995: 35). In the wake of Norman Tebbit's 'cricket test', which was discussed by Brah (1996: 194) and Ghuman 1991, and of Nicholas Tate's exhortations to teachers to foster a common culture, 'what it means to be British' has become a topic for journalists' speculation (Moore, 1995) and for scholarly comment (Jackson, 1997b), and it has been investigated by social scientists (e.g. Short and Carrington, 1995). Tate was speaking as Chief Executive of the School Curriculum and Assessment Authority. Implicit in the debate are equations of citizenship (rights and responsibilities), 'race', 'heritage' (an emotive term for national history and culture) and social and individual identity.

On the basis of research among young British Pakistanis Jacobson distinguished three shifting 'boundaries of Britishness': civic, 'racial' and cultural (1996). All her respondents were British citizens, and so were British in the civic sense, but their racial and cultural identities were more complex. The Coventry data shows that, consistently with this, young Hindus perceive their Britishness as contingent, generation-specific and not necessarily lifelong.

Being Asian

Since 1945 in the UK 'Asian' has increasingly been used to mean 'of South Asian background'. The young Hindus interviewed in Coventry repeatedly used this word, just as Jacobson's Muslim respondents had (1996). However, a Gujarati mathematics student reflected critically:

> I suppose everybody else would class me as Asian, but Asian to me has different implications, different meanings, depending on the context you're using it in.

Similarly, Ambekar's opinion was that 'Asian' is 'too vague and broad' (1997: 39) and cf. Chauhan (1997). Consistently with these young people's reservations Singh-Raud criticised 'Asian' for masking the many axes of diversity (class, ethnicity etc.) (1997); Brah discussed the term in relation to the collective impacts of racism and the arrival of a British-born generation (1996: 17–48) and Baumann presents being Asian as a post-migration identity learned from Afro-Caribbean and white peers (1996: 149–60).

Nonetheless, the young Hindus not only generally accepted it as the term applied by others, but also on occasion applied it to themselves. When they mentioned personal change, for example, this was sometimes in relation to their Asianness. Thus, using 'Asian' as a synonym for showing filial obedience, a Gujarati female student said, 'I've become a lot more Asian . . . if I'm not supposed to do anything I won't do it now.' A Gujarati male student glossed 'Asian' as meaning a 'lack of freedom, by comparison with 'English people'. Two women students described as Asian a more assertive, attention-seeking type of behaviour, which was reactive either to white peers (for example, by parading Punjabi language and *bhangra*) or to parental Asian norms. One of the young women evoked 'the stereotype Asian girl' wearing 'bright lipstick . . . with a few men on her arm'.

In all these cases the label 'Asian' refers to behaviour, although contradictory behaviour, and it is used to differentiate Asian cultural behaviour from what is white, western and English. Recurrently, 'Asian' was an oppositional term, as in a female Punjabi student's observation about her brother that, 'Since he has joined the sixth form he's become very united with other Asians, like us and them.' Jacobson has suggested that 'Asian' culture has more permeable boundaries, overlapping with western youth culture (1997). However, from the Hindu data it is not the permeability of the boundary between Asian, white and black, so much as the clarity of the opposition between Asian and non-Asian which emerges. This supports Baumann's observation among young Southall Punjabis of a cross-religious consciousness of a shared culture defined over against other communities by arranged marriage, caste structure and *bhangra* music (1996).

Unlike the young Pakistanis, the Hindus did not point up differences between what is 'traditional' or 'cultural' on the one hand and what is 'religious' on the other. They did not contrast 'Hindu' with 'Asian' or 'Indian' in the way that Muslim respondents contrasted 'Muslim' with 'Asian' or 'Pakistani'. Rather, for the Hindu respondents, 'Asian' designated a solidarity of those who were not 'western' or 'English'. The term was not, however, used with the pride or intensity with which some individuals expressed their Indianness and Hinduness, nor with any assertion of rights as was the term 'British'.

Being Hindu

I need an identity which allows the concept of my geo-political land being different to that of my socio-cultural. It is at this point that I put forward the assertion that the only identity which satisfies all this is essentially Hindu. (Ambekar 1997: 39)

As scholarly deconstruction of 'Hindu' and 'Hinduism' suggests (e.g. Jackson 1996), 'Hindu' – as compared with 'Muslim' in Jacobson's commentary – has permeable, or shifting, rather than hard boundaries. Numerous communities, beliefs and practices are now subsumed under a western term which misleadingly suggests homogeneity or a system. Moreover, despite the etymological and psychological linkage of 'Hindu' and 'India', the fact that some *sampradaya*s include western devotees suggests that 'Hindu' transcends the category of Indian ethnicity. Nevertheless, like 'Muslim' for Jacobson's respondents, 'Hindu' was a core identity for all the respondents, by contrast with their Britishness or

Asianness and with their parents' Indianness or Africanness. In the words of a Gujarati male sixth former:

> I am a British citizen but I am Hindu at heart basically. That's how I see myself.

Or, in the Punjabi woman trainee's words, 'I am a [sic] British, but deep down I am a Hindu.' This is the obverse of the young Punjabi sixthformer's expression of the impermanence of Britishness, quoted earlier.

One male Punjabi student's narrative below shows how young people's concept of their trans-generational, longitudinal Hindu identity could also grow horizontally through encounters with Hindus from different backgrounds. The reader needs to know that '*om*' is a means for Hindus of invoking and signalling God/ultimate reality. This is true of both the syllable when intoned by a devotee and of the written syllable which resembles the numeral 3 with a tail and with a dot on a concave line above it, in the Devanagari script which is used for writing Sanskrit.

> Usually when I go into an exam I put '*om*' on top of my paper. I was amazed – I talked to a friend about it, who was from Malaysia. He is Indian Malaysian, and I said, 'Do you know, I put '*om*' on my paper?' and he goes [i.e. says], 'No, I thought I was the only person to do that'. And we both laughed that both of us did it. And someone else came in, from Kenya, and said, 'What are you laughing about?' 'Oh, it is just something that we Indians do'. (She is Gujarati . . .), 'something we Punjabis just do'. And she said, 'What's that?' And I said, 'Do you do anything with your exam papers?' and she said, 'Yes, I put '*om*' on the top of it'. And I said, 'That's three of us now do it'. Probably many more do it.

Here identity involves the solidarity that comes from discovering a shared secret, a unifying pattern of behaviour. Rather than starting out with a concept of a universal, unified faith, as Jacobson's Muslims did, the young Hindu experiences and narrates the surprise of gradual discovery of transnational commonalities among Hindus. This instance illustrates Raj's 'experience of Hinduism as a community in moments' which she herself exemplified by the linking of Hindus through a 'chain e-mail wish, fortified by religious Sanskrit prayer' (2003: 102).

Hindu identity is sufficiently elusive for a female Gujarati psychology student to muse:

> But then the question is what is a Hindu? Are you born with Hindu blood? . . . I would say I'm born a Hindu, I'll die a Hindu. But then, maybe, I shouldn't call myself a Hindu in the first place because I don't actually practise Hinduism.

Her tendency to identify with a spiritual path that transcends faith boundaries is not rebellious but rather consistent with the evolving outlook of her fellow devotees of Sathya Sai Baba who emphasise universal human values (Exon 1997). It also concurs with Raj's discovery that '[m]any young Hindu Punjabis I knew did not see themselves as Hindus exclusively but were concerned with what they termed "spirituality"' (2003: 100).

Conclusion

In support of the argument for adopting an ethnographic approach in our teaching and learning, this chapter has, first, illustrated how qualitative methods of fieldwork make it possible to capture and convey something of the nature of identity as an ongoing, complex and affective process. Data collected in this way are a necessary supplement to the account offered by quantitative studies. These indicate, more starkly, the percentages of children who identify themselves, at least in one situation, with a particular religious, cultural or national identity. To give one example: '45% Asian children described themselves as having dual nationality or a singular national identity other than British' (Short and Carrington 1995: 233).

Second, the ethnographic interview data from longitudinal study in Coventry supports an understanding of identity as constituted of interpretative narrations, ongoing and shifting, arising from successive encounters. These include exchanges in classrooms, playgrounds, seminar rooms and corridors.

Similarly, the ethnographic interview itself emerges as one such encounter which, moreover, facilitates, catalyses and exemplifies such self-narration (see Nesbitt 1998a). It allows for expression of the affective element in identity and for seemingly contradictory responses from the same individual. Thus, responses to a single question on a single occasion need not be viewed as definitive, unchanging or exclusive, but as clues to one version of a narrative, a version which needs to be regarded reflexively, with its situationally determined variations (Kehily 1995). Moreover, historical and other contextual knowledge facilitates the process of interpreting the young people's narrative of identity. For example, the influence of Sathya Sai Baba's teaching is crucial in considering the Gujarati Sai devotee's self-questioning.

Although young British Hindus do on occasion use oppositional categories and speak of their relationship to 'two cultures', the data shows binary models to be over-simple. From the study young British Hindus' identity emerges as plural, complex and integrated, rather than as binary or 'between cultures'. It is hybrid (cf. Husain and O'Brien's account of UK Muslims [2001].) As Ballard has suggested, individual respondents' reference to culture conflict may be – at least to some extent – evidence of the impact upon them of the media's construction of their identity (1994). Ahuja (1997) is just one example of how the press perpetuates images of 'entrapment between two cultures', 'split personality', 'the East–West divide' and 'conflict'.

For these young people, Britishness is a civic identity, and one which distinguishes their generation from their parents', while Asian is a primarily cultural identity defining them over against what is 'white', 'western' and 'English'. 'Hindu' emerges as their core identity, a trans-generational narrative thread. Of course, the young people knew the researcher's interest in the Hindu tradition and so 'desired response' must be taken into account. In other words, just as gender 'overdetermined' the personal narratives reported by Kehily (1995: 30), so religion, ethnicity and culture may have been encouraged to overdetermine the young Hindus' accounts.

Paralleling Jacobson's Muslims, the strength of this identification was unaffected by whether or to what extent respondents observed rituals or behavioural norms or knew stories or scriptural teaching. But the young Hindus' strong identification with their faith tradition arises from a signif-icantly different narrative of identity and one which (the Ayodhya reference above suggests) is reactive to the high profile of Muslim identity in media coverage. The activity of a Muslim organisation, Hizb-ut-Tahrir, on British campuses may well be another factor, as this encourages the Vishwa Hindu Parishad and the National Hindu Students' Forum to show pride in being Hindu (Chauhan 1997).

Whereas Islam inspired Jacobson's young Muslims with its universal relevance and clear-cut boundaries (by comparison with the less sharply defined Pakistani or Asian ethnic culture), the boundaries of Hinduism are more 'fuzzy'. That this should be so is unsurprising in the context of scholars' deconstruction of 'Hinduism' and 'Hindu' as terms and concepts which outsiders applied to the indigenous traditions of the Indian sub-continent. Among others, Richard Burghart (1987: 225–8) and von Stietencron (1991: 11–28) discuss the problematic nature of these (western) terms. The young people's identification of themselves as Hindu is not an assertion of returning to 'true teachings' as distinct from ethnic interpretations, but it is an assertion of family continuities. They may iden-tify themselves more tentatively as Hindu than they identify their parents (Raj 2003: 100) but their sense of themselves as Hindu is strengthened by an awareness of the relatively temporary, changing nature of identities based on residence.

Spirituality and Religious Experience

9

Previous chapters have looked at 'religions' in terms of young people's identity and community, and of the supposed boundaries and content of 'religions'. We have looked at the match and varying degrees of mismatch between the representations by insiders (preachers, 'leaders' etc.) and outsiders (including teachers in school) of 'belief' and 'practice', and the less tidy reality of families' hopes, hunches and activities. Young people's spirituality has so far eluded discussion. Yet this is arguably the key aspect of religion. Or, from another angle, religion is a subset of spirituality – a smaller circle within the larger one. Moreover, spirituality has in recent decades shaken off its earlier, sometimes negative, connotations of other worldliness, mysticism and asceticism (see e.g. Mcquarrie 1972) as a minority path within, for example, Christianity; spirituality has become current as a term which affirms humanity at its deepest and most receptive. Indeed, in parallel with the decline in participation in some forms of organised religion, the notion of spirituality – often detached from religious traditions – has gained in prominence and popularity in contexts ranging from counselling (e.g. a conference at the University of East Anglia 2004), health and healing (Cobb and Robshaw 1997) to the ethos of the workplace (e.g. Hicks, forthcoming 2004).

For educationists in England and Wales the upsurge in research and publications on spirituality stems from the statutory requirement that schools provide for pupils' spiritual development (UK Government 1988 1. 1. 2a) and the fact that the government's 'Ofsted' inspectors inspect schools' provision of opportunities for spiritual (as well as moral, social and cultural) development across the entire curriculum (Ofsted 1994) and for the effectiveness of this provision (Ofsted 2004). Teachers have found it hard both to fill the notion of spirituality with content and also to put this into practice.

Current explorations of what spirituality, and spiritual development, entail usually encompass aesthetics (responses to art, music, literature etc); emotion (wonder and tranquillity are often singled out, but more unsettling emotion [Winston 2002: 252–3] is not completely overlooked);

inwardness; a sense of purpose and meaning, as well as ideals and principles. Hay and Nye have developed the understanding of spirituality as
'relational consciousness' (1998). For those who take an eclectic view of
spirituality – and this is true of 'New Age', post-modern takes on spirituality – spiritual development involves increasing pupils' competence in
making a discerning, dependable selection from the numerous traditions
and techniques available, many of which draw upon the philosophy and
devotional practices of faith traditions. For example, stilling exercises,
visualisation and meditation have their origins in Hindu and Buddhist spiritual practice (see e.g. Miller 2002).

Talk of 'spirituality', with its potential for all-inclusiveness, is acceptable
to the religiously unaligned, as well as to the committed adherent of a faith
tradition. (By contrast, 'religion' sits uneasily with many individuals' tacit
or declared secularism, and with the anti-religious stance of some.) But the
young people whose experience is the basis for this chapter do all identify
themselves with a religious label – Christian, Hindu or Sikh. This chapter's
contention is that, given the evident relationship between religions and
spirituality (in its many aspects), research findings on the spiritual dimension of young Christians', Hindus' and Sikhs' lives will repay the attention
of those who work with young people. Moreover our interviewees' experience of nurture within their traditions may well provide pointers for
schools' strategies of spiritual development and for their understanding of
identity formation.

Elsewhere I have outlined methodological issues in researching children's spirituality – especially the part played by reflexivity (Nesbitt
2001b). This chapter's concern will be rather to illustrate the distinctiveness and commonality of spirituality within and across faith communities,
to examine the linkage between children's articulation of religious experience and the formal and informal nurturing that they receive, and to raise
pertinent questions for educationists. These concern schools' understanding and encouragement of spiritual development as well as the
representation of religions in the curriculum. Whereas religions are, in the
UK, chiefly represented in religious education lessons, spiritual development is cross-curricular. Spiritual development is most consciously in
teachers' minds in preparing assemblies ('collective worship') and
personal, social and health education (PSHE) lessons.

Mindful always of Priestley's image for attempting to define the spiritual of sending a child to 'collect wind in a jar so that it can be examined'
(1996: 69), I am allowing my conception of spirituality to be informed by
definitions offered by Wright (1999) and Hay and Nye (1996; Nye and
Hay 1996). Wright suggests 'the developing relationship of the individual,
within community and tradition, to that which is – or which is perceived
to be – of ultimate concern, ultimate value and ultimate truth' (1999: 33)
and Hay and Nye contribute 'awareness sensing, mystery sensing and

value sensing'. The understanding of spirituality underlying this chapter includes what is often termed 'religious experience'. Following James (1960), Hay (1990) and others, 'religious experience' denotes dreams, visions, conversion experiences and memorable sensations understood by the individual concerned as encounters with the divine or with such agencies of a believed-in supernatural order as angels.

Young Christians' religious experience

Although at one time examples of children's 'religious experience' were investigated in the hope that they would shed light on the origins of primitive religion, it has long been understood that, as in adults, these experiences are related to the religious nurturing that the individual has received (Klingberg 1959: 211; Straus 1981), and to the vocabulary and idiom that go with this. Fieldwork in Coventry's Sikh, Hindu and Christian communities allowed for observation of their nurturing in acts of worship, in faith communities' supplementary classes and in the young people's homes, as well as opportunities during interviews to hear their reflective accounts of deep, sustaining and transformative experiences.

In some cases the role of older members for the community was particularly evident. For example, one young man attended a youth group ('Trekkers') at an Anglican church. When the group went to a diocesan retreat centre:

> We stood in a circle and closed our eyes and [the leaders] went round and like saying a prayer on your head. And when anyone touched me I went all cold. They said, 'If you feel the Holy Spirit coming you might get hot, sweaty, and some people might shiver.' And he said when he did it once one person fainted.

Similarly, an 11 year-old Baptist girl described 'asking Jesus into her life' at a Spring Harvest camp which had been organised with the intention of encouraging conversions. Her account of standing up in the gathering because 'the Holy Spirit had touched [her]' clearly showed the influence of Bible study, Evangelical Christian literature, the leader's invitation and the pressure from the crowd on an impressionable young person.

Another example of religious experience fitting a specific religious and emotional context came from the son of a Church of England clergyman who reported:

> In Pathfinders [a church youth group] . . . we went to Crossfire, a Christian rock concert . . . A few of us in the group suddenly felt very happy and we wanted just to run around. We talked about it afterwards and discussed the different ways we thought the Spirit could come upon a person. Sometimes some of us fall down on our knees crying, and some of us feel really happy and get a big grin, laughing.

In some cases young people mentioned no explicit suggestion from their elders that they would have significant experiences, but the context was germane to these occurring. (No one described 'having a vision' or feeling compelled to 'speak in tongues' in the playground, for example.) The language in which children conveyed what they had experienced was specific to the community concerned. Thus a ten year-old Jamaican boy reported a 'vision' which, in his own judgement too, was related to what he had witnessed in church shortly before:

> I had a vision which I can't explain . . . On Sunday night Sister K testified about how she had a vision of all the lights turning off . . . I dreamt that I was in church and all the lights came off. And I told my mum and she said it must be a vision.

Other young Christians spoke of being 'born again', being 'healed' by a saint, and having 'prophecies'. A young member of a New Church 'had two prophecies from different people – both times it was that some people felt God was saying something to them about me'.

One 13 year-old girl from a New Church described 'speaking in tongues', ecstatic utterance that is referred to by theologians as glossolalia. For Pentecostals (see Toulis 1997: 158–60) and other charismatic Christians this experience is a contemporary outpouring of the Holy Spirit, as first reported in the Acts of the Apostles (chapter 2). In this young woman's words:

> It's like a language. You start off with a few words and your vocabulary grows. I probably speak in tongues more at home than I do in church. You can be alone with God.

This experience, like the experience of the rock concert reported above, was one of great joy. When she first spoke in tongues:

> I was really, really happy. It was a lovely feeling. I just wanted to cry with happiness.

In its lack of theological and ecclesiastical language (there is no mention of the Spirit, let alone of 'tongues'), the following description of a profoundly affirming experience is equally clearly consistent with a 14 year-old girl's Quaker environment:

> Sometimes you just get a warm glow inside you and you just feel that everybody loves you and you love everybody. It's kind of a warm glow. Sometimes when you're not doing something else to preoccupy you, like sometimes when I'm just sitting with a best friend and we're not talking, just sitting.

While many accounts bore the hallmark of particular groupings – denominational, ethnic, theological – within the Christian tradition (for example, charismatic, Orthodox etc.), others cut across any such demarcations. Some young people, from a range of backgrounds, mentioned prayer as a prelude, context or element of religious experience. A Jamaican Pentecostal recalled:

> I was in church and felt really heavy, so I went to the altar and prayed and I felt lighter.

Many had 'heard God speak' to them, during their prayers, in a dream, or after 'I'd done something wrong'. Some experiences – for example, young people's dreams of heaven – were common to members of different faiths as well as denominations within a particular faith.

Young Hindus' and Sikhs' spirituality

At the same time the specifics of organisations' formal nurturing, through weekly classes and annual camps, need to be remembered in any overview of young people's spiritual development.

Bal Vikas affords one example (Jackson and Nesbitt 1993: 108, 156–8). Literally 'Child Development', these supplementary classes (currently called Sai Spiritual Education) are organised by followers of Sathya Sai Baba for their children. At the time of fieldwork among eight to 13 year-old Hindus in Coventry the Bal Vikas curriculum included using a *mala* (string of beads) to recite a mantra invoking Sathya Sai Baba plus 'silent sitting' (sitting in line, eyes closed, physically still and focusing on something beautiful), as well as stories and role play concerned wih the 'human values' of truth, love, peace, right conduct and non-violence. Learning to sing *bhajan*s (hymns of devotion) and performing *arati* (circling the lamp reverently in front of Sathya Sai Baba's galanded portrait) were further elements in each Bal Vikas session.

Art-Ong Jumsai Na Ayudhya, Director of the Thailand-based Institute of Sathya Sai Education, who has provided a philosophical basis for Education in Human Values, describes silent sitting's rationale by analogy:

> If you put a piece of paper in the sun nothing will happen, but if you bring a lens in between them, the paper gets burnt. The rays of the sun converge through the lens and develop the power and heat and energy to burn the paper. The paper is like a problem we may have. The lens is the process of silent sitting. (Jumsai 1985: 18)

This practice is consistent with Hindu understanding of yoga and meditation as taught by other gurus. And the Sai devotees' ritualised devotion, focused upon Sathya Sai Baba, is of a piece with the *bhakti* which is integral to spirituality in Hindu (and Sikh) devotion more widely (Nesbitt 2001b). The young Sai devotees focus their attention on words which invoke and exalt Baba, e.g. 'Sai Ram'. Whether used as a greeting or repeated in *bhajans* and meditation, 'Sai Ram' equates Sathya Sai Baba with (God) Ram (Rama). As a visual focus they have photographs of Baba. Similarly, for (other) Hindus and for Sikhs the words and image will encapsulate their particular devotional paths.

For example, for those young Hindus whose families espoused Krishna Consciousness the *mahamantra* [great mantra] which they repeated was:

Hare Krishna Hare Krishna Krishna Krishna Hare Hare
Hare Rama Hare Rama Rama Rama Hare Hare

A 12 year-old boy mentioned that he could jump higher in high jump after repeating these words. More often children reported the peaceful state of mind and the 'good luck' that they noted after reciting a mantra.

Young Hindus described the experience of praying, rather than ritual, as being effective, both in achieving peace of mind and in enabling them to cope with crisis – usually examinations. In each case the young Hindu testified from personal experience. All said that they requested divine help or repeated a mantra to calm themselves. They found that the day then went better. For instance a young Punjabi woman would repeat, 'Please God *om namo shivai*' and feel 'Oh I've prayed, now things will go right for me.' (The words '*om namo shivai*' are an invocation to Lord Shiva.) The Punjabi sixthformer said that she would say a mantra:

and then I say my own few words, what I want to say, how I feel, it's quite calming you know . . . it's like a very calming, soothing effect on your mind just to relax for a bit and take a few deep breaths and just say a prayer to someone, [it's] nice.

The potentially beneficial effects of these techniques for students more widely are revisited below.

The activities for which the young Hindus used the English term 'praying' were various, including repetition of a mantra with the aid of prayer beads, reciting longer prayers such as the *suprabhatam* (the morning prayer which is commended to Sai devotees) and praying in English in petitionary Christian style. A Gujarati male undergraduate explained:

If I find myself in trouble or if I'm frightened or that then I do tend to pray . . . I would probably say *sloka* [verse] or something like that, or if I knew somebody was in trouble then I would sit and pray for them.

The young Sikhs described 'praying' both as personalised petition and, as in the second and third examples below, in terms of repetition of a sacred formula or name for the divine:

I pray to my God every night. [God says] 'Yes, I'll make your wish come true'. (ten year-old girl)

If anybody prays to God all the time they get all powerful. (nine year-old boy)

Do the Guru's prayer and get their God into their minds to remember. They remember it by saying 'Vahiguru' all the time for about ten minutes. (13 year-old boy)

As a visual focus for their devotion Sikhs were familiar with 'photos', i.e. reproductions of artists' impressions of the Gurus, and of Guru Nanak in particular, and – in some families – of a Baba (see chapter 5). For Hindus this focus might be a portrayal of Shivji (Shiva), of Sheranwali Ma (Punjabis' name for the Goddess as 'Mother on the tiger'), of Krishna (as mischievous infant or as flute-playing cowherd or as Arjuna's charioteer on the battle field of Kurukshetra where he uttered the words of the Bhagavad Gita). Alternatively, the focus may be a more recent or living saint-cum-deity. Jalaram Bapa, the nineteenth-century saint (pictured in a white turban) for whose devotion a temple has been built in Leicester, is one example.

Daily prayer from infancy in front of these 'photos' resulted in their becoming mental images (see Lall 1999: 34). Lall quotes her interview with a Sikh girl who would look at her Radhasoami Guru's picture when she was depressed:

The image is always in your mind . . . If you really believe in someone, then you don't need a photo. (1999: 16)

By way of explanation, 'Radhasoami' refers to a religious community, drawn mainly from families of North Indian Sikh and Hindu background, who venerate Gurus in a continuing line (see Juergensmeyer 1987).

Music

Music is recurrently mentioned by young people of different faith backgrounds in connection with heightened awareness and wellbeing. A 12 year-old Gujarati Hindu girl spoke movingly of sitting outside her grandmother's bedroom door listening intently to her morning hymns to the baby Krishna (Jackson and Nesbitt 1993: 116). For the young Anglican quoted above the music precipitating awareness of the Holy Spirit was a Christian rock concert. For Sikhs who are learning *kirtan* (devotional singing the words of the Sikh scriptures, often to the accompaniment of harmonium and tabla) it is a means of interiorising the divine Nam, the divine reality. In the words of one Sikh teenager (not involved in the Coventry studies):

So, how does kirtan differ from singing any other song? The words you sing are from the Guru Granth Sahib. They should be sung in an attitude of prayer and meditation, so that there is something beyond the pleasing melody. Firstly, as the sangat [congregation] sings, the vibrations coming within us and around us have a physical effect on the body . . . kirtan can be soothing, refreshing and uplifting. It leaves us in a state of peace and turns our minds directly and completely to God. Kirtan is therefore a way to experience God. (Babraa 1989: 19)

In the words of a seven year-old Sikh boy *shabad*s (hymns from the scriptures) differ from 'film songs' because 'these are to pray to God so he loves you more inside your heart' (Albans 1999). For young Hindus too *kirtan* can be a spiritual experience – children were encouraged to sing and play musical instruments in congregational worship in the temple, and in ISKCON and Sai *satsang*s (devotional gatherings) (Jackson and Nesbitt 1993: 140–3). It is for this reason that two of the nine points of conduct for Sai devotees are singing *bhajan*s weekly in the family and monthly with members of the Sathya Sai Organisation.

A corporate experience

Young people's – and their elders' – accounts of the benefits of singing together are a reminder that spirituality is not only individual but requires involvement in a community with a shared spiritual focus. Sikh, Hindu and Christian teaching emphasises the importance of congregational worship – for example, the Sikh Gurus use imagery from nature to impress on their hearers the powerful influence of the 'congregation of the righteous' on the individual's spiritual progress. As we have seen, it is in some cases only through an older person's comment that a young person recognises an experience as spiritual – one example was the Pentecostal boy's dream which another's interpretation led him to regard as a 'vision'. Young people's spirituality is affirmed by endorsement and encouraged by company.

Moral commitment

This social aspect of their spiritual development also shapes young people's moral outlook. Their community preaches and practices values which they internalise or reject. Hay and Nye set out 'hallmarks' of spirituality or 'relational consciousness' (1998). Of these one is an 'intense awareness' and, in the case of several young people whom I interviewed, this was strongly ethical in nature (Nesbitt 2001b: 137). Mina (Gujarati Hindu Sai devotee) and Alice (Quaker) spoke out about the environment and about injustice. In Alice's case there was outrage at the idea of war and a strong commitment to pacifism. For Mina non-violence (*ahimsa*) was a value that she espoused from her Bal Vikas classes, and she rejected the caste-based prejudices of her Gujarati Hindu community.

Religious experience

Affirmation of a sense of being at peace shone through many young Hindus' recollections. Religious experience was evident in young people's spirituality, and was mentioned in association with special places and people as well as with deliberate prayer.

A Gujarati man stated: 'If you believe because you've had a direct experience, then your faith is stronger and you will try to better yourself more than someone who is just doing it blindly through tradition'. When questioned about religious experience, such as a sense of divine presence or a religious dream, a number mentioned having experienced a powerful sensation of peace.

Their sense of peace was often associated with a particular place: for one young Gujarati Hindu man it was the sea which nourished his spirituality (cf. Lane 1988). Many of the young people associated spiritual experience with 'sacred architecture' (Jones 2000). Especially powerful is the time of a *darshan* [glimpsing the benedictory gaze of the deity] and the sound of music in the temple. In one young Gujarati woman's words: 'It's really peaceful . . . the songs they sing.' She was referring to her experience in Hindu temples such as the Hare Krishna temple in Mumbai, which she had visited during a brief stay with relatives. Other young people described a similar experience at the Golden Temple in Amritsar (Sikhs' holiest shrine). The young Hindus' and Sikhs' travel in India combined renewing family bonds with a tourism which could equally be described as pilgrimage (see Rountree 2002). The itinerary included major shrines as well as lesser known ones with which the family had a longstanding connection. Three other Hindus reported their sense of overwhelming peace in Christian churches – St Paul's cathedral, Coventry cathedral and a parish church in London. The fact that these were not Hindu places of worship, let alone Hindu shrines in India, was immaterial (see Nye 1998). A Gujarati Hindu student 'went into a church with my friend at home and I felt just as calm as I did when I went to Prashanti' (i.e. Prashanti Nilayam, Sathya Sai Baba's base in south India).

Sacred space and sacred presence were interfused. Some of the sites which they visited were hallowed by a saint or an *avatar* (incarnation) of the divine. So some of the young Hindus referred to their sense of great peace at 'the Shirdi Sai Baba place' (i.e. Shirdi, the home in Maharashtra of the nineteenth-century saint, Sai Baba of Shirdi) and at 'Mathura Vrindavan' (Mathura, in the North Indian state of Uttar Pradesh, is believed to be the birthplace of Krishna; Vrindavan, nearby, is honoured as the place where he played his flute for the cow-girls).

Also contributing to young Hindus' sense of transcendence were encounters with spiritual leaders: several mentioned the impact of meeting Morari Bapu, a celebrated exponent of the *Ramayana*, whose performances in Britain draw audiences of many thousands (Nesbitt 1999b).

Enjoying the religious dimension

Some of the young Christians alluded to 'fear' and 'shaking' in relation to baptism by immersion and experiences involving the Holy Spirit, and one young Hindu woman expressed fear concerning a Mata (a woman possessed by the Goddess), but another emotional strand in young people's narrative was fun and enjoyment. There was both the uncontrollable delight of not being able to stop laughing, the peaceful joy of the young Quaker's 'warm glow' and also some children's relish for organised religious activities.

So a 12 year-old devotee of Sathya Sai Baba described in her 'diary' what happened in the Bal Vikas.

> In Bal Vikas we learn about Religions, God and other Spiritual things, we sing songs have games learn new prayers in different languages. It's real good fun. (21 November 1986).

Some young Christians, Hindus and Sikhs found certain aspects of their communities' religious activity off-putting, but the references to events which they looked forward to were a reminder that the spiritual may also be enjoyable.

Conclusion

Kenneth Hyde reported the variety of 'affective religious happenings' covered by the term 'religious experience' and summarised research in this field (1990: 164–94). The fact that profound religious experiences can occur in the lives of young Christians is not a new discovery (Klingberg 1959). But, although numerous psychological studies of religious experience have been conducted, most (at least in the UK) have involved adults. In some cases the adults recall their childhood experience, but inevitably reinterpret this in the light of intervening years (Hyde 1990: 177). Qualitative studies of young people's articulation of their religious experience and of their spirituality more generally are not only valuable as additions to scholars' insight into religion and childhood. They can challenge current representations of religions in religious education and inform their provision for pupils' spiritual, moral, cultural and social development (SCMS). The data can also help teachers and others who work with children to recognise the significance of religion for many of these young people. This is especially important in view of the fact that in any one school these young people may feel acutely different from their peers (see chapter 3).

Returning the spiritual to religions means, for example, ensuring that Sikhism is not only presented in terms of the 'five Ks'. Moreover, if Sikhism is presented with this focus, pupils must be helped to feel something of the five Ks' wealth of connotation for the observant Khalsa Sikh, and their context in lived experience. Religious education teachers in England and Wales are exhorted to help their students to learn *from* religions as well as *about* them (SCAA 1994: 7). However,

> Curricula for religious education and for religious studies which major on the five Ks in their representation of Sikh tradition may fail to convey the yearning for the divine which pervades Gurbani [the Gurus' utterance, i.e. the Sikh scripture]. An RE syllabus that introduces pupils to the poetic imagery of the Guru Granth Sahib in translation, and to the aesthetic beauty of *shabad kirtan* [singing the words of scripture], can assist Sikh pupils in articulating in English something of their Gurus' inspiration as they encounter expressions of *bhakti* and – in whatever way – make them their own. (Nesbitt 2004)

This approach might also help to counter impressions, such as this from one young Christian, that Sikhism was just a matter of 'Five Ks – tradition, doing things which aren't useful, just for tradition, like carrying swords under your clothes'.

The Coventry studies demonstrate that pupils' spirituality, including their religious experience and how they articulate this, is intrinsic to their *identity*. As we have seen children frequently report experiences in the unmistakable idiom of their particular congregation – those from black-led Pentecostal churches mentioned having a 'vision', 'speaking in tongues'. 'Being born again' and 'prophecy' cropped up in the reflections of young women who belonged to a New Church congregation, and it was a Cypriot Greek Orthodox boy's cousin who was 'visited by a saint'. All the interviewees who spoke in such terms also showed a strong commitment to their Christian self-identity. As Giddens points out:

> A person's identity is not to be found in behaviour, nor – important though this is – in the reactions of others, but in the capacity to *keep a particular narrative going*. (1991: 54)

The narrative of one's story as not only a Hindu but as, say, a follower of Sathya Sai Baba or as a devotee of Krishna is especially sustained by experiences of profound peace, joy, unity and so on that arise during Sai *bhajan*-singing or during a visit to Krishna shrines in India.

Another key area is *friendship*, and several young people mentioned their religious experience and spirituality as a factor in close friendships. For example, an 11 year-old Baptist girl reported that after 'asking Jesus into my life' at an Easter convention (Spring Harvest) she found it easier to talk to a school friend who had also asked Jesus into her life than to relate to her best friend, who had not had this experience. She reported that:

> Even though I go to a Christian school . . . I find it quite difficult to speak about God at school.

Her statement illustrates the difficulty which many people experience in sharing their 'narrative' (Scott 2001: 122). The need to feel at ease talking about God did not limit young people to friendships within their faith community. As mentioned in chapter 7, a young Punjabi Hindu woman, whose family drew inspiration especially from the International Society for Krishna Consciousness, spoke of her friendship with a Christian peer because she too understood what it meant to have a religious faith. This is especially interesting in the context of other researchers' findings among young South Asians, e.g. 'I hang out mainly with Asian girls because they know your feelings' (Shain 2003: 68).

Qualitative data from in-depth research among young people of faith must also contribute to discussion of the religious dimension of some young people's spiritual development. Moreover, *inclusive conceptualisation* of spirituality requires receptive responsiveness to emphases and insights which draw on the range of faith traditions from which our pupils themselves draw. *Bhakti* (loving devotion to God/ Guru) must not be ignored.

This raises the issue of critical alertness in relation to personal faith. Whether the faith concerned is the young Christian's commitment to Christ, in some cases following a conversion experience, or a young Hindu's or Sikh's *bhakti*, acceptance and trust take precedence over analysis and questioning. At the same time teachers' aims in religious education and in furthering spiritual development are likely to include encouraging a *critical awareness*, a facility for exercising informed judgement. Indeed, on the basis of much twentieth-century western psychology, many educationists may regard distancing from – and indeed rejection of – elements of one's home tradition, or the totality of it, as intrinsic to spiritual maturity (Erikson 1968 and Vincent Murray's critique 1989). How teachers resolve this tension between understandings of spiritual development will affect their judgements about individual pupils' spiritual development.

Teachers' own attitudes to faith, too, will affect their provision for pupils' spiritual development (see Feige *et al.* 2000). In consequence, teachers need to be critically aware of their own stance. For the ethnographic researcher who seeks out the spiritual such awareness is also vital (Nesbitt 2001b; 2002).

Alongside the goal of sharpening pupils' critical skills, pragmatically, there is reason for head teachers to welcome concrete suggestions for improving the school's *ethos*, by reducing conflict and increasing attentiveness and receptivity in lessons. Some of our Hindu and Sikh interviewees articulated the feeling of peace that they experienced if, for example, they had recited a mantra. A Bal Vikas guru spoke of children becoming less fidgety as a result of participation in silent sitting. The question which arises for teachers is whether schools can or should (for the welfare of individuals and the whole community) include in their provision similar techniques for helping children to be calmer. Should such provision be on an opt in or an opt out basis? At least two of the values education programmes currently on offer to schools draw to some extent upon their connection with the Hindu tradition (for Living Values: an Educational programme see Arweck and Nesbitt 2003; 2004 and Nesbitt and Arweck 2003). Of these programmes, Sathya Sai Education in Human Values is advertised as resulting in, among other things, 'calmer classes' (SSEHV promotional material 2003). Now that an increasing number of schools (especially primary schools) incorporate practices (e.g. guided visualisation as part of personal, social and health education) in the curriculum, educationists need to consider carefully the relationship between faith communities' and schools' assumptions about spiritual development and between their consequent styles of provision.

To the task of evaluating such initiatives ethnographic research has a contribution to make. Thoroughly researched data are all the more important in order to supplement reporting by promoters (e.g. Devi 2002), supporters (Farrer 2000 on an Oxfordshire primary school's 'quiet revolution' in implementing 'positive values') and by critics and detractors. To take a broadcast example: one interviewee on BBC Radio 4's 'Sunday' programme criticised a Roman Catholic school in Liverpool for setting up a 'quiet place' with cuddly toys, sounds of water, music, colours and the provision of massage, therapy and relaxation to help pupils raise their 'spirituality quotient' (BBC 2002). His grounds for objecting were that such practices are rooted in Hindu tradition.

Young people's readiness to speak about their religious experiences suggests that schools take seriously Scott's concern that there be more space in the curriculum for pupils to connect with and exchange narratives of 'their spiritual lived experiences' (2001: 118). The time to reflect on experiences is itself a contribution to spiritual development. Moreover, some young Hindus' testimony to the help which some practices (for example, reciting a mantra) offer for concentration and improved performance need to be considered receptively by educationists. Devi (2002) reports her primary school pupils asking for the opportunity to have 'silent sitting' before taking their mathematics tests. The field studies not only suggest possibilities for schools' provision for pupils' spiritual development, but (like Farrer 2000) they also indicate connections between this and whole school improvement. It is for heads, governors and staff to evolve and evaluate approaches which are acceptable to staff, parents and pupils in all their diversity of religious and spiritual orientation.

Ethnography as Reflective Practice

10

The ethnographic studies reported in chapters 1 to 9 throw up particular findings which are relevant to religious education, and other subjects, as well as beyond the curriculum. For example, knowing (from chapter 2) about periodic Hindu *vrat*s (fasts) may be useful to the biology teacher or the physical education teacher and for liaising in a sensitive and informed way with a particular family at a particular time. To take another example – being reminded of the different dates on which Christian communities celebrate Easter and Christmas (chapters 3 and 4) may lead to more inclusive teaching and assemblies (acts of collective worship) on the subject of these festivals. Certainly one hope in writing this book has been that the very detail of the reporting will be helpful in just these ways.

This chapter's remit, however, is to tease out the wider range of ways in which ethnography can support the reflective practitioner. First, we look at how field studies influence the ways in which we conceptualise 'religion' and 'culture'. We examine the images which may be helpful, whilst recognising the limitations of all metaphor and analogy. Second, we look at ethnography as a record of young people's lives and we note especially the evidence of the role of schools in the perpetuation (as well as the representation) of religion and culture. We reflect on what the field studies suggest regarding young people's 'plural identity'. Third, we consider the potential value of the ethnographic process for teachers, and we conclude with a commendation of an approach in religious education (and more widely) which is interpretative and dialogic.

Images of cultures and religions

Anthropologists' imaginations have been fertile in providing images for what we mean by culture. In her essay on 'the dynamics of culture' the Swedish anthropologist Lena Gerholm (1993) cites several images of culture – the seamless fabric, the patchwork quilt and Clifford Geertz's octopus 'whose tentacles are in large part separately integrated, neurally quite poorly connected with one another and with what in the octopus passes for a brain, and yet who nonetheless, manages both to get around and to preserve himself, for a while anyway, as a viable if somewhat ungainly entity' (Geertz 1973: 407–8). By choosing this image Geertz is suggesting that we do well to conceive of cultures as internally connected and externally bounded but not strongly so.

Geertz had offered this image in preference to earlier images of the spider's web and the pile of sand (the organised and internally connected and the unbounded, atomic). By pondering data reported from field studies and by attention to the social contexts of one's family, workplace and other membership groups one can consider the usefulness of images such as these and develop one's own understandings of culture. Developing an ethnographic approach, whether or not one has the opportunity to conduct intensive studies of this sort, involves becoming aware of how one visualises 'culture' and 'religion' and trying out other images.

For example, do we think of culture as what people inherit or what they create? The anthropologist Richard Fox suspected that in the past anthropologists had stereotyped 'others' as mere carriers of culture, by 'pressing them pan-cake flat under a tyranny of culture' (1985: xi). In Fox's assessment earlier anthropological 'conceptions of culture all presume that culture exists in advance of human history and action'. Instead he proposes:

> Cultural stability and persistence result only from the successive reproductions of similar fields of forces, they therefore come about because of culture's continuous construction and reconstruction, not because it has stopped and remained stable. (Fox 1985: xi)

We can see this perpetual, successive creation of culture in the particular decisions that individuals make (see Nesbitt 1995b), whether in their choice of words (e.g. to use a Punjabi word or an English one in a particular sentence in a particular context), or in their decisions about the importance of caste distinctions (see chapter 7), or about the likelihood that a baby is crying as a result of *nazar* (the evil eye), or in how they will pray.

Attempts to conceptualise 'religion' raise similar questions. One authority on religious studies, John Bowker, offers a collection of definitions (1997: xv). For example, for the French sociologist Emile Durkheim 'a religion is a unified system of beliefs and practices' and for Geertz a religion is 'a system of symbols'. Bowker proceeds to look at religions as systems and concludes that religions can be recognised but elude definition. Better, he suggests, to follow the eminent phenomenologist Ninian Smart's recommendation of observing religions in terms of their seven different 'dimensions'. These dimensions Smart identified as 'the practical and ritual' and the 'experiential and emotional' as well as the 'narrative or mythical', the 'doctrinal and philosophical', the 'ethical and legal', the 'social and institutional' and the 'material', in which he included art, architecture and sacred places.

In the twentieth century growing awareness that there are many religions, and that they are in closer and closer proximity to each other, precipitated an abundance of images of religions' relationship to each other – favourites being the images of paths winding up a mountain (to the same summit) and as streams pouring down a mountain (from the same pure source). Tree images also flourished. Julius Lipner, among others, visualised the Hindu tradition as a tree – especially as that most bewildering of trees, a banyan (1998: 5). Sometimes the historical relationship between religions is plotted pictorially as branches from a tree (Buddhism, Jainism and Sikhism as branches from the Hindu tree, Christianity and Islam from the Jewish tree). John Hick's suggestion is that the world's faiths are a universe of planets circling around the sun (God) rather than around Christianity (1977). Meanwhile Lat Blaylock, Executive Officer of the Professional Council for Religious Education, has suggested that we picture religions as treasure chests (1999).

My colleague Robert Jackson at the University of Warwick developed a 'three level model' of religion. This consists of the individual, the membership group and the cumulative tradition (Jackson 1997a). His model is an adaptation and development of Wilfred Cantwell Smith's distinction between individuals' personal faith and the cumulative traditions in which the individual is involved. Smith proposed that conceptualising faiths in this way was less misleading than uncritically using the term 'religion' with its fundamentally western and Christian history and connotations (1978). As an example of his three level model Jackson described 'Anita', a young woman, whose 'tradition' is Hindu and whose membership groups included peer groups, ethnic community – her *samaj* (caste) and the wider Gujarati community – as well as a *sampradaya*, i.e. the Sathya Sai Baba movement.

To a varying degree – weaker in the case of Smith's and Jackson's cumulative tradition, stronger in the case of Blaylock's treasure chest – all these images are bounded. As noted in the Introduction, this has been emphasised in the structure of syllabuses and curricula in religious education, which are organised within a framework of distinct world religions (see, for example, SCAA 1994). While Blaylock criticises studying religions 'as if they were separate and "hermetically sealed"' he emphasises that 'the blurring of differences between religions' is to be discouraged (1999: 17). It is anthropologists of religion who protest most powerfully against imposing (or supposing that there are) firm boundaries between, for example, 'Sikhism' and 'Hinduism'. Both Roger Ballard's and Ron Geaves's fieldwork has largely concentrated on expressions of religion in the Punjab and among Punjabis in the UK, and their ethnography leaves no question of the fluidity of popular devotion – evident in the iconography and clientele at pilgrimage places (see Ballard 2003; Geaves 1998b). This makes them deeply uneasy with the premises of boundedness on which so much religious studies in higher education as well as religious education in schools are based (see especially Geaves 1998a). The field studies in Coventry reported in chapters 1 to 9 rang the same alarm bells – see the discussion of 'plural identities' below.

Durkheim's definition of religion as a unified system of belief and practice dominates in religious education. This division raises the question of whether beliefs are what the individual member of a faith tradition should believe (according to some central authority such as scripture) or, rather, what that individual actually believes. It also encourages a tendency to view what members of a faith do as either an expression of what they (should) believe or as an aberration from it. As such, it fosters a judgemental approach to human behaviour. The data reported in chapters 5, 6 and 7 instead support the greater usefulness of Martin Stringer's construct of 'situational belief' (1999) and of Roger Ballard's 'kismetic' dimension of religion (1999). In other words, rather than consciously articulating and adhering to a system of (approved) belief, individuals – and not only those with non-European backgrounds – mobilise particular beliefs in particular situations. These situations are often ones of need because of misfortune, illness and bereavement, and they impel a search for explanations and remedies. Both karma and *nazar* (the evil eye) provide explanations for misfortune, and *amrit* (empowered water) affords one remedy. Prayer variously understood affords another.

By focusing on caste, chapter 7 further problematised the relation of belief and practice. It distinguished between the Gurus' acceptance of caste as a·basis for marriages and their denunciation of it as a source of pride and superiority. At the same time it questioned portrayals of a distinction between Sikhs and Hindus in terms of caste-related belief and practice. Students and teachers need to engage with the question of whether the range of practice (e.g. of attitudes to those of lower castes) indicates a residual or persistent situational belief that is at least as evident among Sikhs as it is among Hindus in the UK.

Ethnography as record: diversity, continuity and change

Over and over again, the field studies indicate the diversity within any supposed category. Whether this be a 'faith community' (e.g. Christians) or a more specific group (such as eight to 13 year-old Black Pentecostal boys in north Coventry), or an activity (for example, celebrating birthdays or Easter) or daily patterns of behaviour (including the dietary choices of young Hindus), ethnographic research dispels any lingering assumptions of homogeneity. The data may reveal stark contradictions within the group, and will certainly show more subtly nuanced variation in individuals' attitudes and practices and in how they articulate these.

Field studies show continuities from one generation to another, with many of the eight to 13 year olds echoing their parents' views on matters of belief and practice; they also capture some clear continuities from one period in an individual's life to another. Thus, some of the young Hindus who participated in the longitudinal study expressed the same idea in almost identical words after a nine-year interval. One example was a Gujarati Hindu who stated on each occasion that 'religion is the most private thing' and a Punjabi Hindu who testified to the power of reciting the Hare Krishna *mahamantra*. As chapter 7 demonstrated, one of these continuities is young Hindus' and Sikhs' sense of caste – internalising the connotations of certain caste designations and knowing that they themselves belong to a particular caste. Caste is an ongoing thread (stronger in some families than in others) in both the families' and individuals' sense of self.

Equally striking is change, such as the divergence of a young person's outlook from her parents' outlook, and also from her own outlook when she was interviewed nine years earlier. The Gujarati psychology student in chapter 9 provides one example. Her personal faith had shifted to some extent from the unquestioning devotion to Sathya Sai Baba which she and her father had shared nine years previously. In chapter 2 the focus on young people in relation to vegetarianism illustrated changes – often changes to and fro within a few years of an individual's experience – and it exposed a range of interacting factors that were at work in these.

Schools' implication in religious socialisation

More soberingly for those of us who are involved in education, fieldwork also reveals the largely uncharted interaction between religious nurturing and young people's encounter in school with their faith traditions. Put another way, the research leaves no doubt that school can be unsettling as well as affirming in terms of individuals' faith tradition and that it contributes to young people's religious socialisation. As will be outlined below, it does this by (a) providing some of their knowledge of the faith with which they identify and ways of articulating it and (b) in some cases triggering pupils' identification of themselves with the particular faith community.

School-based encounter occurs in numerous ways. Obvious occasions of interaction are religious education lessons (including work for public examinations) and collective worship (e.g. the Christmas, Divali and Vaisakhi assemblies of chapter 4), as well as innumerable social interactions with fellow pupils, teachers and other staff. Such interactions include affirmation of young people's faith community and tradition but also dissonances, inconsistencies and contradictions between home and school. These may be potentially hurtful cultural differences and include disjunctions between young people's experience at home and the representation of their 'religions' by teachers and in curriculum materials. To take the cultural differences first: in chapter 2, a teacher's lack of sympathy towards a young Hindu's avoidance of meat during her *vrat* (fast) was – unlike her father's disapproval – suggestive of a deeper dissonance between an aspect of religious tradition and teachers' cultural conditioning. Children's reports of teachers scolding them for attending school with their hands stained with henna after a marriage (not realising its auspicious associations or that it is not just wilful staining of their hands), and a Ukrainian Catholic parent's recollection of a Roman Catholic teacher laughing at a child who had missed school on 7 January 'because it was Christmas', exemplify this sort of gap further. Hence the importance of religious education using children's own knowledge and experience as primary resource material. In this connection, Jackson (2004b) discusses drawing on children's first-hand knowledge and experience through approaches that are interpretive and dialogical.

As regards home experience and the representation of religions in school: chapter 4 referred to teacher-led (though not deliberate) changes to the pronunciation of names and vocabulary from Indian languages. More substantively, chapters 5 and 7 have exemplified how statements about 'God' in curriculum materials on the Sikh tradition, and about castes/*varna* in the context of the Hindu tradition, fit uneasily with experience of many families within the communities concerned.

I have discussed elsewhere the discrepancy between textbook accounts of the five Ks as part and parcel of being a Sikh and young Sikhs' perception that these are markers distinguishing, not Sikh from non-Sikh, but 'proper Sikh' from 'Sikh' (Nesbitt 1999c, 2000). What the curriculum books often do not clarify is that the five Ks are required specifically of Khalsa Sikhs (those who are *amritdhari*, i.e. have been initiated by receiving *amrit* in an *amrit* ceremony), and that only a very small minority of pupils (even in secondary school) will be *amritdhari*.

Ethnography provides just the sort of awareness of a wider social context which is vital if educators are to reflect and implement change (e.g. in religious education materials or in educating pupils and colleagues in cultural sensitivity) in an informed way. Religious education teachers need to be aware of the sorts of dissonance that arise. This is not to rule out the inevitable compressions and simplifications involved in presenting complex material within the constraints of the timetable, but it is to urge caution before generalising about (all) Sikhs, (all) Hindus etc., and to help pupils to understand that individual experience varies.

Ethnography also shows how the interaction between school and an individual's 'faith' includes schools' contribution to individuals' knowledge of their tradition. This is in part because, as some young people's accounts show, school clearly enjoys a privileged status in the minds of some pupils at least, and what a teacher says is accepted as authoritative (or as more authoritative than what a parent says). Thus one Gujarati girl corrected her mother's pronunciation of Indian words and names, insisting that the teacher's (incorrect) versions were correct. A young Punjabi woman (a Ravidasi) recalled learning about the caste system and about reincarnation in her religious education lessons. She said:

> When I heard it at school I believed it. It had a great effect on me because it was my own religion and I thought it was true.

Her receptiveness to the teachers' presentation of the content of her tradition set up an interaction with prior, less articulated awareness of what it meant to be Hindu.

Young people's respect for teachers as authority figures meant, moreover, that teachers' endorsement of their tradition by talking about it gave them a positive feeling about themselves and their tradition. Thus, in recalling the occasion when her religious education teacher quoted from the Bhagavad Gita in assembly, a Punjabi Hindu sixth former in an independent school commented, 'You obviously feel proud when someone talks about your religion.'

What must not be forgotten is the corresponding sense of marginalisation or embarrassment when there is no acknowledgement in school of a pupil's cultural background or when this is presented (though usually not consciously) in a negative, trivial or misleading manner – especially if there are pupils present who will follow this up out of the classroom. One Gujarati girl recalled the amusement of (Punjabi) pupils in the room when her teacher played (as it happened, inappropriate) romantic Indian film songs because it was a Hindu festival. The fact that caste features in so many religious education syllabuses, and that caste is a sensitive issue – especially in the families of colleagues and pupils from historically oppressed castes – underlines the need for sensitivity and skill in handling curriculum material.

The field studies indicated too that, in addition to responding positively to hearing the content of the tradition, whether a belief or a passage of scripture, mediated by a teacher, a young person might even have initially accepted the label for his or her religious identity on a teacher's authority. Thus it was a teacher who, while almost certainly unaware of the interweaving of *sampradaya*s (guru-led devotional groupings) and *zat-biradari* (caste) in the fabric of Punjabi culture, precipitated a Ravidasi girl's identification of herself with a major faith tradition (see below). The girl recalled:

First I used to say [my religion was] Indian, but then my teacher told me that it's not really Indian: it's Sikh. So I start sort of saying, 'It's Sikh'.

The stages by which such an identification might be reached illustrate further the interaction of home and school. In the words of a younger Hindu girl:

I just found out that I'm Hindu. Well, my mum told me because this teacher said, 'Are you a Hindu?' and I said, 'I don't know', so she said, 'Go and ask your mum and tell me.' And when I told her the other day, she said, 'OK' and she wanted to know about Divali, [saying] that you celebrate Divali if you're a Hindu.'

My field notes contain other instances of children and their parents being regarded as resources by the teacher, or at least as channels of information about what the teacher perceives to be aspects of their tradition. As the last quotation illustrates, this is particularly evident in connection with festivals during children's primary school years. As chapter 4 pointed out, in the interactive processes of religious socialisation that take place in the home and the school, the festivals – Christmas, Divali, Easter, Id, Vaisakhi etc. – present teachers with pegs for presenting particular faith traditions, and as opportunities for parents (religious nurturers) and school teachers to interact. As we have seen, schools play a part in the cultural transmission of some minority as well as majority communities.

These examples of parents and teachers reinforcing associations in children's thinking – between an individual, a faith tradition, a country (India, for example) and an annual event – set up a framework for children's understanding of cultural diversity. This must not obscure another finding of these ethnographic studies: the plurality of individuals' identity if set against the simple framework of six 'world religions'.

Plural identities

The field studies show that not only are society, and so its schools, plural in terms of its members' cultural and religious diversity, but individuals are themselves in several senses religiously and culturally plural.

Not fitting the boxes – challenging the boundaries

Chapter 7 in particular mentioned two communities, the Valmikis and Ravidasis. These are the non-disparaging titles for two hereditary (caste-specific) communities. In UK cities including Coventry, Birmingham and London the local Punjabi community includes settled populations from these castes and they have established their own places of public worship (Nesbitt 1990a and b, 1991, 1994). The ways in which young Valmikis and Ravidasis applied the terms 'Hindu' and 'Sikh' to themselves made it clear that any definition of Hindu and Sikh in mutually exclusive terms left out of account families for whom each designation was equally appropriate and equally unsatisfactory. In one sense these families are both Hindu and Sikh; in another they are no more plural than other Punjabi families. This is because it can be argued that they do not span the Hindu–Sikh boundary because in practice there is no such boundary.

Similarly, the finding that some Sikhs from other castes (including Jats), venerate the Goddess, that at Divali some Ramgarhia Sikhs venerate the God Vishvakarma, or that Hindus may include a picture of Guru Nanak in their domestic shrine, need not be read as signs of cultural plurality in terms of spanning or mixing 'different faiths', but as evidence of the inappropriateness of trying to represent Sikhism and Hinduism as such distinct entities. Instead one can read such data as evidence of the continuing cultural fluidity of Punjab in the twenty-first century as well as in earlier centuries (see Oberoi 1994) and can begin to question the appropriateness of boxing individuals by supposedly distinct religious affiliation. The diagram on page 147 provides one way of conceptualising this continuum of 'belief' and 'practice'.

The fact that, for example, Sikh spokespeople present their faith with such a firm boundary needs to be balanced by the ethnographic reports and children's experiences that unsettle this – see for example Lall (1999) for a Sikh teacher's sharing of the diversity of young Sikhs' experiences of religious devotion. Reading about the history and politics of religion in the Punjab will also deepen understanding of the movements among Sikhs towards presenting a strongly separate identity (Oberoi 1994; Juergensmeyer 1982). Teachers and others need to be aware of differences of stance, to be open to different perspectives and to question statements in curriculum books and syllabuses critically.

To take another example of apparent plurality, the fact (observed in chapter 4) that Hindus may venerate the infant Jesus at Christmas can be read as an indication of the encompassing character of Hindu tradition as well as of the convergence of two religions or cultures. The identity of the worshipper as a Hindu is not changed by this catholicity in worship, although – as the young Gujarati woman from a family of Sai devotees explained – one's identity could be primarily universalist rather than (more narrowly) Hindu.

Mixed faith and dual heritage

Increasing numbers of families are plural in the sense that parents identify themselves with different ethnic, cultural or religious communities and this influences the way in which their children experience and articulate their own identities (Alibhai-Brown 2001; Ata 2003; Katz 1996;

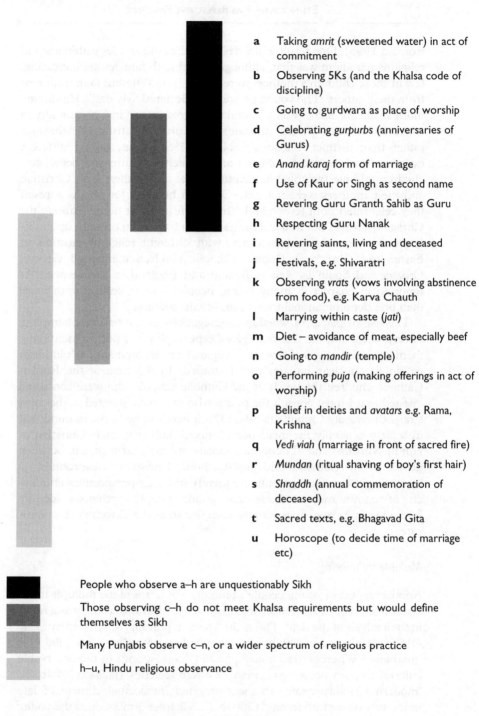

a   Taking *amrit* (sweetened water) in act of commitment

b   Observing 5Ks (and the Khalsa code of discipline)

c   Going to gurdwara as place of worship

d   Celebrating *gurpurbs* (anniversaries of Gurus)

e   *Anand karaj* form of marriage

f   Use of Kaur or Singh as second name

g   Revering Guru Granth Sahib as Guru

h   Respecting Guru Nanak

i   Revering saints, living and deceased

j   Festivals, e.g. Shivaratri

k   Observing *vrats* (vows involving abstinence from food), e.g. Karva Chauth

l   Marrying within caste (*jati*)

m   Diet – avoidance of meat, especially beef

n   Going to *mandir* (temple)

o   Performing *puja* (making offerings in act of worship)

p   Belief in deities and *avatars* e.g. Rama, Krishna

q   *Vedi viah* (marriage in front of sacred fire)

r   *Mundan* (ritual shaving of boy's first hair)

s   *Shraddh* (annual commemoration of deceased)

t   Sacred texts, e.g. Bhagavad Gita

u   Horoscope (to decide time of marriage etc)

People who observe a–h are unquestionably Sikh

Those observing c–h do not meet Khalsa requirements but would define themselves as Sikh

Many Punjabis observe c–n, or a wider spectrum of religious practice

h–u, Hindu religious observance

Figure 1   The Hindu–Sikh continuum of belief and practice

Note: This diagram is intended to show the approximate relationship between individuals' religious practices and whether they identify themselves as 'Hindu' or 'Sikh'. The categories should not be interpreted too rigidly.

Romain 1996). One result of the design of the field studies within a world religions paradigm was that, although mixed faith families are increasing, few of these children's mothers were in fact from different faith traditions from their fathers. The young person who declared 'My dad's Hindu, my mum's side are Sikhs' was a Valmiki (i.e. growing up in a community in which 'Sikh' and 'Hindu' indicate points on a spectrum of behaviour rather than distinct 'religions') (Nesbitt 1991). But, raising different questions with regard to religion and ethnicity, culture and belief, two children told me (as noted in chapter 3) that their fathers were Christian and their mothers were not only Christian but also Jewish. As a result they celebrated both Jewish and Christian festivals at home. Among the Christians, it was not unusual for parents to have been brought up in different countries from each other, with different religious customs at Easter and Christmas. Roman Catholic children mentioned Greece, Croatia and Spain as well as Ireland and England in this respect. As reported in chapter 2, many young people were in contact with more than one denominational expression of Christianity.

The use of places of worship/congregations as the basis for sampling interviewees, and the fact that 'gate-keepers' played a part in identifying them, reduced the incidence of religious or denominational pluralism within the nuclear families that I studied. In the case of the Roman Catholic children the heads of the Catholic schools who were contacted insisted that I must consult the priest, who may have pointed to the most straightforwardly Catholic families. But it needs to be borne in mind that in society generally the incidence of mixed faith (e.g. Sikh–Christian or Hindu–Muslim) and of denominationally 'mixed' marriage, e.g. between people from Catholic and non-Catholic Christian backgrounds, is increasing. Moreover, parents' frequently differing perspectives and levels of commitment suggest that young people's religious identity formation is in many cases more complex than the Coventry data indicate.

Multiple influencing

Another aspect of young people's plurality – in terms of the multiple influences which they experience – did however recur more strongly as a motif in the analysis of the data. This is the 'modern plurality' discussed by Skeie (1995) and Jackson (2004b) and described evocatively by Eck (2000) as 'marbling'. Whereas 'traditional' plurality 'corresponds to the observable cultural diversity presented in many Western societies' (Jackson 2004b: 8), 'modern plurality relates to the variegated intellectual climate of late modernity or postmodernity' (2004b: 8). Chapter 3 mentioned the young Christians who had encountered ideas of reincarnation and chapter 6 introduced the young Hindus who were engaging simultaneously with ideas that they met through their families, through the media and at school – for example different accounts of the creation of the universe or of what the optimum diet is, or regarding romantic love and marriage.

Elsewhere I have used the term 'plural spirituality' to convey something of this 'modern plurality' (Nesbitt 2003), as at the deepest level of questing, enquiry and experience individuals encounter images, ideals and idioms from (what are in some ways and according to dominant perceptions) different sources: Christian and Hindu, European and African, sacred and secular.

In Wendy Doniger O'Flaherty's terms, more and more individuals are simultaneously orthoprax and heterodox – they remain within their cultural norms, e.g. following their religion's rituals, while benefiting 'in their heads' from the myths of many cultures (1999: 344).

Plural identity

Increasingly complex patterns of individual identity result from 'tradi-tional' plurality (Skeie 1995). Chapter 8 highlighted some of the various ways in which individuals – all of them 'Hindu' by one self-definition – may identify themselves in different contexts. They may also identify as Asian and as British, for example. As Raj (2003) shows, other identities such as Black or 'of Indian origin' may also come into play for these same young people. Self-identifications as Gujarati (or Punjabi, Bengali etc.) according to their ethnicity and ancestral region in India; as a Vaishnav, or as a devotee of the Mother Goddess or of Krishna (according to their *sampradaya* or devotional grouping); or as a Khatri or a Brahmin (their caste solidarity), or as coming from a Kenyan family (because their parents and grand parents had lived there before coming to the UK) surfaced strongly in certain situations (see Nesbitt 2004b).

Ethnographic studies disclose identity forming through successive encounters with 'others' (Tajfel 1981). Identity is itself processual, forming in definition and redefinition through contact with groupings that in some respects differ from one's own and in other respects overlap with it. It involves ongoing processes of categorising, feeling affirmed and feeling excluded, e.g. through others' racist behaviour. As chapter 8 illus-trated, self-awareness is a matter of interpretation, of telling a coherent life story (Jackson 2004b discussing Meijer 1995).

One clear acknowledgement of the gap that is widening between the simple world religions categories of much religious education and the experience of many individuals comes from the eminent religious educa-tionist, John Hull:

> It is clear that religious education is moving away from the phenomenology of religion toward the phenomenology of the life-world . . . Constructs such as 'Muslims' and 'Protestants' are no longer useful unless they are presented as a

contribution to the formation of identity, a subjective development in which both religious diversity in the culture and implicit in the lived world of the young person will be combined. This 'living religion' of the life-world is not the same as the actual religion of the old traditions. (Hull 2003)

Ethnography as process

Ethnography, too, is better understood as processual. It is not simply the set of methods, the qualitative approach, that is employed in obtaining data through sustained academic study. Ethnography itself consists of interactive processes. As the Introduction explained, ethnography requires us to be reflexive, because the ethnographer affects, and is affected by, the field. As chapter 8 noted, the researcher's in-depth, one to one interviews with young people facilitated some young people's articulation of who they are and how they perceive themselves in relation to others. The interviews were intrinsic to this self-narration.

Involvement in the research stimulated young people's responses to their experience. From a 20 year-old Gujarati Hindu man comes evidence of how an earlier phase of our study had made an impact on his religious development:

> I think I just got involved with what you were doing [i.e. the research] so that helped a lot as well. It opened up what I thought as well. I found that helped a great deal. I remember you asking me to keep a diary . . . I remember my mum helping me write down . . . I was finding I became a lot more interested in my own religion . . . I found a lot more about Hinduism.

Similarly, a young Christian and a young Hindu woman admitted that the experience of taking part in the field studies had encouraged their choice of study at university— theology and religious education respectively. Such admissions require the researcher to reflect conscientiously on the reflexive character of ethnography – the impact of the participants on the researcher as well as the influence of the research process on the participants.

It is just this sort of awareness, as well as the open curiosity and the scepticism of generalisations, that can best further the intentions of intercultural education. Through adopting ethnography as process all who are engaged in social interaction, and schools in particular, can deepen their understanding and enhance their professional skills. This is the message of Dell Hymes and Celia Roberts among others, who advocate ethnography as 'continuous with ordinary life' and as 'a general possession' (Hymes 1980: 98–9 as cited in Roberts 2002). The point is not that 'we should all strive to become professional ethnographers but rather that we should use ethnography to pursue our particular interests and careers' (Roberts 2002:

115). Roberts quotes Hymes' vision of a democratic society as one in which ethnography would be seen:

> as a general possession, although differentially cultivated. At one pole would be a certain number of people trained in ethnography as a profession. At the other pole would be the general population, respected . . . as having a knowledge of their worlds, intricate and subtle in many ways . . . and as having come to this knowledge by a process ethnographic in character. In between would be those able to combine some disciplined understanding of ethnographic inquiry with the pursuit of their vocation whatever that might be. (Hymes 1980: 99 quoted in Roberts 2002: 115)

Such an awareness can inform pastoral care and deepen teachers' representations of religious and cultural diversity. This is in part because it involves training oneself to see, to avoid observer blindness, especially where one's own background, assumptions and behaviour are concerned. One writer on research methodology tells the story of the observer who sees each day a peasant man crossing the frontier one way between two countries. Each day the peasant is with his donkey and the observer becomes convinced that he must be engaged in smuggling. Try as he may, he cannot figure out what the contraband is – until the day when he learns that the man is smuggling donkeys.

An ethnographic alertness helps us to see the world differently – this may mean recognising the cultural assumptions embedded in taking it for granted that birthday celebrations are part of every child's entitlement if not of their experience. It may mean perceiving commonalities of experience where previously cultural difference had seemed to dominate. It may mean listening to the way in which a parent actually pronounces a child's name and recognising the importance of doing so each time one meets a child whose name is unfamiliar.

Of course the interactive, dynamic quality of ethnography may more deeply affect teachers who are able to conduct even small-scale field studies and this experience informs their teaching. As part of the MA in Religious Education course at the University of Warwick, for example, students – most of whom are teachers – engage as ethnographers in field studies of religions. The teachers concerned have the transforming experience of assuming a different role, in some cases *vis-à-vis* their own pupils (Cochran-Smith and Lytle 1993; Gillespie 1995: 67ff). Their understanding of faith traditions, and so of the relationship between pupils' religious nurture and the representation of their tradition in religious education, changes. For example, a Leicester secondary school teacher's study of Swadhyaya, a Hindu self-study group, brought him insight into some of his pupils' distinctive nurturing and its contribution to how they approached their studies in general and religious education in particular (Bennett 1997).

Teachers' ethnographic insight can, especially when coupled with a long-standing association with a faith community, inform their production of curriculum materials, so narrowing the gap further. Elizabeth Wayne's ethnographic work had, together with her involvement in the local Hindu community, familiarised her with the importance of the summer festival of Raksha Bandhan. This, like Divali, is celebrated by a wide spectrum of Hindus (and by many Sikhs). However, unlike Divali, probably because it falls in the summer holidays, it receives much less attention in schools. Wayne's understanding of how the festival strengthened bonds between siblings and cousins, regardless of geographical distance, enabled her to explore this aspect confidently when she was teaching. This classroom experience, in turn, was the basis for material in a curriculum book (Wayne et al. 1996: 40–1).

Indeed it was the ethnographic studies reported in this book which provided an empirical basis for the interpretive approach (sometimes referred to as the Warwick approach) which Robert Jackson developed (1997a, 2000) and for the curriculum materials which it generated (e.g. Barratt 1994a, b, c; Barratt and Price 1996; Everington 1996; Robson 1995; Wayne et al. 1996). The relationship between fieldwork and curriculum books is discussed by Judith Everington (1993). The materials aimed to set up a dialogue between pupils and the young people of their age whom the materials presented. In this process the pupils are helped to build 'bridges' between their own experience and the experience of these young people. This involves the pupils acquiring the ethnographic skills of (a) reflecting on what they are learning about the young Hindu's or United Reformed Church child's experience and concepts in the light of their own and (b) reflecting on their own experience and concepts in the light of the young Hindu's or United Reformed Church child's. Other educationists have developed variations of the approach – see e.g. Cush (1999). Denise Cush's concern is that concepts such as reincarnation may in fact be exoticised and distanced from young people if they are presented through the experience of young people from unfamiliar religious and cultural backgrounds.

In addition to studies of communities there is also potential for concerted ethnographic study of educational initiatives. For example, a series of small-scale studies at the University of Warwick is providing insights into values education programmes that are running in some mainstream schools (see Nesbitt and Henderson 2003; Arweck and Nesbitt 2003, 2004; Nesbitt and Arweck 2003). These programmes were formulated and are promoted under the auspices of religious organisations – in two cases Hindu-related new religious movements, the Sathya Sai Organisation and the Brahma Kumaris World Spiritual University. Some schools have adopted the programmes as part of the statutory provision for pupils' spiritual, moral, social and cultural development (SMSC). The ethnographic style of the research allows for observation of lessons and assemblies, conversation with the teachers and pupils involved and with the organisations that are promoting the programmes. The data can be collected and analysed with reference to personal, social and health education in the school and the school's ethos and provision for pupils' spiritual, moral, social and cultural development. Such research provides a context, and raises questions, to help teachers in deciding whether to adopt (or at least select from) programmes such as Sathya Sai Education in Human Values and Living Values: An Educational Program.

In conclusion

Religion and culture are at the heart of worldwide changes in a plural society and so awareness of them drives associated developments in the curriculum in the direction of a more radically intercultural education. In the UK these include the introduction of citizenship education and the requirement of cross-curricular provision for pupils SMSC development. Even so, the centrality of representing religions and cultures in religious education can obscure the need for teachers more generally and others to deepen their understanding.

Ethnography challenges us to question our assumptions about religion and culture and about particular religions and cultures. Educationists need to be on guard for tendencies to harden or soften boundaries by the ways in which they generalise or emphasise distinctions between groups. In acknowledging culture and religion, schools must beware of becoming enmeshed in a retrospective 'nostalgia for culture' (Raj 2003) which stereotypes and locks individuals into labelled boxes as 'Hindu', 'Muslim', 'Chinese' or 'Irish' with timeless ways of being – and celebrating.

Moves towards a more dialogic approach to religious education are one way forward. These include the initiative of Julia Ipgrave in facilitating primary school children's e-mail dialogue with peers from other backgrounds (2001; Ipgrave's work is discussed in Jackson 2004b ch. 6) and Joyce Miller's organisation of meetings between secondary school pupils of different faiths in Bradford (2003). This virtual and face to face exchange of ideas continues the 'interpretive approach'.

Field workers live with the excitement of continually learning and unlearning, formulating and reformulating pictures of how individuals and groups are connected and how identities evolve, including their own identities. Pupils' religious and cultural literacy stands to benefit from education that is imbued with this spirit of discovery.

Appendix: Practical Guidelines for Teachers – Cultural Diversity and the School

These notes are relevant to primary and later stages of education, and were trialled with BA (QTS) students in the Institute of Education, University of Warwick as part of their module on Core Professional Studies. They raise points which have largely arisen from the research that this book reports, and provide some practical responses to them. Most important is the general emphasis on *listening and observing*, being *imaginatively open-minded* and always being *prepared to go on adapting* what you do to your particular situation. Reference is made to several articles in *Multicultural Teaching*, a journal which has been relaunched as *Race Equality Teaching* (ISSN 1478-8497). Copies of the issues mentioned below are available from Trentham Books, 734 London Road, Stoke on Trent, UK, ST4 5NP.

Objectives

These notes are intended to help you to:

- identify opportunities for cultural sensitivity in relation to parents and pupils
- contribute to staff awareness of cultural and minority issues
- select and design materials to promote the cultural development of pupils
- suggest ways of countering racism in school

Pastoral care

It is easy to concentrate on curricular issues to the exclusion of other vital dimensions of pupils' experience. Much of what you discover about cultural diversity, particularly as it relates to individuals in your school, will enhance your sensitivity to the outlooks and needs of pupils and their families. The insights that you bring to bear in supporting individuals will not necessarily or directly feed into curriculum design and content. But the ongoing process of bringing together your 'knowledge' to date on cultural issues and your sensitive openness to individuals and situations will influence your professional practice as a whole. One example is the need to understand differing patterns of fasting and avoidance of certain foods at certain times – see below. Pastoral care also includes understanding the demands on children out of school hours, such as working in the family business (Chan 1995) or attending Qur'an classes in the mosque, and also the particular difficulties that refugee children may experience (Spafford and Bolloten 1995).

Racism

Police statistics published in *Leicester Mercury* (19 June 1997) showed that 11–14 year olds are responsible for the majority of racial abuse incidents in Leicester. During their years at primary school (but one hopes not as a result of primary school) patterns of prejudice and victimisation develop. Race and racism are contested terms, but bullying often involves racism in the sense that pupils label each other in terms of difference in pigmentation/ethnicity/national origin/religious allegiance. Schools' policies on racism – and their swift, impartial implementation – can play a key role. Remember too that 'ethnic groups' are not homogeneous. For example, the 'Asians' in a school might be Indian, Pakistani, Bangladeshi and Sri Lankan (parental homeland), Punjabi, Bengali, Tamil (regional, cultural, linguistic identities which span these national borders), Sikh, Muslim, Christian, Hindu or Buddhist (religious affiliation) and they may be from hereditary groups ('castes') with connotations of prestige or oppression. Prejudice and name-calling need not be just between 'black' and 'white'.

It is for teachers to explore ways of counteracting the racism endemic in society and to offer means of conflict resolution. The pain of the victim may find expression through expressive activities such as Kiran Chahal's (1997) piece of creative writing:

They call you names for the fun of it
To make your insides weak
To injure all your happiness
And tell you you're a Sikh

Local, global and globalised

Wherever you are teaching you are engaging with a unique local community in helping pupils to understand the world. Try to build up your knowledge of the local community – its particular history of settlement and migration (e.g. of an Irish or Scottish workforce), its dynamics (e.g. families identifying with their weaver or miner forebears) and its organisations, social networks and places of worship.

At the same time keep a critical eye on how more distant societies are portrayed, e.g. in the media – sometimes because of war or other catastrophe – and in school. (I recall a visiting Inuit's puzzlement at always being asked about igloos – she said that she had no experience of these – and shortly afterwards I spotted a display of Eskimos and igloos in a local school.) Be especially attentive to the connections that pupils will make between themselves/local groups, football teams etc. and the societies or events that you present. This does not necessarily mean that, for example, the Crusades cannot be taught because they have for so long been presented with a particular, anti-Muslim bias, but it does call for serious attention to how they are introduced and discussed. Consider too the messages about, for example, India and African countries that fund-raising publicity may convey, and the implications for pupils' attitudes. Keep your ears open for connections that pupils (or rather parents) make between current events and their peers. For example, Coventry parents supported their son for beating up a boy from a Kurdish refugee family because he was Turkish (at a time when football supporters' anti-Turkish prejudices were high). During the 'Iran crisis' some Sikhs in American schools suffered because others confused them with Iranians, and since 11 September 2001 turban-wearing Sikhs in Europe as well as the USA have been assumed to belong to the Taliban/al-Qaeda and have been assaulted. Be on the look out for anti-Muslim and anti-Semitic/anti-Israeli feelings.

Individuals and minorities

It is easy to characterise a school catchment area as 'white' or as mainly Bangladeshi etc. These assumptions can result in some minorities (often minorities of one) feeling marginalised or excluded. Remember that the experience of being the only Hindu in your year or the only boy wearing a turban in the school is very different from being part of a larger group of Hindus or Sikhs. Some children will feel embarrassed and ashamed of their 'different' culture whereas others may prefer feeling special – like two mixed heritage, Goan/English sisters I know who asserted their Englishness in a school where most pupils were from South Asian or African Caribbean families, and enjoyed demonstrating Indian dress and dance in their next, mainly white school.

Of course both 'black' and 'white' cover a wide spectrum of cultural, national, political and religious identities. They include families who strictly follow the discipline expected of, for example, Jehovah's Witnesses or Exclusive Brethren. Some pupils too may well be spending holidays with close relatives – perhaps a parent – overseas, like the Coventry children who told me about Christmases in Barcelona and Easters in Croatia. It is easy to overlook the fact that a family of South Asian origin may be Christian or to assume that a 'westernised' pupil does not share cultural sensitivities with less 'westernised' pupils. It may be that individual pupils would feel affirmed by 'coming out' about their background in an organised activity – or they might be devastated. It is for the teacher to make tactful soundings in each case.

It is easy to overlook the situation of Travelling children and their families – see Bohan (1996) for ideas. Check books for images of Gypsies.

Parents

Awareness of cultural diversity includes respecting parents' experience and understanding their assumptions about teachers' and parents' roles (Dhasmana 1994). Those who grew up in societies where parents were only called to school if a child had committed some misdemeanour may be initially uneasy with teacher–parent contact. This may be especially true of parents who received little or no formal education themselves and/or find difficulty in communicating in English. Consider whether your school uses the most effective means for involving these parents and what provision there is for translating and interpreting (does everything depend on the child as interpreter?) One area is the importance of sensitivity to the perceptions of minority parents regarding 'special needs' (see Shah and Abrol 1990).

Parents from some backgrounds may be suspicious of learning activities which appear to be 'just playing', and may feel reassured by evidence of more 'traditional' methods. They may also regard corporal punishment as an important sanction in turning children into disciplined members of society.

Remember that refugee parents, although initially housed in difficult inner city areas, may be highly qualified professionals with high aspirations for their children's educational achievement.

By virtue of, for example, their overseas upbringing some parents may be invaluable as resources if sensitively approached and well-briefed. Contributing to the education of others can be a deeply affirming experience for people who often feel marginalised. But this will also require you to prepare colleagues and pupils to make them welcome in an appropriate way. Reflect on whether colleagues shaking hands with them, pupils addressing them by first or last name or some other form of address (e.g. 'Auntie') will be most appreciated.

Names

'Surnames'

Don't be embarrassed to enquire how parents wish you to address them: in many societies the use of the personal name suggests great familiarity or a lack of due respect. Don't assume that Mr Singh's wife is Mrs Singh as she's more likely – if she is a Sikh – to be Mrs Kaur.

Among Hindus of North Indian background 'Devi', 'Rani' and 'Kumari' (literally 'goddess', 'queen' and 'unmarried girl' are the second part of many girls' given names, but may be used for official purposes as surnames. Brothers and parents will usually be using a different name as their surname. Similarly, 'Begum' is a way of addressing a Muslim woman. If a girl is using this as her surname, you must make sure that you check what surname her parents are using before you address them.

South Indians and people from other parts of Asia may have their family name first, preceding their given name. For example, Rukmani might be a Tamil woman's final name and Rajendran might be a Tamil man's final name, which they use, in the West at least, as 'surnames', but Rukmani and Rajendran are not likely to be their family names.

Pronunciation and meaning

Think how you feel if your names are constantly mispronounced. Teachers (including pre-school teachers') mispronunciation of a young person's name may determine how most people pronounce it for the rest of his/her life. South Asian children are frequently known at home by an affectionate nickname, so may be unused to hearing their official name, and too in awe of the teacher to try to improve her pronunciation. Make it clear to parents that you wish to imitate their pronunciation as closely as possible, and ask them to repeat names slowly a few times, allowing you to listen carefully for which syllable is stressed etc. Pronounced differently the name loses its meaning.

Most pupils' names – both given names and family names – have meanings. In many cases the given names are of religious significance. Your pupils' names, the reasons for them and the way in which they were conferred provide a rich resource for pupils to learn about cultural patterns and individuals' heritages. Many schools have pupils whose names conform to different naming systems. You need to confirm, for example, that a Muslim child Muhammad Siddiq is to be called Siddiq rather than by the religious title, Muhammad.

Languages

Names evolve within different language systems. In many schools the majority of the teachers are competent in only one language (English) while many of their pupils are using two or more. (Think of, for example, the young Pakistanis who speak Mirpuri to grandparents, watch Hindi/Urdu movies and learn to recite the Qu'ran in Arabic at the mosque class.) Richard Yeomans has commented on their evident competence in calligraphy (1993a and b; 1994), and being tuned in to several languages gives pupils an advantage when learning languages in school. But you will frequently hear multilingual children described negatively in terms of being or presenting problems. Affirming pupils involves affirming languages. In the UK some school notice boards have the school's name in Gujarati, Hindi, Bengali, Punjabi and Urdu scripts. Even if all the South Asian parents (though not so many of the grandparents) are more literate in English than in any South Asian language, and even if their children do not know these alphabets, what comes across to them is that the school is aware of these languages and takes them seriously.

Remember that when you are teaching about, for example, Islam or Hinduism, or doing a project on Pakistan or China, there may well be parents who can give you confidence in pronouncing key terms in a way that is meaningful to children from the communities concerned.

Think of appropriate ways of providing language support for speakers of other languages – and consult with ESOL (English for Speakers of Other Languages) specialists if possible. Rigour in repeating words, assisting with spelling and emphasising patterns in spoken and written English will help pupils more generally. The implications of bi- and multi-lingualism for pupils' assessment mustn't be forgotten (Gravelle 1990).

Body language

Language is more than words. There are still teachers who reprimand a boy for not looking his teacher in the eye when she speaks to him. In many Asian societies one shows respect to elders – especially of the opposite sex – by lowering the gaze. Other possible differences in expected behaviour relate to the preparing, serving and eating of food. Traditionally in South Asian societies the right hand is regarded as more appropriate for handling food, whether for offering it to someone else or for lifting food to one's own mouth. Pupils can be introduced to accepting difference by looking at what they already take for granted about behaving differently in different places (classroom, beach, a place of worship). Drama and religious education (for example, when preparing to visit a mosque or temple) provide opportunities for role play.

Calendars

You can buy copies of Shap Calendar of Religious Festivals from The Shap Working Party, PO Box 38580, London SW1P 3XF, tel. 00 44 [0]20 7898 1494, website: www.shap.org. Accompanying the calendar are notes on each festival. By referring to this calendar teachers can plan appropriate acts of collective worship, make a point of acknowledging the major days in a pupil's religious year and show understanding if Muslims are absent for Id celebrations or if Gujarati Hindus are tired and excited during the days of Navaratri, the nine-night autumn festival (see e.g. Jackson and Nesbitt 1993). Most importantly you, and your pupils, discover that calendars are worked out on different principles. For instance, the Jewish and the Hindu are largely lunar, with an inter-calated month to keep them in line with the seasons and the solar year, whereas the Islamic calendar is totally lunar. The result is that Muslim festivals and the month of fasting are not tied to a particular season as the lunar year is shorter than the 365/6 day year.

Remember that for Orthodox (e.g. Cypriot) families Easter usually does not coincide with 'western' Easter, and that some Orthodox (and Ukrainian Catholic) communities – and Rastafarians – celebrate Christmas on 6–7 January (25 December by the older Julian calendar). Should the primary school schedule be so rigid that a Ukrainian child cannot be allowed a day off for a family celebration?

Most Muslim and Hindu pupils will be unsure of the dates of their festivals as, like both western and eastern Easter the dates are – by the dominant Gregorian calendar – different each year. You need to check with the Shap calendar, and if possible with the relevant communities, so that you are prepared for festivals such as Divali well in advance. In 2003 a new Sikh calendar was adopted. This means that most Sikh festivals – but not Guru Nanak's Birthday – do not change their date on the secular calendar.

Very importantly for developing students' understanding, avoid speaking as if there is only one calendar (the Gregorian, secular calendar) which is consistent from year to year, while 'other' communities have festivals that 'move'. Chinese, Jewish, Muslim, Hindu and other festivals and fasts are no less regular, and the calendars concerned are no less reasonable. It is only the difference between the calendars concerned that makes the significant days of one calendar appear to move if one is using a different calendar. Help pupils to understand this.

Celebrations

Celebrations provide a wealth of material for discussion and activity work, but also require sensitive handling. For instance, Divali is an opportunity for trying out Indian sweets and savouries and acting out the story of Ram and Sita, but Muslim, Jewish and Christian/Jehovah's Witness parents will need reassurance that what is set up is a learning experience for pupils, not an expectation that they celebrate as if they were Hindus.

Birthdays are an excellent springboard in primary school, but don't forget the Jehovah's Witness view of birthdays (Redbridge SACRE 1997a). It is all too easy to assume that birthdays have similar significance and that birthday parties take the same form cross-culturally. Of course there are some dominant trends which increasingly determine how families mark the day, regardless of parental background. As teachers are we happy to assume that majority practice is the norm, or do we encourage children to share with confidence their different experiences?

Perhaps the recent fashion for *mehndi* (henna patterns) has made teachers more aware of why South Asian girls sometimes come to school with their hands stained and patterned in terracotta. If teachers show an affirming interest in marriage practices, South Asian girls need not be humiliated by uncomprehending teachers telling them to 'Go and wash that stuff off your hands!'

Some relatively long-established British dates, or the ways in which they are marked, may be unacceptable or difficult for some families. For instance, Halloween parties are condemned by many concerned Christians. One Coventry teacher reported last year that fireworks for Guy Fawkes caused distress to refugee children whose families had recent experience of living in a war zone.

Don't forget the diversity of celebration within a single faith community. Some books show Christmas 'overseas', but what about the diversity of Christmases and Easters in society generally, and in your own school or locality (Nesbitt 1993b)?

Christmas – the autumn term of most primary schools is dominated by the build up to Christmas. Is this appropriate in all schools? How should the sensibilities of, for example, Jewish and Muslim parents be respected? One school organised a nativity play in which pupils (including Muslims) were asked to play the part of pigs. How was this multiply inappropriate?

Seeing everything as an educational opportunity

Some families will take their children out of school for several months so that they can spend time with relatives overseas. For instance, pupils may disappear to Pakistan or India to stay with grandparents. They usually return with a much improved command of their 'mother tongue'. Naturally teachers are concerned by the interruption to their schooling, but some manage to turn these visits to good eductional advantage by equipping the child with a diary. This can be adapted to the age of the pupil and can consist of questions/activities relating to the journeys, places of special interest, members of the extended family, marriages and festivals, pleasant and unpleasant experiences, plants, animals etc.

Diet

Dietary requirements can be a particularly challenging area for the teacher who is concerned with both nutrition and pupils'/parents' moral or religious requirements. The pressures on school catering services are many (including under-staffing and lack of time) and some major decisions (e.g. not to provide *halal* meat) will be made at a higher level (by the Local Education Authority in the UK). In the UK widespread changes in diet have made it possible to provide meals which offend a minimum of religious scruples. However baked beans and English versions of 'curry' will not necessarily attract those pupils whose dietary needs are for vegetarian, kosher or *halal* food. Discovering, for example, that a Hindu pupil's refusal to eat non-vegetarian foods on particular days results from a family's observance of a *vrat* (vow/fast) or weekly pattern of abstention may enable you to clear up misunderstandings about the child's apparently inconsistent behaviour. During Ramadan some Muslim pupils may undertake to go without food and drink between sunrise and sunset, and you may need to make allowances for changed behaviour or energy levels. (Redbridge SACRE 1997b gives useful guidance.)

Gender

Some parents – not only Muslims – will have concerns about nudity (e.g. showering), dress (e.g. exposing the legs) and lack of segregation between the sexes. With pupils of secondary school age the issues are felt to be more important than with pupils who have not yet reached puberty. But respect for parents' values requires primary schools too to consider carefully policies on, for example, acceptable sportswear and the provision of sex education. Sarvar (1994) is a helpful document to consult on practical ways forward.

Dress

This is a good place to mention Sikhs – in relation both to the prohibition for boys from many committed families to cut their hair and to the religious significance of wearing a *kara* (steel wrist bangle). Do recommend your schools to get hold of the London Borough of Redbridge's briefing paper, *Sikh Appearance and Identity* (Redbridge SACRE 1999). Does your school needlessly upset the sensitivities of, for example, Exclusive Brethren or Muslims by ruling out headscarves, or insisting that girls wear trousers, or that they must not wear trousers? Where there are regulations about uniform, how can agreement be reached non-confrontationally with parents or pupils who object on religious or cultural grounds?

Curriculum areas

The Qualifications and Curriculum Authority (QCA) provides useful principles as well as teachers' practical suggestions for encouraging 'respect for all' in all areas of the curriculum.[1] This website is a must for all teachers, but it, and the brief suggestions below, must be treated cautiously. Read carefully Geneva Gay's advice on 'Effective Multicultural Teaching Practices' (2001). Always ask yourself whether a particular strategy or lesson content is just a tokenistic add-on to the curriculum, or whether it is challenging assumptions and frameworks which enshrine some cultural practices and frameworks as 'normal' and some as 'different'.

Every curriculum area is an opportunity for affirming cultural diversity, although some allow more scope than others. At the same time constant alertness to inappropriate representation of aspects of people's experience is necessary. The following notes are simply illustrative of possible content and your particular pupils' difficulties and interests need to be taken into account in deciding design and delivery. Some items given under one heading would contribute equally to one or more other subjects.

Literacy: Are pupils encouraged (by library resourcing etc.) to engage with culturally diverse literature? Are books tokenistic, stereotypical or misinformed? Is our concern with alerting pupils to spelling, grammar, punctuation, style and genre balanced by encouraging pupils' engagement with relevant social and cultural issues? We need to be aware of imperialist assumptions in the 'classics' and sensitive to parental concerns – for example, many Muslim parents' dislike of the inclusion of dogs and pigs in primary school reading material.

Drama: Read Neelands (1998) on the 'green children', and Winston (2000 and 2004) to be fired with ways of exercising pupils' imaginations. Working with ideas in Winston (2000), see how primary school pupils' ideas on 'belonging' and difference, and their capacity for respect and empathy, evolve through responding to the Celtic story of 'The Sea Woman', or (2004) what it was like to be an asylum seeker in Victorian Britain.

Numeracy: Have you thought of why our number system is 'Arabic'? Introduce pupils to the fact that what the Arabs brought to Europe was a modified version of a system (including the zero) which had evolved in India. Never think that mathematics is culturally neutral. Joseph (1990) and Kassem (2001) should enable you to aim for an 'anti-racist' mathematics. Bishop (2001), Cotton (2001) and Winter (2001) suggest how mathematics teachers can promote justice, inclusiveness and moral, social and cultural awareness in their classes.

Science: Include mention of non-European contributions. Try to use pictures of people of non-European background in laboratories etc. Consider the relationship between scientific 'advance' and the environment.

ICT: Consider the opportunities of the internet for exploring websites and encouraging pupils' critical response to how, for example, a group with which they identify is represented; remember that there may also be opportunities for intranet links between schools with pupils from culturally dissimilar backgrounds (see Ipgrave 2001).

Design and Technology: Include articles, buildings etc. from as wide a cultural base as possible. The range is wide – for example, younger primary school pupils can design a shoe-rack (for a place of worship such as a Hindu temple) or make a *chauri* (the 'fan' used in a gurdwara), older pupils can design a mosque (see Yeomans 1993a and b; 1994). For 'early years' children there are plenty of examples in Wood *et al.* 1998). Or help children to look at the many ways in which, for example, the coconut palm is used – from ladles and cups made from half coconuts, to thatch and fencing from leaves and canoes from trunks. 'Appropriate' technology offers excellent examples of problem-solving in specific situations.

Modern languages: From the start learners can be helped to realise that languages do not consist of one to one equivalents, but involve different ways of understanding and communicating experience. Exploring the cultural context of language, without building up stereotypes, is vital. The learner's experience of being 'out of one's depth' is an excellent basis for developing empathy with people who are insecure in pupils' own language(s).

History: Vigilance in ensuring that material (for example, on migration or battles or cultural achievements) challenges pupils to question stereotypes and encourages them to appreciate diversity. Encourage writing, drama etc. that includes contrasting perspectives, and help pupils to understand why the past is interpreted and represented in different ways. (Indian and Pakistani textbooks, for instance, differ on important aspects of their shared history.)

Geography: Pupils can see how places in different parts of the world are connected – because of migration, trade, language etc. Examine curriculum materials carefully: some convey a message of the 'backwardness' of overseas societies with which many British pupils are closely associated. Some material is misleading because it is so out of date.

Introduce affirmatively the merits (e.g. sustainability) of some 'traditional' types of agriculture etc. Look creatively at themes from physical geography. Rivers, for example, offer an opportunity to explore how they are used in different periods and regions.

Religious Education (RE) **and** *collective worship:* concern with promoting understanding of cultural diversity is central to many publications and resources. Ipgrave (1998) provides suggestions for building on the experience of one group – Muslim pupils. Ipgrave (2001) provides excellent ideas for 'pupil-to-pupil dialogue'. Religious education is an opportunity to organise visits (to places of worship, for example) and to invite in visitors (for example, an imam or a rabbi; a member of support staff who can share her experience of Shabbat as a Jewish mother; a pupil who is happy to answer questions about celebrating Divali). Build up a bank of contacts. Some reconnoitring, plus careful briefing of the host/ visitor and sensitive preparation of the pupils are vital for a relaxed, illuminating, fruitful encounter.

Art: Yeomans (1993a and b; 1994) illustrates matching a culturally specific theme (the mosque) to Muslim pupils' particular experience. Examine the cultural base from which your ideas and examples are coming – and widen it. The 'respect for all' website[1] lists key principles to inform teaching and learning. For example, in a particular tradition is the human figure represented? If not, why not? If so, is the relative size of the figures down to perspective or relative status?

Music: Introduce children to a wide range of musical instruments and expression. Help them to appreciate how particular music evolved within a particular community. Which continents are not represented by your resources? There may be pupils in your school who are developing proficiency in playing, for example, a tabla or a harmonium (these are played in Sikh and Hindu places of worship), and who would be willing to play their instrument in school, and to answer questions.

Physical Education (PE) provides opportunities for individuals from different backgrounds to co-operate. PE is a crucial area for teachers to show sensitivity re dress and gender. See Fleming (1992) for a discussion that raises issues far wider than South Asian dance. Can you incorporate minority sports such as the Punjabi (and now international) *kabaddi*? Many exercises are integral to yoga – pupils can be helped to understand that physical techniques (how they breathe, for instance) can affect their ability to concentrate, and they can be made aware of the Indian origins of yoga. Take account of pupils who are fasting, especially of Muslim pupils during Ramadan – see Redbridge SACRE 1997b.)

Citizenship and Personal Social and Health Education (PSHE) are non-statutory areas for Key Stages 1 and 2, i.e. for 5–11 year olds. Progression in citizenship involves pupils showing that they understand concepts such as fairness and respect for others, and using their 'imagination to understand other people's experiences'. This is an excellent opportunity for introducing examples of diversity. All the above subject areas can contribute to these areas – e.g. Winston (2004 – see Drama above).

Repeated warning! All suggestions need to be treated cautiously – remembering the damage that can be done by the 'saris, samosas and steel band' style of multiculturalism.

Note

1   For practical ideas across the curriculum visit 'Respect for all: valuing diversity and challenging racism through the curriculum' at www.qca.org.uk/ages 3–14/inclusion/ 301.html.

Glossary

Words which have a capital in their English translation are capitalised.

A = Arabic, G = Gujarati, H = Hindi, Heb = Hebrew, P = Punjabi, S = Sanskrit, U = Ukrainian.

Note: Most of the Indian words are common or very similar in several languages, but in many cases only one or two languages have been indicated.

ahimsa (S, H)	non-violence.
Akal Purakh (P)	God (Sikh title literally meaning Timeless One).
akhand path (P)	continuous, approximately 48-hour long, reading of the Sikh scriptures.
Allah (A)	God.
amrit, amritjal (P)	literally 'undying', holy water, the sweetened water used in Sikh rite of initiation into the Khalsa (q.v.).
amrit chhakana (P)	to partake of *amrit*, i.e. in the rite of initiation as a Khalsa Sikh.
Anand karaj	Sikh marriage ceremony centred on circumambulation of the Guru Granth Sahib.
Anglican	belonging to the diverse international Christian denomination, which draws on both Catholicism and the European Reformation, and which is in communion with the Church of England.
Annakut (G)	day following Divali day, when Gujarati Hindus make impressive offerings of food to the gods.
Antarayami (H)	God in the sense of one's inner guide.
arati (H)	Hindu worship in which a wick light and other items are circled in front of a representation of a deity.
Ardas (P)	formal Sikh congregational prayer.
Arya Samaj (H, P)	literally 'Aryan Society', a Hindu movement begun in the nineteenth century by Swami Dayananda Saraswati.
ashrama (s)	stage of life (in Hindu tradition), e.g. as a celibate student, married householder, etc.
avatar (H)	literally 'descent' (i.e. to earth), an incarnation of God, usually referring to Vishnu's appearance in forms including Rama and Krishna.
Baba, Babaji (P, H)	respectful title for revered man, often used in place of the name of a Sikh religious leader or *sant* (see below).

Baba Balak Nath	figure who is worshipped by some North Indians – an immortal blue-skinned youth.
Baisakhi	= Vaisakhi (q.v.)
Bal Vikas (H)	child development; name (in the 1980s) for classes organised by Sathya Sai Baba's followers.
Baptist	Protestant Christian denomination which emphasises the requirement that only 'believers' (i.e. not infants) may be baptised.
Bar Mitzvah	(Heb: son of the commandment) rite which marks a Jewish boy's reaching adulthood at 13.
Bat Chayil	(Heb: daughter of valour) celebration which marks an Orthodox Jewish girl's religious maturity at 13.
Bat Mitzvah	(Heb: daughter of the commandment) Rite which – for Progressive Jews – marks a girl's religious coming of age at 12.
bhagati (P)	= *bhakti* religious devotion.
Bhagavad Gita (S)	lit. song of the Lord, popular Hindu scripture – Krishna's sermon to Arjuna delivered on the battlefield at Kurukshetra in North India.
Bhagvan (H)	God, Lord.
bhai (H, P)	brother; term used as a respectful title for, e.g., a Sikh religious leader.
Bhai Bij (G)	day soon after Divali when brothers visit their married sisters for a meal.
Bhaia Duj (P)	= Bhai Bij (q.v.)
bhajan (H)	devotional song
bhakti (H)	religious devotion.
bhangra (P)	folk dance of Punjab, and the contemporary hybrid music and dance that developed from it.
Bhatra (P)	the Sikh caste-based community that was first to settle in UK cities.
Brahma (S)	(For Hindus) God as creator.
Brahmin (S, H)	member of the priestly caste.
Catholic	(from Greek *katholikos*, universal) usually referring to Churches which are in communion with the Pope, i.e. 'Roman Catholic'.
Chamar (P, H)	member of caste traditionally associated with skinning and tanning.
Charismatic	term denoting Christians who emphasise the contemporary activity of the Holy Spirit in giving 'gifts', notably of 'speaking in tongues', i.e. using words in a language unknown to the speaker. The Charismatic movement formed in the 1960s.
Chasidic	= Hasidic, relating to a Jewish devotional movement that started in late eighteenth-century Europe.
chauri (P)	Indian symbol of authority, now typically Sikh. Usually made from white tail hair of a horse or a yak.
chhitta (P)	splashing, i.e. of holy water.

Chuhra, pl. Chuhre (P)	member(s) of caste traditionally associated with removing refuse.
Church of England	the Anglican (see above) Christian denomination which, in England, has the privilege of being 'by law established'.
Dalit (H)	oppressed, member of lowest castes.
Darzi (G, H, P)	member of tailor caste.
Dasahra (H)	tenth day, i.e. of autumn festival; Hindus celebrate the defeat of Ravana by Rama.
dhann (P)	great, blessed.
dharma (S)	'religion', appropriate conduct, righteousness.
Dhobi (H, P, G)	member of washerman caste.
dhup (H)	incense.
Divali (H)	all-Indian festival of light celebrated in late October/ early November.
Eastern Rite	term for Christians (e.g. the Ukrainian Catholics) who accept the primacy of the Pope but follow Orthodox (see below), not Catholic forms of worship.
Eid	= Id (A) (q.v.)
epitaphios (Greek)	wooden stand, representing Jesus' tomb, in Greek Orthodox churches on Holy Friday.
Evangelical	term for Protestant Christians who stress the need for personal conversion, and regard the Bible as the only authority in matters of faith.
five Ks	five external signs of Sikh allegiance, required of Khalsa Sikhs.
Ganesh Chauth	annual day dedicated to Ganesh, the elephant-headed Hindu God of wisdom and new enterprises.
Ganga jal (H)	water from Ganga (River Ganges).
Gaumata (H)	Hindu title of respect for the cow as our mother who gives us milk.
glossolalia	speaking 'in tongues', believed by many Christians to be a gift of the Holy Spirit, unintelligible utterances.
granthi (P)	person attending to the Sikh scriptures.
Gujarati	person, language etc. originating from the area covered by the present Indian state of Gujarat in western India.
guna (S)	lit. cord, strand; quality.
gurdwara (P)	Sikhs' place of worship.
Gurmukhi (P)	the script of the Sikh scriptures, also used for modern Punjabi.
gurpurb (P)	Sikh festival associated with an event in the Gurus' lives.
guru (S, H, P, G)	For Hindus a teacher, especially a religious teacher. For Sikhs, one of the ten Gurus from Guru Nanak, b. 1469, to Guru Gobind Singh, d. 1708.
Guru Granth Sahib (P)	the Sikhs' scriptures.
halal (A)	what is permitted according to Islamic law, particularly meat of an animal slaughtered in the permitted way.

Hanukkah (Heb)	lit: dedication; Jewish eight-day winter festival of lights, commemorating Judas Maccabee's purification of the temple in Jerusalem after its desecration.
Hanuman Chalisa	40 verses in praise of Hindu monkey-headed god Hanuman, as the ideal devotee of Rama.
Hari (H, P)	Lord, God (Hindu, Sikh).
Holy Spirit	in Christian theology this is the third 'person' of the 'Trinity', i.e. God as Father, Son and Holy Spirit/ Holy Ghost.
Holy Week	the week preceding Easter day.
Id, Eid (A)	festival; the Muslim festivals Id al-Fitr (which breaks the fast of Ramadan) and of Id al-Adha during the month of pilgrimage.
ik oankar (P)	(in Sikh scripture) the statement 'God (or reality) is one' written as numeral and syllable.
ISKCON	International Society for Krishna Consciousness, the title of the 'Hare Krishna Movement'.
jadu (H, P)	magic, black magic.
jal (H, P)	water.
Jalaram Baba	a saint, now worshipped by some Gujarati Hindus.
jalebi (H)	Indian sweet made by deep-frying batter and dunking in sugar syrup
janam sakhi (P)	lit. birth witness; the stories of Guru Nanak's life.
Janmashthami (S, H)	annual Hindu festival of Krishna's birth.
japan (P)	to repeat, i.e. (for Sikhs) to remember the name of God.
Jat (P)	caste of peasant landowners, economically dominant in Punjab, and forming the majority of the Sikh community.
jati (H)	endogamous community (united in the past at least by a shared occupation), caste.
Jaya Parvati (G)	a *vrat* (see below) kept by Gujarati women and girls.
Jehovah's Witness	Christianity-related community that emphasises the imminent coming of the kingdom of God.
jutha (H)	food (potentially) contaminated by another's saliva, impure.
kala tika (H)	black mark – often a smudge on the face – to avert the evil eye.
kankotri (G)	red powder.
kanku (G)	red powder (H. *kumkum*) used in Hindu worship and for marking the face.
kara (P)	steel circle worn by Sikhs on right wrist as one of the five Ks. (q.v.)
karah prashad (P)	*karah* = iron bowl; *prashad/ prasada* = blessed food offering; among Sikhs the sweet food (made of wheat flour, butter, sugar, water) shared by worshippers.
karma (S, H)	(primarily Hindu) cosmic moral law of cause and effect.
Karva Chauth	a *vrat* (see below) observed by women and girls about 11 days before Divali (see above).
katha (H)	homily, story, public rendering of, e.g., *Mahabharata* (q.v.).

kesh (P)	uncut hair (one of Sikhs' five Ks [q.v.]).
Khalsa (P)	(lit.'pure' or 'owing allegiance to no intermediary') = Sikh, and in particular, Sikh who has been initiated with *amrit* (q.v.).
khanda (P)	two-edged sword used for stirring *amrit* (q.v.); the Sikh emblem consisting of this, together with two *kirpan*s and a circle.
Khatri (P)	a Punjabi caste usually regarded as Kshatriya, and traditionally associated with accountancy.
Khuda (Persian, P)	God.
kirpan (P)	poniard, sword (one of Sikhs' five Ks [q.v.]).
kirtan (H, P)	(Sikh) hymn-singing.
kistka (U)	'pen' used by Ukrainians – preparing for Easter – for drawing (in molten wax) on eggs.
kosher	(Heb. kasher) fit (for consumption) according to Jewish law.
Krishna	(S. Krsna = black) the eighth incarnation of God Vishnu.
Kshatriya (S)	warrior class (*varna*), in second position in the *varna* hierarchy.
kurta (H, P)	shirt, worn over trousers.
Lakshmi (S)	Goddess of wealth and good fortune.
Lohana (G)	a Gujarati caste, associated with trading.
Mahabharat(a) (H, S)	Hindu epic which includes Krishna's sermon, the Bhagavad Gita.
mahamantra (S, H)	great mantra, e.g. the 'Hare Krishna' mantra.
mala (H)	rosary, prayer beads (usually 108).
Mata (H)	goddess; woman renowned for spiritual powers.
Methodist	a Protestant Christian denomination, resulting from the preaching of John and Charles Wesley.
mithai (H)	generally fudge-like sweetmeats made from milk, sugar, chickpea flour, nuts etc.
mukti (H, P)	liberation (from cycle of death and rebirth).
mul mantar (P)	basic sacred formula; the opening of Sikh scriptures; Guru Nanak's statement of belief in one God and of God's qualities.
murti (H)	image of deity (focus of Hindu worship).
Mykolaj (U)	Nicholas, the saint whose day is 19 December.
Nam (S, H, P)	name, God's name, encapsulating the nature of God (a key term in Sikh theology).
nam simaran (P)	remembering the name, recitation of God's name, e.g. 'Vahiguru Satnam', e.g. with a *mala* (q.v.).
Navaratri (S)	Hindus' nine-night festival which starts one lunar month before Divali. Gujaratis celebrate with nightly dances.
nazar lage (H, P)	inflicting the evil eye.
New Church	term sometimes used for the Christian congregations from 1960 onwards which worship in a very informal manner and proclaim the 'kingship' of Christ.
nishan sahib	Sikhs' flagpole and pennant, marked with *khanda* emblem (q.v.).

Norta (G)	= Navaratri (q.v.)
oankar (P)	one reality/one God (the sacred syllable 'om'). See *ik oankar* above.
om (S)	sacred syllable used in meditation.
om namo shivai (S)	invocation of God Shiva.
Orthodox	major, international Christian denomination, which sees itself as the direct descendant from the church of the first century CE.
Orthodox Judaism	traditional Judaism (as distinct from Progressive Judaism [q.v.]).
pagri (H)	turban.
pakora (H)	savoury, spicy vegetable fritter made with chickpea batter.
palki (P)	stand (usually made of wood) for the Sikh scriptures.
panj piare (P)	'five beloved', the first five Sikhs to be initiated in 1699, the five Khalsa Sikhs who initiate others into the Khalsa in the *amrit* (q.v.) ceremony.
Panth (P)	the Sikh community.
Paramatma (P)	Supreme Spirit, God (one of the titles used by Sikhs).
path (P, H)	reading (e.g. of Sikh scriptures), also used for recitation of a short passage.
Pentecostal	refers to Christians who emphasise the manifestation of the Holy Spirit at the (Jewish) festival of Pentecost (see New Testament, Acts 2) and to the Holy Spirit's continuing activity. (Modern) Pentecostal movements began forming from *c.* 1900.
Prajapati	title of Gujarati Hindus from traditionally artisan castes.
Progressive Judaism	a modern interpretation of Judaism, less traditional than Orthodox Judaism.
Protestant	belonging to a Christian denomination other than Catholic or Orthodox.
puja (H)	Hindu worship involving offerings.
Punjabi	belonging to Punjab, an area spanning the Pakistan-India border; the language of Punjab (the land of five rivers).
purana (S)	collection of Hindu stories.
Pushtimarg (H, G)	literally way of grace; a Gujarati *sampradaya* (q.v.) devoted to the infant Krishna.
Pushtimargi (H, G)	Hindu devotee who follows Pushtimarg (q.v.).
pysanky (U)	patterned egg.
Quaker	usual name for member of Religious Society of Friends, a Protestant denomination whose worship is – in the UK – largely silent.
Rabb (P)	God (a Sikh name for God).
Radhasoami (P, H)	an international movement, led by North Indian spiritual masters. Followers practise meditation and are strictly vegetarian.
Rahit maryada (P)	Sikhs' code of practice.
Rajput (H, P)	name for a caste often equated with *kshatriya*.

Raksha Bandhan (H) Hindus' August festival in which brothers receive a special wrist-thread from their sisters.

Ram (H), Rama (S) hero of the Hindu epic, *Ramayana*, venerated as incarnation of God Vishnu.

Ram(a)lila (S, H) annual reenactment of the story of Rama and Sita during the first ten days of the lunar month before Divali.

Ram(a)navami
(S, H) Hindu Spring festival marking the birth of Rama (see above).

Ramgarhia (P) title for Sikhs from castes specialising traditionally in carpentry, brick-laying, masonry and iron-work.

Ravana (S) (pronounced to rhyme with 'carven') Demon-king of Lanka who abducted Rama's wife, Sita.

Ravidasi (P, H) follower of the mediaeval saint, Ravidas. Followers are from his (Chamar [q.v.]) caste community.

Roman Catholic Christian denomination led by the Pope (bishop of Rome).

roti (H, P) chapati, circular yeastless wheat bread cooked on griddle.

sadhana (S, H) (Hindu, Buddhist) particular spiritual practices such as reciting mantras.

Salvation Army Christian denomination founded 1865 for evangelism and social work.

samaj (H) lit. society; a religious or caste organisation.

samosa (H, P, G) a deep-fried triangular spicy vegetable pasty.

sampradaya (S, H) religious group following a succession of gurus.

sangat (P) Sikh congregation.

sant (P, H) a Punjabi religious leader.

Satguru (P) true Guru, title for God and for Guru (among Sikhs).

Satnam (P) true name – Sikhs refer to God in this way.

satsang (H, P, G) religious gathering.

Sathya Sai Baba South Indian God-man, b. 1926.

Scheduled Caste term used in India for disadvantaged castes that were once termed 'untouchable'.

shabad (P) 'word'; any hymn from the Guru Granth Sahib (q.v.).

shabad kirtan (P) singing of *shabad* (q.v.).

Shabbat (Heb.) Sabbath, i.e., Saturday (from Friday sunset to Saturday sunset)

shastra (S, H) Hindu law code.

Sheranvali Ma (P) Hindus' Goddess Durga, lit. the mother on a tiger.

Shirdi Sai Baba holy man from town in South West India.

Shravan (H) a lunar month of the Hindu calendar – approximately August.

Shudra (S, H, P) the lowest *varna* (q.v.) in the Hindu *varna* system, consisting of artisan castes.

simaran (P) to remember – repetition of the name of God.

Sita (S) the virtuous wife of Rama.

sloka (S) sacred verse, verse of scripture.

Soni (G) member of Gujarati goldsmith caste.

Sukhmani path (P) a reading of Sukhmani Sahib (q.v.).

Sukhmani Sahib (P)	'Hymn of Peace', popular composition by Guru Arjan.
suprabhatam (S)	lit. good morning; early morning prayer, e.g. one recited daily by devotees of Sathya Sai Baba (q.v.).
Sviat vechir, sviata vechera (U)	Holy Supper, Christmas Eve meal of 12 meatless dishes.
Swami (S, H)	Lord, God.
Swaminarayan (H, G)	'Lord God': title for a Hindu religious movement with many Gujarati adherents and for its founder, Sahajananda, worshipped as an incarnation of God.
tamasik (H)	dull; *tamasik* substances such as meat and alcohol are believed to have a dulling effect on the consumer.
tantra (S, H)	term loosely used for Hindu texts related to the occult.
tayaji (P, H)	respectful address for one's father's elder brother, uncle.
Uniat(e)	Eastern Rite Catholic, i.e. Ukrainian and other churches which recognise the Pope's primacy but retain distinctive practices of Orthodox (q.v.) Christians.
United Reformed Church (URC)	Protestant Christian denomination formed in 1972 from the Congregational Church of England and the Presbyterian Church of England and joined in 1983 by the Churches of Christ.
Vahiguru (P)	(originally an exclamation in praise of the Guru) currently Sikh word for God.
Vaikunth(a) S, H)	Vishnu's home, heaven (Hindu term).
Vaisakhi (P, H)	Spring harvest festival of Punjab, Sikhs' commemoration (April 14) of the creation of the Khalsa (q.v.).
Vaishnav(a) (S, H)	(Hindu) worshipper of God as Vishnu, e.g. in the form of Rama or Krishna.
Valmiki (P)	member of the Punjabi caste which has suffered most discrimination, a worshipper of Valmiki, composer of the *Ramayana*.
varna (S)	lit. colour; one of the four classes into which Hindu society is classically divided
varnashramadharma (S)	Hindu understanding of a man's duty being determined by his *varna* and *ashrama*.
vidhi (S)	(Hindu) ritual.
Vishvakarma	(from S: 'all-creating') Divine architect of the universe, especially revered by Hindus and Sikhs from castes associated with construction.
vrat (H, G)	religious vow, often involving abstention from certain foods, observed on particular days.
zat biradari (P)	people of one caste who interact socially.

Bibliography

Adiraja dasa (1984) *The Hare Krishna Book of Vegetarian Cooking*, Letchmore Heath: Bhaktivedanta Book Trust.

Ahuja, A. (1997) 'Caught in the Culture Trap', *Times*, 7 April.

Albans, P. (1999) 'A Field Study of Faith Nurture in Young Sikh Children', unpublished MA essay, Institute of Education, University of Warwick.

Alibhai, Y. (1987) 'A White Christmas', *New Society*, 18, December, 15–17.

Alibhai-Brown, Y. (2001) *Mixed Feelings: The Complex Lives of Mixed Race Britons*, London: Women's Press.

Aloneftis, V. (1990) *We're Different, We're Greeks from London not Cyprus*, unpublished MPhil thesis, Brunel University.

Alred, G, Byram, M. and Fleming, M. (2003) (eds), *Intercultural Experience and Education*, Clevedon: Multicultural Matters.

Ambekar, J. (1997) 'Searching for Identity', *World Religions in Education*, 38–40.

Anwar, M. (1976) 'Young Asians between Two Cultures', *New Society*, 38, December, 563–5.

Anwar, M. (1998) *Between Cultures: Continuity and Change in the Lives of Young Asians*, London: Routledge.

Arweck, E. and Nesbitt, E. (2003) 'Values Education: The Development and Classroom Use of an Educational Programme', *British Educational Research Journal*.

Arweck, E. and Nesbitt, E. (2004) 'Living Values: An Educational Programme – From Initiative to Uptake', *British Journal of Religious Education*, 26 (2), 133–49.

Arweck, E. and Stringer, M. D. (2002) *Theorizing Faith: The Insider/Outsider Problem in the Study of Ritual*, Birmingham: University of Birmingham Press.

Ata, A. W. (2003) *Christian–Muslim Intermarriage in Australia: Identity, Social Cohesion and Cultural Fragmentation*, Ringwood, Australia: David Lovell.

Babraa, D. K. (1989) *Religions through Festivals*, London: Longman.

Bailey, D. (1989) *My Birthday Party*, London: Macmillan.

Ballard, R. (1994) *Desh Pardesh: The South Asian Presence in Britain*, London: Hurst.

—— (1999) 'Panth Kismet Dharm te Qaum: Continuity and Change in Four Dimensions of Punjabi Religion', in P. Singh and S. S. Thandi (eds), *Punjabi Identity in a Global Context*, New Delhi: Oxford University Press, pp. 7–38.

Ballard, R. (2003) 'Challenging Paradigms: Popular Religion in Punjab', www.art.man.ac.uk/CASAS/pages/presentations.ht, accessed 17 June 2003.

Barratt, M. (1994a) *Something to Share*, Oxford: Heinemann.

—— (1994b) *An Egg for Babcha*, Oxford: Heinemann.

—— (1994c) *Lucy's Sunday*, Oxford: Heinemann.

Barratt, M. and Price, J. (1996) *Meeting Christians Book One*, Oxford: Heinemann.

Barth, F. (ed.) (1969) *Ethnic Groups and Boundaries*, London: Allen and Unwin.

Baumann, G. (1992) 'Ritual Implicates "Others": Rereading Durkheim in a Plural Society' in D. de Coppier (ed.), *Understanding Rituals*, London: Routledge, pp. 97–116.

—— (1994) '"The Lamps are Many but the Light is One"? Processes of Syncretisation in a Multi-Ethnic Suburb of London' in G. Ajmer (ed.), *Syncretism and the Commerce of Symbols*, Gothenburg: University of Gothenburg Press, pp. 1–8.

—— (1996) *Contesting Culture: Discourses of identity in Multi-Ethnic London*, Cambridge: Cambridge University Press.

—— (1999) *The Multicultural Riddle: Rethinking National, Ethnic and Religious Identities*, London: Routledge.

BBC (2002) 'Sunday', Radio 4, 24 March.

BBC (2003a) 'Birthdays – Primary School': http://www.bbc.co.uk/ parenting/ family/celeb_primary.shtml (accessed 29 September 2003).

BBC (2003b) 'Caste Divide', Radio 4, 1 April.

Beardsworth, A. and Keil. T. (1992) 'The Vegetarian Option: Varieties, Conversions, Motives and Careers', *Sociological Review*, 40 (2), May, 253–93.

Bennett, D. (1997) 'A Field Study of Religious Nurture in a Swadhyaya Group', University of Warwick: unpublished MA assignment.

Bennett, O. (1989) *Our New Home*, London: Hamish Hamilton.

Bhabha, H. K. (1994) *The Location of Culture*, New York: Routledge.

Bhachu, P. (1985) *Twice Migrants: East African Sikh Settlers in Britain*, London: Tavistock.

Bhatti, G. (1999) *Asian Children at Home and at School: An Ethnographic Study*, London: Routledge.

Bishop, A. (2001) 'What Values do *You* Teach when You Teach Mathematics?' in P. Gates (ed.), *Issues in Mathematics Teaching*, London: Routledge, pp. 93–104.

Blair, M. and J. Bourne with C. Coffin, A. Creese and C. Kenner (1998) *Making the Difference: Teaching and Learning Strategies in Successful Multi-Ethnic Schools*, London: DfEE.

Blaylock, L. (1999) '"The Space between is Holy": Inter-Faith Issues in Religious Education', *Resource*, 21 (2), 15–19.

Bohan, J. (1996) 'Traveller Children and Resources in Schools', *Multicultural Teaching*, 15 (1), 39–43.

Bowker, J. (1997) 'Religion' in J. Bowker (ed.), *The Oxford Dictionary of World Religions*, Oxford: Oxford University Press, pp. xv–xxiv.

Bowman, M. (1994) 'Islam, Adat and Multiculturalism in Malaysia', *DISKUS*, 2 (1), 15–27 http://www.uni-marburg.de/religionswissenschaft/ journal/diskus/ bowman. html

Brah, A. (1996) *Cartographies of Diaspora: Contesting Identities*, London: Routledge.

Brockington, J. L. (1981) *The Sacred Thread: Hinduism in its Continuity and Diversity*, Edinburgh: Edinburgh University Press.

Bullivant, B. M. (1978) *The Way of Tradition: Life in an Orthodox Jewish School*, Hawthorn: Australian Council for Educational Research.

Bunting, M. (1998) 'Coming of Age', G2, *The Guardian*, 8 October, 2–3.

Burghart, R. (1987) (ed.), *Hinduism in Great Britain: The Perpetuation of Religion in an Alien Milieu*, London: Tavistock.

Butler, R. (1993) *Themes in Religion: Sikhism*, London: Longman.

Census 2001 (2004) http://www.statistics.gov.uk/census2001/default.asp (accessed 1 March 2004).

Chadha, G. and Bhachu, P. (1996) '"Ruptured and Sutured" Identities: Gurinder Chadha and Parminder Bhachu discuss their lives and work', *Sojourner: The Women's Forum*, 15–17.

Chahal, K. (1997) poem, *Runnymede Bulletin*, 304, 9.

Chan, Y. M. (1995) 'Chinese Children and Education in Britain', *Multicultural Teaching*, 13 (2), 11–14.

Chauhan, K. (1997) 'Hindu Students Forum and the Quest for Roots', *The Asian Age*, 27 November.

Chidester, D. (2000) *Christianity: A Global History*, London: Penguin.

Cobb, M. and Robshaw, V. (1997) *The Spiritual Challenge of Health Care*, Churchill Livingstone.

Cochran-Smith, M. and Lytle, S. L. (1993) *Inside Outside: Teacher Research and Knowledge*, New York: Teachers College Press.

Cohen, R. (1995) 'Fuzzy Frontiers of Identity: The British Case', *Social Identities*, 1 (1), 35–62.

Cole, W. O. and Sambhi, P. S. (1986) *Baisakhi*, Exeter: Religious and Moral Education Press.

Cole, W.O. and Sambhi, P.S. (1990) *A Popular Dictionary of Sikhism*, London: Curzon.

Coniaris, A. M. (1981) *These are the Sacraments: The Life-Giving Mysteries of the Orthodox Church*, Minneapolis: Light and Life Publishing Co.

Connelly, M. (1999) *Christmas A Social History*, London: I. B. Tauris.

Constantinides, P. (1977) 'The Greek Cypriots: Factors in Maintenance of Ethnic Identity' in J. L. Watson (ed.), *Between Two Cultures: Migrants and Minorities in Britain*, Oxford: Blackwell, pp. 269–300.

Cotton, T. (2001) 'Mathematics Teaching in the Real World' in P. Gates (ed.), *Issues in Mathematics Teaching*, London: Routledge Falmer, pp. 23–37.

Creedon, J. (1998) 'The Age of Do-It-Yourself Religion', The Editor, *The Guardian*, 5 September, 12–13.

Cush, D. (1999) '"Learning From" the Concept and Concepts of a Religious Tradition: Jainism in the RE Curriculum', *Journal of Beliefs and Values*, 20 (1), 60–74.

Dandelion, B. P. (1996) *A Sociological Analysis of the Theology of Quakers*, Lampeter: Edwin Mellen Press.

Das, R. (2002) *The Heart of Hinduism: A Comprehensive Guide for Teachers and Professionals*, Aldenham: ISKCON Educational Services.

Devi, A. (2002) 'It's All in the Mind: A Paper to Discuss the Impact of Silent Sitting, as Part of the Sathya Sai EHV Programme on Maths Attainment and Self-Esteem'. Paper presented to the 9th Annual International Conference on 'Education, Spirituality and the Whole Child', Roehampton.

Dhanjal, B. (1987) *Sarah's Birthday Surprise*, London: Hamish Hamilton.

—— (1987) *Sikhism*, London: Batsford.

—— (1993) *Amritsar*, London: Evans.

Dhasmana, L. (1994) 'Asian Parents' Perceptions and Experiences about Inner

City Schools – A Local Perspective', *Multicultural Teaching*, 12 (2), 24–8.

Diversity in Health (2003) Online. http://www.diversity in health.com/regions/ middleeast/kurdish/htm and http://www.diversity in health.com/regions/africa/ somalis.htm (accessed 29 September 2003).

Donaldson, J. (1994) *Birthday Surprise*, Aylesbury: Ginn.

Dosanjh, J. S. and Ghuman, P. A. S. (1996) *Child-rearing in Ethnic Minorities*, Clevedon: Multilingual Matters.

Draycott, P. (1996) *Sikhism A New Approach*, London: Hodder and Stoughton.

Drury, B. (1989) *Ethnicity amongst Second Generation Sikh Girls: A Case Study in Nottingham*, unpublished Ph.D. thesis, University of Nottingham.

Dwyer, J. T., Mayer, L. D. V. H., Dowd, K., Kandel, R. F. and Mayer, J. (1974) 'The New Vegetarians: The Natural High?' *Journal of the American Dietetic Association*, 65, 529–36.

Easton, B. (1999) 'Aspects of the Experience of Young Ravidasis in Wolverhampton: A Field Study', University of Warwick: unpublished MA assignment.

Eck, D. (2000) 'Dialogue and Method: reconstructing the Study of Religion' in K. Patten and B. Ray (eds), *A Magic Still Dwells: Comparative Religion in the Postmodern Age*, Berkeley: University of California Press, pp. 131–49.

Erikson, E. H. (1968) *Identity, Youth and Crisis*, New York: Norton.

Everington, J. (1993) 'Bridging Fieldwork and Classwork: The Development of Curriculum Materials within the Religious Education and Community Project', *Resource*, 16 (1), 7–10.

—— (1996) *Meeting Christians Book Two*, Oxford: Heinemann.

Exon, B. (1997) 'Autonomous Agents and Divine Stage Managers: Models of (Self)Determination amongst Western Devotees of Two Modern Hindu Religious Movements', *Scottish Journal of Religious Studies*, 18 (2), 163–79.

Farrer, F. (2000) *A Quiet Revolution: Encouraging Positive Values in our Children*, London: Rider.

Feige, A., Dressler, B., Lukatis, W. and Schöll, A. (2000) *'Religion' bei ReligionslehrerInnen. Religions-pädagogische Zielvorstellungen und religioses Selbstverstandnis in empirisch-soziologischen Zugangen. Berufsbiographische Fallanalysen und eine repräsentative Meinungserhebung unter evangelischen ReligionslehrerInnen in Niedersachsen*, Münster u.a.: LIT-Verlag.

Fenton, J. Y. (1991) 'Academic Study of Religion and Asian Indian-American College Students' in R. B. Williams (ed.), *A Sacred Thread: Modern Transmission of Hindu Tradition in India and Abroad*, Chambersburg: Anima, pp. 258–77.

Fetterman, D. M. (1998) *Ethnography Step by Step*, London: Sage.

Figueroa, P. (1998) 'Intercultural Education in Britain' in K. Cushner (ed.), *International Perspectives on Intercultural Education*, Mahwah, New Jersey: Lawrence Erlbaum Associates, pp. 122–44.

Firth, S. (1997) *Dying, Death and Bereavement in a British Hindu Community*, Kampen: Kok Pharos.

Fitzgerald, T. (1990) 'Hinduism and the 'World Religion' Fallacy', *Religion*, 20, 101–18.

Fleming, S. (1992) 'Multiculturalism in the Physical Education Curriculum: The Case of the South Asian Male Youth, Dance and South Asian Dance', *Multicultural Teaching*, 11 (1).

Foucault, M. (1971) *Madness and Civilisation*, London: Tavistock.

Fournier, C. (1997–2002) 'Celebrating Name Days' http://www.domestic-church.com/CONTENT.DCC/19980101/ARTICLES/NAMEDAYS (accessed 30 September 2003).

Fox, R. G. (1985) *Lions of the Punjab: Culture in the Making*, Berkeley: University of California Press.

Friederichs, J. O'Brien and Gupta, A. Sen (1995) 'International Education in a Multicultural Environment: An Analysis of the Impact on Individual Identity and Group Relations and a Discussion of the Important Aspects', *European Journal of Intercultural Studies*, 6 (1), 25–36.

Garala, R. and Nesbitt, E. 'I Enjoy Study of All Faiths', *Coventry Evening Telegraph*, 12 November.

Gardner, P. (2001) *Teaching and Learning in Multicultural Classrooms*, London: David Fulton.

Gardner, K. and Shukur, A. (1994) '"I'm Bengali, I'm Asian,and I'm Living Here": The Changing Identity of British Bengalis' in R. Ballard (ed.), *Desh Pardesh: The South Asian Presence in Britain*, London: Hurst, pp. 142–64.

Gates, B. (1976) *The Language of Life and Death: Religion in the Developing World of Children and Young People*, unpublished Ph.D. thesis, University of Lancaster.

Gay, G. (2001) 'Effective Multicultural Teaching Practices' in C. F. Diaz (ed.) *Multicultural Teaching for the 21st Century*, New York: Longman, pp. 23–41.

Geaves, R. (1998a) 'The Borders between Religions: A Challenge to the World Religions Approach to Religious Education', *British Journal of Religious Education*, 21 (1), 20–31.

—— (1998b) 'The Worship of Baba Balaknath', *International Journal of Punjab Studies*, 5 (1) pp. 75–86.

Geertz, C. (1973) *The Interpretation of Cultures*, New York: Basic Books.

—— (1983) *Local Knowledge: Further Essays in Interpretive Anthropology*, New York: Basic Books.

Gerholm, L. (1993) 'The Dynamics of Culture', http://www.etn.lu.se/ethscand/text/1993/1993_13–24.PDF (accessed 5 March 2004).

Ghuman, P. A. S. (1991) 'Have they Passed the Cricket Test? A Qualitative Study of Asian Adolescents', *Journal of Multilingual and Multicultural Development*, 12, 327–46.

—— (1994) *Coping with Two Cultures: A study of British Asians and Indo-Canadian Adolescents*, Clevedon: Multilingual Matters.

—— (1999) *Asian Adolescents in the West*, Leicester: BPS Books.

—— (2003) *South Asian Adolescents in the West*, Cardiff: University of Wales Press.

Giddens, A. (1991) *Modernity and Self-Identity: Self and Society in the Late Modern Age*, Oxford: Polity.

Gillespie, M. (1995) *Television, Ethnicity and Cultural Change*, London: Routledge.

Gravelle, M. (1990) 'Assessment and Bilingual Pupils', *Multicultural Teaching*, 9 (1), 13–15.

Hall, K. D. (2002) *Lives in Translation: Sikh Youth as British Citizens*, Philadelphia: University of Pennsylvania Press.

Hammersley, M. and Atkinson, P. (1995) *Ethnography Principles in Practice*, London: Routledge.

Haug, F. (1987) *Female Sexualisation*, London: Verso.

Haw, K. (1998) *Educating Muslim Girls: Shifting Discourse*, Buckingham: Open University Press.

Hay, D. (1990) *Religious Experience Today: Studying the Facts*, London: Mowbray.

Hay, D. and Nye, R. (1996) 'Investigating Spirituality: The Need for a Fruitful Hypothesis', *The International Journal of Children's Spirituality*, 1 (1), 6–16.

—— (1998) *The Spirit of the Child*, London: Fount Books.

Heelas, P. (1996) *The New Age Movement: The Celebration of the Self and the Sacralization of Modernity*, Oxford: Blackwell.

Henley, J. (2003) 'MPs Urge French Ban on Religious Symbols', *The Guardian*, 14 November, 19.

Hick, J. (1977) *God and the Universe of Faiths: Essays in the Philosophy of Religion*, London: Fount.

Hicks, D. A. (forthcoming 2004) *Religion in the Workplace: Pluralism, Spirituality and Leadership*, Cambridge: Cambridge University Press.

Homan, R. (1991) '"Toil and Trouble": Halloween as an Educational Theme and Political Issues', *British Journal of Religious Education*, 14 (1), 9–15.

Home Office (2001a) *Community Cohesion: A Report of the Independent Review Team chaired by Ted Cantle*, December, London: Home Office.

Home Office (2001b) *Building Cohesive Communities: A Report of the Ministerial Group on Public Order and Community Cohesion*, December, London: Home Office.

Home Office Faith Communities Unit (2004) *Working Together: Co-operation between Government and Faith Communities*, London: Home Office. http://www.homeoffice.gov.uk/docs3/workingtog_faith040329.pdf (accessed 3 May 2004).

Hornsby-Smith, M. P. (1986) 'The Immigrant Background of Roman Catholics in England and Wales: A Research Note', *New Community*, 13 (1), 79–85.

—— (1989) 'The Roman Catholic Church in Britain since the Second World War' in P. Badham (ed.), Religion, *State and Society in Modern Britain*, Lampeter: The Edwin Mellen Press, pp. 85–98.

Hull, J. (1991) *Mishmash: Religious Education in Multi-Cultural Britain A Study in Metaphor*, Birmingham Papers in Religious Education No. 3, Derby, The University of Birmingham and the Christian Education Movement.

—— (2003) review of *Towards Religious Competence: Diversity as a Challenge for Education in Europe* in *British Journal of Religious Education*, 25 (3), 251–3.

Husain, F. and O'Brian, M. (2001) 'Muslims in Britain: Faith, Family and Community' in C. D. H. Harvey (ed.), *Maintaining our Differences: Minority Families in Multicultural Societies*, Aldershot: Ashgate, pp. 15–28.

Husselbee, L. A. and Thomas, D. M. (n.d.) *Children in Communion?* London: The United Reformed Church.

Hyde, K. (1990) *Religion in Childhood and Adolescence: A Comprehensive Review of the Research*, Birmingham, Alabama: Religious Education Press.

Hymes, D. (1980) *Language in Education: Ethnolinguistic Essays*, Washington: Centre for Applied Linguistics.

Indiaweekly (1999) 'Lakshmi Puja Goes Hi-Tech', *Indiaweekly*, 18 November, 9.

Ions, V. (1967) *Indian Mythology*, London: Hamlyn.

Ipgrave, J. (1998) 'Religious Education and Muslim Students', London: Teacher Training Agency.

—— (2001) *Pupil-to-Pupil Dialogue in the Classroom as a Tool for Religious Education*, Coventry: Warwick Religions and Education Research Unit, Institute of Education, University of Warwick.

Jackson, R. (1976) 'Holi in North India and in an English City: Some Adaptations and Anomalies', *New Community*, 5 (3), Autumn, 203–10.

—— (1996) 'The Construction of "Hinduism" and its Impact on Religious Education in England and Wales, *Panorama: International Journal of Comparative Religious Education and Values*, 6 (1), 115–30.

—— (1997a) *Religious Education: An Interpretive Approach*, London: Hodder and Stoughton.

—— (1997b) 'Editorial', *British Journal of Religious Education*, 19 (3), 130–2.

—— (1997c) 'Seas of Faith Flow Together, *TES*, 24 October, p. 19.

—— (2000) 'The Warwick Religious Education Project: The Interpretive Approach to Religious Education' in M. Grimmitt (ed.), *Pedagogies of Religious Education: Case Studies in the Research and Development of Good Pedagogic Practice in RE*, Great Wakering: McCrimmons, pp. 130–52.

—— (2003) *International Perspectives on Citizenship, Education and Religious Diversity*, London: Routledge Falmer.

—— (2004a) 'Intercultural Education and Recent European Pedagogies of Religious Education', *Intercultural Education*.

——. (2004b) *Rethinking Religious Education and Plurality: Issues in Diversity and Pedagogy*, London: Routledge Falmer.

Jackson, R. and Nesbitt, E. (1992) 'The Diversity of Experience in the Religious Upbringing of Children from Christian Families in Britain', *British Journal of Religious Education*, 15 (1), 19–28.

—— (1993) *Hindu Children in Britain*, Stoke on Trent: Trentham.

Jacobson, J. (1996) 'Perceptions of Britishness', unpublished paper, Conference on 'Multicultural Competence: A Resource for Tomorrow', Hogskolen i Bergen, August.

—— (1997) 'Religion and Ethnicity: Dual and Alternative Sources of Identity among Young British Pakistanis, *Ethnic and Racial Studies*, 20, 238–56.

—— (1998) *Islam in Transition: Religion and Identity among British Pakistani Youth*, London: Routledge.

Jaffrey, M. (1985) *Seasons of Splendour*, London: Pavilion.

James, W. (1960) *The Varieties of Religious Experience*, London: Fontana.

Joly, D. (1995) *Britannia's Crescent: Making a Place for Muslims in British Society*, Aldershot: Avebury.

Jones, L. (2000) *The Hermeneutics of Sacred Architecture: Experience, Interpretation, Comparison*, London: Harvard University Press.

Joseph, G. (1990) 'The Politics of Anti-Racist Mathematics', *Multicultural Teaching*, 9 (1), 31–3.

Juergensmeyer, M. (1982) *Religion as Social Vision: The Movement against Untouchability in 20th Century Punjab*, Berkeley: University of California Press.

—— (1987) 'The Radhasoami Revival of the Sant Tradition' in K. Schomer and W. H. McLeod (eds), *The Sants: Studies in a Devotional Tradition in India*, Delhi: Motilal Banarsidas, pp. 265–80.

Jumsai, A-O, (1985) 'Exposition of the Basic Human Values', *Education in Human Values Journal*, 2, 9–26.

Kalsi, S. S. (1992) *The Evolution of a Sikh Community in Britain: Religious and Social Change among the Sikhs of Leeds and Bradford*, Leeds: Community Religions Project, Department of Theology and Religious Studies, University of Leeds.

Kanitkar, V. P. (Hemant) (1991) 'Hinduism' in W. O. Cole (ed.), *Moral Issues in Six Religions*, Oxford: Heinemann, pp. 78–113.

Kanitkar, V. P. (Hemant) and Cole, W. O. (1995) *Hinduism, Teach Yourself*, London: Hodder Headline.

Kapoor, S. S. (1986) *Sikh Festivals*, Hove: Wayland.

Karian, S. (1994) 'Food for a Change: Our Animal-Centred Food System Harms People, Animals and the Environment' *Dollars and Sense*, 193, May–June, 30–1, 41.

Kassem, D. (2001) 'Ethnicity and Mathematics Education' in P. Gates (ed.), *Issues in Mathematics Teaching*, London: Routledge Falmer, pp. 64–76.

Katz, I. (1996) *Construction of Racial Identity in Children of Mixed Marriage*, London: Jessica Kingsley.

Kaur-Singh, K. (1994) 'Sikhism' in J. Holm and J. Bowker (eds), *Women in Religion*, London: Pinter, pp. 141–57.

Keene. M. (1993) *Seekers after Truth: Hinduism, Buddhism, Sikhism*, Cambridge: University of Cambridge Press.

Kehily, M. J. (1995) 'Self-Narration, Autobiography and Identity Construction, *Gender and Education*, 7 (1), 23–31.

Killingley, D. (1991) ' Varna and Caste in Hindu Apologetic' in D. Killingley, W. Menski and S. Firth, *Hindu Ritual and Society*, Newcastle upon Tyne: S. Y. Killingley, pp. 7–31.

Klingberg, G. (1959) 'A Study of Religious Experience in Children from 9 to 13 Years of Age', *Religious Education*, 54 (3), 211–16.

Kotsoni, K. (1990) *The Greek Orthodox Community in Leeds*, Community Religions Project Research Papers [New Series], Leeds: Department of Theology and Religous Studies, University of Leeds.

Kuper, A. (1993) 'The English Christmas and the Family: Time Out and Alternative Realities' in D. Miller (ed.), *Unwrapping Christmas*, Oxford: Clarendon, pp. 157–75.

Kurtz, S. N. (1992) *All the Mothers are One: Hindu India and the Cultural Reshaping of Psychoanalysis*, New York: Columbia University Press.

Lall, S. (1999) *'I Know who God is': A Study of Sikh Children's Spirituality within Various Expressions of Sikhism*, Oxford: Farmington Institute for Christian Studies.

Lane, B. C. (1988) *Landscapes of the Sacred: Geography and Narrative in American Spirituality*, New York: Paulist Press.

Leganger-Krogstad, H. (2001) 'Religious Education in a Global Perspective: A Contextual Approach' in H-G. Heimbrock, C. Th. Scheilke and P. Schreiner (eds), *Towards Religious Competence: Diversity as a Challenge for Education in Europe*, Muenster: Lit Verlag, pp. 53–73.

Leicester, M. (1992) 'Antiracism versus the New Multiculturalism: Moving beyond the Interminable Debate' in J. Lynch, C. Modgil and S. Modgil (eds), *Cultural Diversity and the Schools: Equity or Excellence? Education and Cultural Reproduction*, London: Falmer.

Leslie, J. (2003) *Authority and Meaning in Indian Religions: Hinduism and the Case of Valmiki*, Aldershot: Ashgate.

Lewis, P. (1994) *Islamic Britain: Religion, Politics and Identity among British Muslims*, London: I. B. Tauris.

Lipner, J. (1999) *Hindus: Their Religious Beliefs and Practices*, London: Routledge.

Logan, P. (1988) 'Practising Religion: British Hindu Children and the Navaratri Festival', *British Journal of Religious Education*, 10 (3), 160–9.

Macauliffe, M. A. (rep. 1985) *The Sikh Religion Its Gurus, Sacred Writings and Authors*, Vols V and VI, New Delhi: Oxford University Press.

McCann, V. (2002) 'Jehovah's Witnesses and the Issue of Birthdays, Spotlight Ministries, http://www.spotlightministries.org.uk/birthdays.htm (accessed 29 September 2003).

McConnell, A. (n. d.) (ed.) *The Christ We Share A World Church Resource for Local Mission*, London: Church Mission Society, United Society for the Propagation of the Gospel, The Methodist Church.

McCutcheon, R. (1999) (ed.), *The Insider/Outsider Problem in the Study of Religion*, London: Cassell.

McGee, M. (1991) 'Desired Fruits: Motive and Intention in the Votive Rites of Hindu Women' in J. Leslie (ed.), *Roles and Rituals for Hindu Women*, London: Pinter, pp. 71–88.

McLeod, W. H. (1976) *The Evolution of the Sikh Community*, Oxford: Clarendon.

—— (1995) *Historical Dictionary of Sikhs*, Lanham MD and London: Scarecrow.

—— (2000) *Exploring Sikhism: Aspects of Sikh Identity, Culture and Thought*, New Delhi: Oxford University Press.

McLeod, W. H. (2003) *Sikhs of the Khalsa: A History of the Khalsa Rahit*, New Delhi: Oxford University Press.

Mcquarrie, J. (1972) *Paths in Spirituality*, London: SCM Press.

Malinowski, B. (1922) *Argonauts of the Western Pacific, An Account of Native Enterprise and Adventure in the Archipelagoes of Melanesian New Guinea*, London: Routledge and Kegan Paul.

Marriott, Mc Kim (n.d.) 'Changing Channels of Cultural Transmission in Indian Civilization' in L. P. Vidyarthi (ed.), *Aspects of Religion in Indian Society*, Meerut: Kedar Nath Ram Nath.

—— (1966) 'The Feast of Love' in Milton Singer (ed.), *Krishna, Myths, Rites and Attitudes*, Chicago: University of Chicago Press, pp. 200–31.

Meijer, W. (1995) 'The Plural Self: A Hermeneutical View on Identity and Plurality', *British Journal of Religious Education*, 17 (2), 92–9.

Melucci, A. (1997) 'Identity and Difference in a Globalised World' in P. Werbner and T. Modood (eds), *Debating Cultural Hybridity: Multi-Cultural Identities and the Politics of Anti-Racism*, London: Zed pp. 58–69.

Menski, W. (1996) 'Hinduism' in P. Morgan and C. Lawton (eds), *Ethical Issues in Six Religious Traditions*, Edinburgh: Edinburgh University Press, pp. 1–54.

Meyerhoff, B. (1978) *Number our Days*, New York: Simon and Schuster.

Michaelson, M. (1987) 'Domestic Hinduism in a Gujarati Trading Caste' in R. Burghart (ed.), *Hinduism in Great Britain: The Perpetuation of Religion in an Alien Cultural Milieu*, London: Tavistock, pp. 32–49.

Miller, J. (2002) Review of C. Erricker and J. Erricker (eds), *Meditation in Schools*, *British Journal of Religious Education* 25 (1), 72–5.

—— (2003) 'Faith and Belonging in Bradford', *RE Today*, 20 (3), 34.

Miller, L. F. and Widener, S. (2003) 'Birthdays, Jewishly'. http://www.ritualwell.org: 10030/Rituals/ritual.html?docid=936 (accessed 30 September 2003).

Modood, T. (1988) Who's Defining Who? *New Society*, 4 March, 4–5.

Modood, T., Beishon., S. and Virdee, S. (1994) *Changing Ethnic Identities*, London: Policy Studies Institute.

Modood, T., Berthoud, R., Lakey, J., Smith, P., Virdee, S. and Beishon, S. (1997) *Ethnic Minorities in Britain: Diversity and Disadvantage: The Fourth National Survey of Ethnic Minorities*, London: Policy Studies Institute.

Moore, S. (1995) 'Flying the Flag of Convenience', *The Guardian*, 20 July.

Morrish, I, (1971) *The Background of Immigrant Children*, London: Allen and Unwin.

Mukta, P. (1997) 'New Hinduism – Teaching Intolerance, Practicing Aggression', *Resource: Journal of the Professional Council for Religious Education*, 20 (1), 9–14.

Murray, V. (1989) 'Catholic and Sikh Sixth Formers – Education for Different Identities', *Sikh Bulletin*, 9, 1–6.

Neelands, J. (1998) *Beginning Drama 11–14*, London: David Fulton.

Nesbitt, E. (1980) *Aspects of Sikh Tradition in Nottingham*, unpublished MPhil thesis, University of Nottingham.

—— (1981) 'A Note on Bhatra Sikhs', *New Community*, 9 (1), 70–2.

—— (1985) 'The Nanaksar Movement', *Religion*, 15, 67–79.

—— (1990a) 'Pitfalls in Religious Taxonomy: Hindus and Sikhs, Valmikis and Ravidasis', *Religion Today*, 6 (1), 9–12.

—— (1990b) 'Religion and Identity: The Valmiki Community in Coventry', *New Community*, 16 (2), 261–74.

—— (1991) 'My Dad's Hindu, My Mum's Side are Sikhs': Issues in Religious identity [Arts, Culture, Education research Paper] Charlbury: National Foundation for Arts Education.

—— (1993a) 'The Transmission of Christian Tradition in an Ethnically Diverse Society' in R. Barot (ed.), *Religion and Ethnicity: Minorities and Social Change in the Metropolis*, Kampen: Kok Pharos, pp. 156–69.

—— (1993b) 'Drawing on the Ethnic Diversity of Christian Tradition in Britain', *Multicultural Teaching*, 11 (2), 9–11.

—— (1993c) 'Children and the World to Come: The Views of Children Aged Eight to Fourteen on Life after Death', *Religion Today*, 8 (3), 10–13.

—— (1994) 'Valmikis in Coventry: The Revival and Reconstruction of a Community' in R. Ballard (ed.), *Desh Pardesh: The South Asian Presence in Britain*, London: Hurst, pp. 117–41.

—— (1995a) 'Many Happy Returns: Some British South Asian Children's Birthday Parties', *Multicultural Teaching*, 14 (1), 34–5 and 40.

—— (1995b) 'Punjabis in Britain: Cultural History and Cultural Choices', *South Asia Research*, 15 (2), 221–40.

—— (1997) '"Splashed with Goodness": The Many Meanings of *Amrit* for Young British Sikhs', *Journal of Contemporary Religion*, 12 (1), 17–33.

—— (1998a) 'British, Asian and Hindu: Identity, Self-Narration and the Ethnographic Interview, *Journal of Beliefs and Values: Studies in Religion and Education*, 19 (2), 189–200.

—— (1998b) 'How Culture Changes: British Sikh Children and the Vaisakhi

Festival', *Journal of Sikh Studies*, 22 (1), 95–118.

—— (1998c) 'Bridging the Gap between Young People's Experience of their Religious Tradition at Home and School: The Contribution of Ethnographic Research', *British Journal of Religious Education*, 20 (2), 98–110.

—— (1999a) '"Being Religious Shows in your Food": Young British Hindus and Vegetarianism' in T. S. Rukmani (ed.), *Hindu Diaspora: Global Perspectives*, Montreal: Chair in Hindu Studies, Department of Religion, Concordia University, pp. 397–426.

—— (1999b) 'The Impact of Morari Bapu's *Kathas* on Britain's Young Hindus', *Scottish Journal of Religious Studies*, 20 (2), 177–92.

—— (1999c) 'Sikhs and Proper Sikhs: The Representation of Sikhism in Curriculum Books and Young British Sikhs' Perceptions of their Identity' in P. Singh and N. G. Barrier (eds), *Sikh Identity: Continuity and Change*, New Delhi: Oxford University Press, pp. 315–34.

—— (2000) *The Religious Lives of Sikh Children: A Coventry Based Study*, Leeds: Community Religions Project, University of Leeds.

—— (2001a) 'Ethnographic Research at Warwick: Some Methodological Issues', *British Journal of Religious Education*, 23 (3), 144–55.

—— (2001b) 'Religious Nurture and Young People's Spirituality: Reflections on Research at the University of Warwick', in J. Erricker, C. Ota and C. Erricker (eds), *Spiritual Education Cultural, Religious and Social Differences: New Perspectives for the 21st Century*, Brighton and Portland: Sussex Academic Press, pp. 130–42.

—— (2002) '"Quaker Ethnographers: A Reflexive Approach' in E. Arweck and M. Stringer (eds), *Theorizing Faith: The Insider/Outsider Problem in the Study of Ritual*, Birmingham: University of Birmingham Press, pp. 133–54.

—— (2003) *Interfaith Pilgrims*, London: Quaker Books.

—— (2004a forthcoming) 'Young British Sikhs and Religious Devotion' in A. King and J. Brockington (eds), *The Intimate Other*, New Delhi: Orient Longman.

—— (2004b) '"I'm a Gujarati Lohana and a Vaishnav as Well": Religious Identity Formation among Young Coventrian Punjabis and Gujaratis' in S. Coleman and P. Collins (eds), *Religion, Identity and Change: British Perspectives on Global Transformations*, London: Ashgate, pp. 174–90.

—— (2004c forthcoming) *Sikhism*, PRS-LTSN Subject Centre Faith Guides, Leeds: PRS-LTSN, Department of Theology and Religious Studies, University of Leeds.

Nesbitt, E. and Arweck, E. (2003) 'Researching a New Interface between Religions and Publicly Funded Schools in the UK', *International Journal for Children's Spirituality*, 8 (3), 239–54.

Nesbitt, E. and Henderson, A. (2003) 'Religious Organisations in the UK and Values Education Programmes for Schools', *Journal of Beliefs and Values*, 24 (1), 75–88.

Nesbitt, E. and Jackson, R. (1992) 'Christian and Hindu Children: Their Perceptions of their own and Others' Religious Traditions', *Journal of Empirical Theology*, 5 (2), 39–62.

—— (1995) 'Sikh Children's Use of "God": Ethnographic Fieldwork and Religious Education', *British Journal of Religious Education*, 17 (2), 108–20.

Nickolds, A. (1999) 'What Is He On?', G2, *The Guardian*, 2 February, 2–3.

Nye, M. (1998) 'Hindus Old and New: Problems of Sacred Space in Britain' in E. Barker and M. Warburg (eds), *New Religions and New Religiosity*, Aarhus: Aarhus University Press, pp. 222–42.

Nye, R. and Hay, D. (1996) 'Identifying Children's Spirituality: How do you Start without a Starting Point?' *British Journal of Religious Education*, 18 (3), 144–54.

Oberoi, H. S. (1994) *The Construction of Religious Boundaries: Culture, Identity and Diversity in the Sikh Tradition*, Delhi: Oxford University Press.

O'Flaherty, W. D. (1975) *Hindu Myths*, Harmondsworth: Penguin.

—— (1999) 'The Uses and Misuses of Other People's Myths' in R. McCutcheon (ed.), *The Insider/Outsider Problem in the Study of Religion: A Reader*, London: Cassell, pp. 331–49.

Ofsted (Office for Standards in Education) (1994) *Spiritual, Moral, Social and Cultural Development: A Discussion Paper*, London: Ofsted.

—— (Office for Standards in Education) (2004) *Promoting and Evaluating Pupils' Spiritual, Moral, Social and Cultural Development*, www.ofsted.gov.uk

Orans, M. (1965) *The Santal*, Detroit: Wayne State University Press.

Østberg, S. (2003) *Pakistani Children in Norway: Islamic Nurture in a Secular Context*, Leeds: Community Religions Project, Department of Theology and Religious Studies, University of Leeds.

Ota, C. (1997) 'Learning to Juggle – The Experience of Muslim and Sikh Children Coping with Different Value Systems', *Journal of Beliefs and Values: Studies in Religions and Education*, 18 (2), 227–34.

Parekh, B. (2000) *The Future of Multi-Ethnic Britain*, London: The Runnymede Trust.

Parker-Jenkins, M. (1995) *Children of Islam: A Teacher's Guide to Meeting the Needs of Muslim Pupils*, Stoke on Trent: Trentham.

Parsons, G. (1989) 'The Rise of Religious Pluralism in the Church of England' in P. Badham (ed.), *Religion, State and Society in Modern Britain*, Lampeter: The Edwin Mellen Press, pp. 1–22.

Pettigrew, J. (1972) Some Notes on the Social System of the Sikh Jats', *New Community*, 1(5), 354–63.

Priestley, J. (1996) Review, *International Journal of Children's Spirituality*, 1 (1), 69.

Prinja, N. K. (1996) *Explaining Hindu Dharma*, Norwich: Religious and Moral Education Press.

Raj, D. S. (2003) *Where are you from? Middle-class Migrants in the Modern World*, Berkeley: University of California Press.

Rattansi, A. (1992) 'Changing the Subject: Racism, Culture and Education' in J. Donald and A. Rattansi (eds), *Race, Culture and Difference*, London: Sage in association with the Open University, pp. 11–48.

Redbridge SACRE (1997a) *Briefing Paper 2 Jehovah's Witnesses and the School*, London Borough of Redbridge, Standing Advisory Council on Religious Education. Available from Advisory Service Office, Lynton House, 255–259 High Road, Ilford, Essex IG1 1NN, UK.

—— (1997b) *Briefing Paper 1, Ramadan and Its Implications for Schools*, London Borough of Redbridge, Standing Advisory Council on Reliigous Education. (For availability see previous entry.)

—— (1999) *Briefing Paper 3 Sikh Appearance and Identity*, London Borough of

Redbridge, Standing Advisory Council on Religious Education. (Available as above.)

Rex, J. (1997) 'Multiculturalism and Antiracism Reconsidered' in P. Sikes and F. Rizvi (eds), *Researching Race and Social Justice in Education: Essays in Honour of Barry Troyna*, Stoke on Trent: Trentham, pp. 109–18.

Ricoeur, P. (1988) *Time and Narrative*, Vol. 3 (Chicago and London, Chicago University Press) (translation of *Temps et Récit*, 3).

Roberts, C. (2002) 'Ethnography and Cultural Practice: Ways of Learning during Residence Abroad' in G. Alred, M. Byram and M. Fleming, M. (eds), *Intercultural Experience and Education*, Clevedon: Multilingual Matters, pp. 114–30.

Robson, G. (1995) *Christians*, Oxford: Heinemann.

Romain, J. A. (1996) *Till Faith Us Do Part*, London: Fount.

Roman, A. (2003) 'Celebrating our Name Days', http://www.unicorne.org/ orthodoxy/articles/alex roman/celebrating.htm (accessed 30 September 2003).

Rosen, H. (1988) 'The Voices of Communities and Language in Classrooms: A review of *Ways with Words* in N. Mercier (ed.), *Language and Literacy from an Educational Perspective*, Milton Keynes: Open University Press.

Rountree, K. (2002) 'Goddess Pilgrims as Tourists: Inscribing the Body through Sacred Travel', *Sociology of Religion* 63 (4), 475–96.

Rudge, L. (1998) '"I am Nothing – Does it Matter?" A Critique of Current Religious Education Policy and Practice in England on behalf of the Silent Majority', *British Journal of Religious Education*, 20 (3), 155–65.

Saberwal, S. (1976) *Mobile Men: Limits to Social Change in Urban Punjab*, New Delhi: Vikas.

Said, E. (1989) 'Representing the Colonised: Anthropology's Interlocutors', *Critical Enquiry*, 15 (2), 205–25.

Sambhi, P. S. (1991) 'Sikhism' in W. O. Cole (ed.), *Moral Issues in Six Religions*, Oxford: Heinemann, pp. 186–220.

Santosh, R. and Bhanot, S. (2003) *The Hindu Youth Research Project 2001*, Oxford: Oxford Centre for Hindu Studies. http://www.ochs.org.uk/research/youth-survey.html (accessed 3 May 2004).

Sarvar, G. (1994) *British Muslims and Schools*, London: The Muslim Educational Trust.

SCAA (1994) *Model Syllabuses for Religious Education Model 1: Living Faiths Today*, London: School Curriculum and Assessment Authority.

Scholefield, L. (2004) 'Bagels, Schnitzels and McDonald's: "Fuzzy Frontiers" of Jewish Identity in an English Jewish Secondary School', *British Journal of Religious Education*, 26 (3).

Scott, D. (2001) 'Storytelling, Voice and Qualitative Research: Spirituality as a Site of Ambiguity and Difficulty' in J. Erricker, C. Ota and C. Erricker (eds), *Spiritual Education Cultural, Religious and Social Differences: New Perspectives for the 21st Century*, Brighton and Portland: Sussex Academic Press, pp. 118–29.

Searle-Chatterjee, M. (1993) 'Christmas Cards and the Construction of Social Relations in Britain Today' in D. Miller (ed.), *Unwrapping Christmas*, Oxford: Clarendon, pp. 176–92.

—— (2000) '"World Religions" and "Ethnic Groups": Do these Paradigms Lend themselves to the Cause of Hindu Nationalism?' *Ethnic and Racial Studies*, 23 (3), 497–515.

Searle-Chatterjee, M. and Sharma, U. (1994) *Contextualising Caste: Post-Dumontian Approaches*, Oxford: Blackwell.

Shah, S. and Abrol, S. (1990) 'Not so Special: The National Curriculum and Children of Asian Origin', *Multicultural Teaching*, 9, 4–6.

Shaikh 'Abdul 'Aziz bin 'Abdullah bin Baaz (2003) in 'Celebrating Birthdays Sunnah or Bidah?' http://members.tripod.com/dawaa/birthdays.html (accessed 29 September 2003).

Shain, F. (2003) *The Schooling and Identity of Asian Girls*, Stoke on Trent: Trentham.

Shaw, A. (1994) 'The Pakistani community in Oxford' in R. Ballard (ed.), *Desh Pardesh*, London: Hurst and Co., pp. 35–57.

—— (2000) *Kinship and Continuity: Pakistani Families in Britain*, Amsterdam: Harwood.

Short, G. and Carrington, B. (1995) 'What Makes a Person British? Children's Conceptions of their National Culture and Identity, *Educational Studies*, 21, 217–38.

Shukra, A. (1994) 'Caste – A Personal Perspective' in M. Searle-Chatterjee and U. Sharma (eds), *Contextualising Caste: Post-Dumontian Approaches*, Oxford: Blackwell, pp. 169–78.

Singh, Kapur (1989) *Parasaprasna: An Enquiry into the Genesis and Unique Character of the Order of the Khalsa with an Exposition of the Sikh Tenets*, Amritsar: Guru Nanak Dev University.

Singh, Khushwant (1977) *A History of the Sikhs Volume 2 1839–1974*, Delhi: Oxford University Press.

Singh, Nikky-Guninder K. (1995) *The Name of My Beloved: Verses of the Sikh Gurus*, San Francisco: HarperSanFrancisco.

—— (2003) 'Sikh Sacred Aesthetics and the Arabesques of Inter-Religious Understanding', unpublished paper presented at international conference on 'Sikhism and Inter-Religious Dialogue' University of Birmingham with Hofstra University (New York), 25–26 October.

Singh, Patwant (1988) *The Golden Temple*, New Delhi: Time Books International.

Singh, R. N. (2003) (ed.), *Social Philosophy and Social Transformation of Sikhs*, New Delhi: Commonwealth.

Singh-Raud, H. (1997) 'Educating Sita: The Education of British Asian Girls', paper presented at the British Educational Research Association, York, 11 September.

Skeie, G. (1995) 'Plurality and Pluralism: A Challenge for Religious Education', *British Journal of Religious Education*, 17 (2), 84–91.

Slovensko.com (2003) http://www.slovensko.com/slovakia/calendar.htm_(accessed 30 September 2003).

Smith, D. (1993) 'The Pre-Modern and the Post-Modern – Some Parallels, with Special Reference to Hinduism, *Religion*, 23, 157–65.

Smith, D. (1999) *Hinduism and Modernity*, Oxford: Blackwell.

Smith, W. C. (1978) *The Meaning and End of Religion*, London: SPCK.

Spafford, T. and Bolloten, B. (1995) 'The Admission and Induction of Refugee Children into School', *Multicultural Teaching*, 14 (1), 7–10.

Spradley, J. (1980) *Participant Observation*, New York: Holt, Rinehart and Winston.

Srinivas, M. N. (1967) *Social Change in Modern India*, Berkeley: University of California Press.

Steedman, C. (1985) '"Listen How the Caged Bird Sings": Amarjit's Song' in C. Steedman, C. Urwin and V. Walkerdine (eds), *Language, Gender and Childhood*, London: Routledge, pp. 137–63.

Straus, R. A. (1981) 'The Social-Psychology of Religious Experience: A Naturalistic Approach, *Sociological Analysis*, 42, 57–67.

Stringer, M. (1999) *On the Perception of Worship: The Ethnography of Worship in Four Christian Congregations in Manchester*, Birmingham: University of Birmingham Press.

Subramuniyaswami, Satguru Sivaya (1993) *Dancing with Siva: Hinduism's Contemporary Catechism*, California: Himalayan Academy.

Sugirtharajah, S. (1997) 'Talking about Hinduism "Till the Sacred Cows Come Home": A Response to "Hinduism and Ecology" by Catherine Robinson and Denise Cush', *Journal of Beliefs and Values*, 18 (1), 39–45.

Syal, M. (1996) *Anita and Me*, London: HarperCollins.

—— (1997) 'And I Bet you have Curried Turkey as well . . . ', *The Guardian*, 27 December.

Tajfel, H. (1981) *Human Groups and Social Categories*, Cambridge: Cambridge University Press.

Tatla, D. S. (1992) 'Nurturing the Faithful: The Role of the Sant among Britain's Sikhs', *Religion*, 22 (4), 349–74.

Taylor, J. H. (1976) *The Half-Way Generation*, Basingstoke: NFER.

Taylor, M. J. and Hegarty, S. (1985) *The Best of Both Worlds . . . ?* (Windsor, NFER-Nelson).

The Teacher (2001) 'Children, Terror and War', London: National Union of Teachers, November, 3.

Toulis, N. R. (1997) *Believing Identity: Pentecostalism and the Mediation of Jamaican Ethnicity and Gender in England*, Oxford: Berg.

Treacy-Cole, D. (2001) 'Spirituality and Healing in a Scientific Age' in U. King (ed.), *Spirituality and Society in the New Millennium*, Brighton and Portland: Sussex Academic Press.

Troyna, B. (1983) 'Multicultural Education: Just Another Brick in the Wall?' *New Community* 10, 424–8.

—— (1986) 'Beyond Multiculturalism: Towards the Enactment of Anti-Racist Education in Policy, Provision and Pedagogy', *Oxford Review of Education*, 13 (3), 301–20.

Twigg, J. (1979) 'Food for Thought: Purity and Vegetarianism', *Religion*, 9 (l), 13–35.

UK Government (1988) *Education Reform Act*, London: HMSO.

Ukrainian Women's Association of Canada, Daughters of Ukraine Branch (1987) *Ukrainian Daughters Cook Book*, Regina: Saskatchewan.

Vertovec, S. (1996) 'On the Reproduction and Representation of "Hinduism" in Britain' in T. Ranger, Y. Samad and O. Stuart (eds), *Culture, Identity and Politics: Ethnic Minorities in Britain*, Aldershot: Avebury, pp. 77–89.

von Stietencron, H. (1991) 'Hinduism: On the Proper Use of a Deceptive Term' in G. D. Sontheimer and H. Kulke (eds), *Hinduism Reconsidered*, Delhi: Manohar, pp. 11–27.

Ward, C. M. (2001) *The Meat-Eating Vegetarian*, Leicester: Islamic Foundation.

Wardekker, W. L. and Miedema, S. (2001) 'Religious Identity Formation between Participation and Distantiation' in H.-G.Heimbrock, C. Th. Scheilke and P. Schreiner (eds), *Towards Religious Competence: Diversity as a Challenge for Education in Europe*, Münster: Lit Verlag, pp. 23–33.

Watson, J. L. (1977) (ed.) *Between Two Cultures*, Oxford: Blackwell.

Wayne, E., Everington, J. with Kadodwala, D. and Nesbitt, E. (1996) *Hindus* (Interpreting Religions Key Stage 3), Oxford: Heinemann.

Weeks, J. (1987) 'Questions of Identity' in R. Caplan (ed.), *The Cultural Construction of Sexuality*, London: Routledge.

Weller, P. (2001) *Religions in the UK Directory 2001–03*, Derby: University of Derby in association with the Inter Faith Network for the United Kingdom.

—— (2004) 'Identity, Politics, and the Future(s) of Religion in the UK: The Case of the Religion Questions in the 2001 Decennial Census', *Journal of Contemporary Religion*, 19 (1), 3–21.

Werbner, P. and Modood, T. (1997) *Debating Cultural Hybridity: Multi-Cultural Identities and the Politics of Anti-Racism*, London: Zed.

Whiting, R. (rep. 1991) *Religions for Today*, Cheltenham: Stanley Thornes.

Williams, R. B. (1984) *A New Face of Hinduism: The Swaminarayan Religion*, Cambridge: Cambridge University Press.

Winston, J. (2000) *Drama, Literacy and Moral Education 5–11*, London: David Fulton.

—— (2002) 'Drama, Spirituality and the Curriculum', *International Journal of Children's Spirituality*, 7 (3), 241–55.

—— (2003) 'This is the Logbook of the Starship TEMPEST: Shakespeare within a Context of "Multiple Cultural Competence', *Drama Australia Journal*, 27 (2), 37–52.

—— (2004) *Drama and English at the Heart of the Curriculum*, London: David Fulton.

Winter, J. (2001) 'Personal, Spiritual, Moral, Social and Cultural Issues in Teaching Mathematics' in P. Gates (ed.), *Issues in Mathematics Teaching*, London: Routledge Falmer, pp. 197–214.

Wood, A. with Oxley, J., Prior, L. and Sims, P. (1998) *Homing In: A Practical Resource for Religious Education*, Stoke on Trent: Trentham.

Wright, A. (1999) *Discerning the Spirit: Teaching Spirituality in the Religious Education Classroom*, Abingdon: Culham College Institute.

—— (2000) 'Cultivating Spiritual and Religious Literacy through a Critical Pedagogy of Religious Education' in M. Grimmitt (ed.), *Pedagogies of Religious Education: Case Studies in the Research and Development of Good Pedagogic Practice in RE*, Great Wakering: McCrimmons, pp. 170–87.

Yeomans, R. (1993a) 'Islamic Art in the Primary Classroom', *Resource*, 15 (2), 5–7.

—— (1993b) 'Islamic Art in the Primary School', *RE Today*, 10 (2), 10–11.

—— (1994) 'Islamic Art in the Primary Classroom', *Muslim Education Quarterly*, 11 (2), 52–6.

Index

Shudra, 100, 101
Shukra, A., 108
Shukur, A., 114, 119
Sikh Appearance and Identity, 163
Sikh Code of Discipline, 74
Sikh communities
    belief and practice, 11, 66–80
    birthdays, 16–17, 18, 19
    calendars, 56, 57, 160
    caste, 11, 98–102, 107–12, 141, 142
    Christmas, 50, 52, 53, 63
    continuities, 142
    diet, 27
    Divali, 56, 146
    dress, 162–3
    five Ks, 21, 57, 75, 135, 143
    God/gods, 66–73, 79, 143
    Hindu-Sikh continuum of belief and
        practice, 147
    image of Sikhism, 140
    kesh (uncut hair), 2, 24, 57, 162
    multiple identities, 114
    music, 131–2
    pilgrimage places, 76
    plural identity, 145–6
    prayer, 68, 70, 130–1
    religious experience, 133
    spirituality, 12, 129–31, 135
    stereotyping, 2, 21
    western attitudes, 2
    see also amrit; Baba, Babaji; gurdwaras;
        Vaisakhi
silent sitting, 129, 137
simaran, 67
Singh, Baba Ajit, 75, 76, 77, 78, 79
Singh, Kapur, 74
Singh, Khushwant, 62, 108
Singh, Nikky-Guninder Kaur, 2, 67
Singh, Patwant, 74, 76
Singh-Raud, H., 120
Sita, 54, 55–6
Skeie, G., 82, 148, 149
sloka, 130
Slovak calendar, 15
Slovensko.com, 15
Smart, Ninian, 139–40
Smith, D., 81, 96
Smith, William Cantwell, 140
Socrates, 88
Somali communities, 14
Soni caste, 101, 102, 105, 106, 107
Spafford, T., 155
spells, 85–6

spirituality, 125–37
    Hindu communities, 123, 129–31
    inclusive conceptualization of, 136
    moral commitment, 132
    schools, 12, 125–6, 134–5, 136–7
    Sikh communities, 12, 129–31, 135
    social aspect of, 132
    and vegetarianism, 30
Spradley, J., 72
Srinivas, M. N., 32
stereotypes, 2, 21, 34, 64
stilling exercises, 126
Straus, R. A., 127
Stringer, Martin, 5, 36, 53, 141
Subramuniyaswami, Satguru Sivaya,
    23–4
Sugirtharajah, S., 23
Sukhmani *path*, 16
Sukhmani Sahib, 16
superstitions, 11, 80, 85, 95
suprabhatam, 130
surnames, 158
Swadhyaya, 151
Swami, 83
Swaminarayan, 24, 26
Syal, Meera, 63, 117
syncretization by convergence, 63

tabla, 60
Tajfel, Henri, 115, 116, 149
tamasik, 31
tantra, 85
Tarkhan caste, 107, 108
Tate, Nicholas, 119–20
Tatla, D. S., 71
tayaji, 93
Taylor, J. H., 113
Taylor, M. J., 113
The Teacher, 2
teachers
    birthdays, 13, 19–20, 161
    caste, 1, 98
    Christian communities, 48–9
    as ethnographers, 5–7, 151–2
    intrafaith diversity, 49
    names of parents and pupils, 158
    and parents, 157, 162
    pastoral care, 1, 6, 154–5
    practical guidelines, 12, 154–66
    racism policies, 155
    religious socialisation, 142–5
    Sikh beliefs and practices, 80
    spiritual development, 12, 125–6,